To Dr. Duane L. Blake,
an educator among educators

Culture Meets Culture in the Movies

An Analysis East, West, North and South, with Filmographies

DAVID H. BUDD

McFarland & Company, Inc., Publishers
Jefferson, North Carolina, and London

791. 4301 BUD

Library of Congress Cataloguing-in-Publication Data

Budd, David H., 1950–
    Culture meets culture in the movies : an analysis East, West,
North and South, with filmographies / David H. Budd.
        p.   cm.
    Includes bibliographical references and index.
    ISBN 0-7864-1095-7 (softcover : 50# alkaline paper) ∞
    1. Intercultural communication in motion pictures.   I. Title.

    PN1995.9.I55B83   2002
    791.43'655—dc21   2001044074

British Library cataloguing data are available

On the cover: Anthony Quinn and Keanu Reeves in
A Walk in the Clouds (1995)

Manufactured in the United States of America

McFarland & Company, Inc., Publishers
  Box 611, Jefferson, North Carolina 28640
    www.mcfarlandpub.com

TABLE OF CONTENTS

INTRODUCTION

"I write every day about this place. I write about the economy. I write about the politics. And yet I understand zilch, nothing."
Chinese Box

"His eyes seemed to see right through me ... a soft American who'd always had it easy."
Iron and Silk

"I'm speaking from experience. People stick to their own kind. You're forced to accept that when you grow older."
Mississippi Masala

This book is about the interaction of persons from different cultures as portrayed in popular film, especially relatively modern, commonly available Western film. This study could not encompass the prodigious output of Western television drama per se, but numerous films discussed were originally made for TV, and like cream rising, the best of these find their way into the video market.

Two premises drive this book: the poignant importance of understanding by and about members of differing cultures, and the outstanding potential of film to foster rich characterizations or shallow stereotypes, empathy or hostility, to impart humor, horror, pain, sadness, and optimism across the gamut of human stories. For much of the populace of modern societies, film still constitutes their chief exposure to other cultural groups. A typical North American, for example, has never met a Russian, a Japanese, or a South African, or for that matter a resident of a Native American reservation. He or she is far more likely to have encountered cultural-others in films or televised drama, and to have formed impressions of them almost as surely as if they had been next-door neighbors.

The importance of intercultural awareness and understanding is so clearly compelling that it needs little re-emphasis here. From the obvious instances (war between ethnic or religious or national groups throughout recorded history) to the subtle (international treaties on the complexities of environmental management), understanding between peoples is a matter of high stakes. Clearly, such understanding has broad significance, but what may be less clear is the contribution that film analysis can make. The value of that contribution depends, in large measure, on the extent to which we accept that images and myths influence everyday consciousness. Increasingly, the dominant minds in both the humanities and social sciences argue that we mediate reality through acquired or "constructed" frames of thinking, feeling, and expressiveness. Clifford Geertz and others hold strongly with the axiom of Max Weber that the human animal is "suspended in webs of significance he himself has spun." What does film—the medium of fantasy and glitz and escapism—have to do with a need for sharper understanding of culturally molded significance, across cultural frontiers?

Alone, in the Dark

The Big Screen has touched most of the lives on earth in our times, and has been as emblematic of modernity as any other innovation. In all film-watching societies it has created pop heroes and slang, styles of dress and behavior, images of peoples and places—in short, it has molded while it has reflected contemporary culture.

It has done so in ways at once quite broad and infinitely personal. Alone in the dark, each viewer, constructs a distinctly different reality from the communally viewed story. Alone in the dark, each viewer engages in what often functions as a powerful waking fantasy. Who has not emerged from a movie experience somewhat disoriented at first with the abrupt return to the "real" world? Yet paradoxically this extremely private, individualized experience is quite communal. It serves to construct collective fantasy, emotion, and meaning, which are shared through the currency of clichéd questions: "Your favorite movie star? Your favorite movie of all time?" Film allusions are traded in everyday conversation. Robert Redford, Sidney Poitier, Vanessa Redgrave, Anthony Hopkins, Gerard Depardieu, Jean-Paul Belmondo, all in their own fashion and time have come into U.S. American, British, and French lives much like impressive next-door neighbors, real and palpable, familiar in their personas, molding our expectations of our societies and ourselves across a comfortable backyard fence of perception.

Subliminal messages presumably register in deeper realms of the psyche, and Jungians may argue that the imagery of our visual mass media enters into the primal "collective unconscious." If culture is most fundamentally defined (with apology to cultural anthropologists and ethnographers for condensing their increasingly sophisticated analyses) as the values, beliefs, meanings, and emotions collectively (and often extra-consciously) held, then culture has much in common with the experience of popular film, and film goes far in defining culture.

More Than Meets the Eye

A medium so powerfully interwoven with our cultural selves may justly qualify as "popular" but not as "popularized" in the pejorative sense, as beneath serious study. In fact, the film-analysis course in an English or Communications department of the university has gone in a few years from exception to rule, and some measure of film analysis accompanies the previews in such widely-viewed programs as "Siskel and Ebert" in the United States. Full-time film critics still compose a quite small profession, but it *is* a profession.

Even those films (admittedly the overwhelming majority) that play fast and loose with day-to-day "reality" may suggest the stuff of myth and fantasy, or may shape stereotypes and misunderstandings, and thus be meaningful grist for analysis. Thus we may speak of the "reality" of the preposterous "Rambo" and Superman movies: the man who transcends social impotence speaks to the frustrated male in all epochs, and especially so in a time of declining personal and cultural power in the Western world.[1] Until recent years, film portraits of the American Indian were so laughably wooden (and downright inaccurate) as to nicely illustrate the construction of Old-West fantasy. And the absence of realistic, dignified Latin Americans in North American film proves highly instructive in its own right. What's more, many a mediocre film hides diamonds among the weeds, featuring isolated, brilliant moments which nicely encapsulate key themes. Hopelessly offbeat and brokering little substance, *The Golden Child* (1986) offers a brief but noteworthy dialectic on the "American character," while *Dragon: The Bruce Lee Story* (1993) brings a few points of laser-like focus to the intersection of cultures. Even soft, superficial films can merit a close look for scenes that sharply illustrate larger issues.

A still highly popular yet subtly-crafted type of film may serve for quite meaningful, even copious analysis. Consider the interest in Japanese prowess in business that was common in North America during the last two decades. Often discussed were the roots of Japanese hegemony in age-old cultural traditions (including traditions related to alliances and

loyalty in business), the insinuation of Japanese presence into other industrialized countries, the Japanese penchant for borrowing elements of culture and technology, and overall Japan's complex, ambivalent relationship
to the West. The slick and fast-paced *Rising Sun* (1993) evokes facets of
every one of these issues, if not directly through dialogue then indirectly
through cinematographic suggestion. In the first seven and a half minutes
alone, it portrays many aspects of the Japanese as seen by Americans: their
image as "ants," competing with the United States culture of rugged individualism; their fascination with Americana and especially the mythology
of the Old West and the freedom of the "open range"; the attraction of
their men to American women; their negotiating styles; their ascendancy
in high-tech including high-tech for industrial espionage; their "inscrutability" in both business and personal settings; their contemporary economic
power; and their fundamental greetings, protocols, and customs. It also
engages American journalistic and popular notions of Japanese involvement in world affairs, including trade policy, Japan's post–Cold War role,
and the phenomenon of "Japan bashing." This is impressive range for a
"pure entertainment" film, all within the opening minutes! Notwithstanding predictable (and perhaps valid) charges of an outrageously "Hollywood" approach, *Rising Sun* offers remarkably rich material for analysis
of the ongoing Japanese-American drama.

For the most part films like *Rising Sun*, contemporary in theme, feel,
and scope, and commonly available, are my focus here. Films produced in
the last quarter century receive most of the attention for two reasons—they
are the more accessible at even the "corner video store," and also, in most
cases, afford a greater sense of authenticity in their cultural depictions than
do older films.

A Film Genre Apart

Films that portray not only a single culture, but the complexity of the
interplay between cultures, deserve, even demand, a challenging analysis.
First of all they carry high impact with their easily politicized images. Not
only is there acute contemporary sensitivity toward (and controversy about)
such images, but there is some reason to believe they substantially matter:
a significant thread of research has always suggested high (and quite logical) correlations between the images projected by film and those we inter-
nalize. [2] Currently, and into the foreseeable future, we live amid debate
about the "politically correct" way to portray, even refer to, diverse groups—
so much so that any socio-cultural commentary runs the risk of seeming

ethnocentric, chauvinistic. Hopefully, an awareness of the snares waiting for any analysis of ethnicity will characterize this book. At one and the same time the current vehemence concerning subgroups may underscore the point that we need enlightenment from whatever sources available, including intercultural film.

For the purposes of this book, "intercultural" films are those animated by significant levels of interaction among persons from distinctly different cultural or ethnic backgrounds. More specifically, the large, overarching differences in national culture (Japan vis-à-vis the West) and stark differences in ethnic or cultural identity (Native Americans vis-à-vis the Anglo culture) serve as the primary focus. The chapter on Multicultural America, addressing numerous subgroups within the larger North American society, represents the clear exception.

Nonetheless, classifying intercultural film, like the classification of cultures themselves, often proves difficult. This study focuses on major, recognizable national (or ethnic) differences for numerous reasons, not the least of which is limiting an enormous subject to manageable scope. Women, as a subgroup within all national groups, receive special attention here in various chapters but surely not as much as deserved, and it remains for an author with solid feminist credentials to expand that vein of analysis. Other groups as well can and should insist that attention be paid to their particularity. However, in the modern political climate, the number of groups with claims to a distinct identity continues to grow, and responding to every such claim is beyond the reach of any single treatment. In the broadest reach, an enormously wide range of films fit under the "intercultural" umbrella. A somewhat different but prominent example is much of science fiction, for the genre almost by definition imagines strange new worlds and new cultures. In fact, so rich and varied has the field become that sci-fi film deserves its own, full-length study.

Under one highly inclusive definition virtually all films deal in some fashion with a clash of cultures or subcultures—in other words, protagonists in conflict with other humans holding values highly different from their own. In this sense, the garden-variety crime thriller, or a Western, presents the clash of the culture of the badge versus the culture of lawlessness. Yet such a point of view tends to confuse those persons who occupy, often by some measure of choice, diametrically different "roles" within a society with persons who come from different cultures. It confuses persons who choose to embrace or reject a set of commonly understood beliefs and rules with persons who were socialized in the milieu of sharply different beliefs and rules, persons who truly are culturally distinct.

In another sense, even the monocultural film becomes intercultural when representatives of a second culture react to it. It constitutes a type of cross-cultural encounter, if perhaps an additional step removed, with the director as facilitator. Few Westerners personally know Taiwanese, yet large non–Chinese audiences engaged with their everyday lives in *Eat, Drink, Man, Woman* (1994). And *Shall We Dance?* (1997), looking into the soul of Japanese culture through the lens of universal experience, surely becomes a bridge for Westerners into little known territory. Such films serve as effective vehicles for travel into other societies, as introductions to difference with a sympathetic face. "Understanding a people's culture," advises Clifford Geertz, "exposes their normalness without reducing their particularity." This large body of international, though not intercultural, film merits it own exhaustive study that goes far beyond the possible scope of this book.

Films that deal with intercultural communication and conflict are among the most genuinely refreshing, engaging, and important of all, and perhaps are quite disproportionately represented among excellent films. They elicit responses to the most fundamental dilemmas and challenge the most fundamental perceptions. Alongside them, the stock patterns of cops and crooks, sheriffs and gunslingers, or rich men and beautiful women seem insipid and predictable (and these stock films are produced in virtually every filmmaking country). Only when the characters or circumstances or both are truly extraordinary do these standard films escape being painfully ordinary, whereas the meeting of different cultures may involve everyday characters in relatively mundane circumstances, and still tease mind, imagination, and understanding and invoke humor and pathos while imparting insight.

It is, after all, a classic dimension of the storytelling arts: phenomena extraordinary enough or unpredictable enough to create tension, or engage deeper levels of curiosity, imagination, and passion. In "monocultural" stories the circumstances must be extraordinary and the actors must draw on special reserves in their characters or the story is flat and our reactions grow jaded, while in intercultural films the very crosstalk of cultures may provide sufficient interest and tension to engage the viewer.

One minor caveat: the depths of character that drive arresting monocultural films may prove hard to gauge in the intercultural context. For example, if we are not familiar with the culture, how are we to distinguish transcendent, extraordinary acts by Chinese from merely "being Chinese"? And one corollary: the further from our base of knowledge and experience a given portrayal is, ironically the more "real" it may seem and the more credulous we may be. Thus a light comedy about telling off our boss may pass as only stress-releasing fantasy—we know our own lives well enough to know we can't behave that way—but a fanciful portrayal of the unfamiliar may be taken literally.

A Few Caveats, and Many Strengths

If intercultural interplay drives many of the best films, it is equally true that film provides an extremely appropriate medium for the study of the intercultural experience. Film has the potential to effectively elicit a sense of the layered dimensions of culture, and thus of the inner as well as outward motivations of its members. Language and dialogue and the showcasing of social activity are especially, dramatically the province of film, as are the nature of hierarchy and the social structure, and the uses of work and leisure. These factors, among those which illuminate and define culture, appear even more salient when culture meets culture.[3]

Such critical areas as religion, mythology, and national self-image may also, however, be compellingly evoked through the medium with its strength in portraying the visual and symbolic, or in recreating the historical experience that grounds the present-day collective psyche (as in *Seven Years in Tibet* [1997], which also offers a rich visual presence to go with vague Western images of Tibet). As well, contrasts between myths and realities evident within and between societies may be effectively evoked (as in *The Mission* [1986], which contrasts Europeans' sixteenth-century dogma with their behavior in the New World).

If effective intercultural understanding means transcending stereotypes, exploring new facets of individuals and grasping experiences in their full context, then film stands out as a critically useful medium. It can make a sympathetic character of unlikely candidates, or give a fully human backdrop to an inhuman situation (as with the violent Geronimo and his fading Apaches in several film versions). Well-crafted film can give a sympathetic face to even those characters whose beliefs and behaviors are so different that the audience's empathy is difficult to achieve (from young Vietnamese and Cambodians in *Which Way Home?* [1990] to the Inuit in *Shadow of the Wolf* [1986]). The same qualities of film may serve to show both or multiple sides of conflicts that stem from divergent realities, effectively illustrating the distinct sets of perceptions.

Writing or teaching about cultural difference and film portrayals presents one special challenge: while the large, obvious differences are relatively easy to describe, subtler differences are harder to convey. Indeed, the literally and figuratively black and white differences are the stuff movies are made of—the racial divide in South Africa, the stark contrasts between Westerners and Japanese. Film will much more often portray the yawning chasms, and the sharply drawn conflicts, rather than the delicate differences between, say, U.S. American and Canadian thinking, or lingering East versus West German attitudes, or the subtly varying customs that French and Italians find appropriate in business and social settings. The subtler differences, if even understood by filmmakers, are difficult to bring to compelling life on screen. Nonetheless certain types of screenplay, especially the closely written comedy, may produce more stories at these delicate intersections in the future.

The key strength of the film medium, of course, is that it vividly depicts setting, action and immediate emotion, and as such film may convey the essence of characters in action and in interaction more clearly than their underlying philosophies, or what is sometimes called "cosmic view." If, as Marshall McLuhan suggested, the medium is itself the core of the message, film is more adept at portraying action than reflection, more suited to the portrayal of "doing" than of "being." Unfortunately, characters who represent being versus doing cultures may be reduced to more doing, with the "beingness" of their existence seriously underportrayed. The only inherent weakness of film may be its limited capacity for conveying the subtler, philosophical side of a culture. Nonetheless, several films set in the East such as *Beyond Rangoon* (1995) and *Seven Years in Tibet* strive hard, with some success, to elicit the contemplative, spiritual underpinnings of these cultures while telling lively, Western stories.

If the essence of experiencing relationships, and especially of experiencing an entire milieu, is being there, then film comes closer than most media in getting us there, or in giving us the *illusion* of being there. Therein lies the rub. The subjectivity of story, camera, and style in the medium has long demonstrated its unique power to create a reality apart. When the viewer is drawn into unfamiliar territory the potential for confusion between having been there and acquired sophistication, and merely having experienced the world apart created by the director, is significant.

The saving grace, however, resides in the power of film to compellingly engage our interests, to elicit emotional as well as intellectual responses across the range of human personality. Artfully and honestly crafted, film is probably as fine a medium as we have to portray cultures interacting with other cultures. Naturally partisans of other art forms, especially the novel, may rush to challenge such an eminence. In fact, many readers of *A Passage to India* (1924) or *Empire of the Sun* (1984), for example, may suffer disappointment with the film versions, albeit expertly crafted. No film of marketable length can render every observation, nuance, or line of dialogue in a full-bodied novel. Yet the high impact of film is such that a two-hour experience may more forcefully imprint a lasting understanding than the most masterful novel.

Film, on its surface, appears to offer its impact more artfully than intellectually. To derive the most from it the viewer clearly needs to go beyond the surface, to engage in critical or analytical thinking. Paradoxically a medium that permits the brain to idle in neutral, that can lull the critical senses to sleep, invites, even requires, the most thorough and challenging review. Film and its "data" are properly the subject of serious, reflective, qualitative research, and intercultural film offers the viewer almost limitless range of dialogue, gesture, and context as analytical grist.

Mental Focus

Intercultural analysis is ultimately, and almost infinitely, interdisciplinary—especially so in that each of its constituent fields is informed by several others. The Western-defined disciplines of communication, anthropology, psychology and social psychology, sociology, religion and cosmology, to name only the most obvious, enter into the analysis of exchange across cultures; film criticism calls into play many of those disciplines as well as literary studies and the technical qualities of the medium itself. The discussions in the following chapters will interact with these disciplines, but without resort to the highly theoretical debates among specialists, and remaining approachable for the generally educated reader. The real, practical world of intercultural interaction, as explored in film, remains the focus. Illuminating the wisdom embedded in the film stories, not the art form of film, is the primary goal.

One of the brightest lights of the modern study of culture, Edward T. Hall, has warned that though we have learned much about culture in recent generations, we still understand relatively little about the intersection of cultures. I focus here on that intersection. One common label for that focus is "intercultural communication," which defines narrowly at least my primary expertise and interest.

At first blush it might appear, then, that this analysis would manageably snap into a focus solely on communication, both verbal and nonverbal. "He said, his mother added, and his bride replied with that shrug of the shoulders so characteristic of her people," and so on. Would that any meaningful analysis might ever be so simple! The bare bones of communication between members of different cultures has meaning only in a larger context, the context provided by the ever widening concentric circles of family and extended family, by societal and historical realities as well as by the universal or "cosmic" view. When the chief Ten Bears reveals to Lieutenant Dunbar in *Dances with Wolves* (1990), "You are the only white man I have ever seen. I have studied you more than you know," his deceivingly bland comment springs from the knowledge that understanding of whites is essential for the survival of his people; more broadly, it resonates with the sense of conflict, confusion, and mystery that clouded Native and New American encounters for generations. When the Vietnamese girl insists to the protagonist of *Good Morning, Vietnam* (1988) that a female in her society and an American soldier cannot simply be friends ("No friends. No friends."), her resolve is rooted not only in the recent American and the longer-term presence of foreigners in her country, but also in basic mores and even in a Buddhist world view which accepts a grand order, often an immutable order, to human activity. When Katya in *The Russia House* (1991) suggests in halting English that dinner with a Western man would not be "convenient" she reveals more than a shared word for "convenient" and "appropriate" in Russian; she also reveals layers of delicacy for Russians openly engaging with foreigners. This study did not set out to specifically address historical and political factors, but they constitute a solid presence, like bones beneath flesh, in any intercultural exchange. To study the meeting of cultures is to study context.

Whose Point of View?

Clearly, films that depict intercultural interaction will never suffer from a lack of challenging perspectives. The messages conveyed by the setting itself constitute rich material, including both the physical architecture and the "cultural architecture" in play. The unique point of view of the director will manifest itself most obviously in choice of scenes, shaping of those scenes, even choice of camera techniques. Point of view is self-propagating: by mid-film a viewer's "point of view" has been established and is part of the equation thereafter. More broadly, the director's point of view includes historical setting, choice of underlying character in protagonists, and both the obvious and subtle turns in plot.

An illustrative case is *Dances with Wolves*, perhaps the most famous of the genuinely sympathetic treatments of the American Indian. Analysis may begin with the sharp break from the stock Westerns and their portrayal of heroism solely in white man's terms. But we note that the star of a film that aims to present the "horse-culture Lakota Sioux" is an Anglo, and his co-star a white woman adopted by Indians as a child. We are meant to engage, and do, with the Lakota, but upon close examination, Indians are on the screen a relatively small percentage of time without one of the white characters. Does the director consider us incapable of engaging primarily with the Lakota, even when so sympathetically depicted? And why do we not glimpse even a shred of humanity in the Pawnee? Does even a supposedly breakthrough Western need the traditional additive of "bad Indians" in its tank to fuel raw entertainment value? We can explore whether a story written by, produced by, directed by, and starring whites can ultimately achieve an empathetic treatment of Indians, and whether it convinces objective historians or Native Americans with roots in the plains Lakota culture. We may also focus on the aspects of tribal life featured—kids in mischief fearing parental rebuke, romantic gossip around the village—and wonder if the familiar has not been stressed to the exclusion of activities more difficult for the Anglo audience to relate to. We may examine whether the story squarely portrays frontier whites in contact with Lakota, or relies on the artifice of a bridge—a bicultural and bilingual white woman. We may even conclude that the drama engages less the meeting of European and indigenous cultures than the meeting of the New Americans with conditions of wilderness. The striking cinematography captures landscapes like paintings, but is it seen through "white" or "Indian"-conditioned eyes? The musical score leaves no doubt: it clearly brings a European symphonic majesty, not a sense of Native music, to the drama on the open plains. Nonetheless, much heartening communication does occur between Dunbar and the tribe. What lessons are to be learned, perhaps the efficacy of Dunbar's humility, his self-effacing mimes, his willingness to meet at least halfway? What does his final status as a pariah in his native society tell us, and what is the next "frontier" in white–Indian relations?

Even this brief sketch of analytical avenues should resoundingly make the point: film provides a gamut of perspective on human character within its cultural context, and myriad ways of viewing interactions. Each film is a prism, producing a colorful spectrum of messages—one small turn of the analytical wrist and strikingly different visions show through the kaleidoscope. No analysis of key scenes and possible interpretations could satisfy every analyst, nor should it: another interpreter, after carefully reviewing the same films, might choose to highlight substantially different content and overriding messages. That would only reinforce my core contention, that the intellectual resource holds almost unlimited depth and potential.

Objective Subjectivity

As the following chapters will reveal, this study is largely limited to Western although not exclusively North American popular films, most produced in the last quarter-century. It is in many ways also limited to Western perspectives, that is, to an analysis that is itself the product of Western conditioning. The irony may be bittersweet: an overarching truth which emerges from the study of intercultural interplay is the subjectivity of the cultural lens—all cultures tend to shape information and reality in at least slightly different ways—and by extension even the most sensitive and best intentioned analyses will succumb to some tendency to be of, by, and for a given cultural perspective.

The other trap of subjectivity lies in the materials for analysis, the films themselves. In overwhelming majority they are Western films, written, produced, and directed by Westerners who cannot totally transcend their cultural grounding, however elevated their intentions. Although discussion of the different clusters of film will revisit these issues, the broad-brush picture is one of Western protagonists as the locus of interest in intercultural films, and of stories told through primarily Western voices. Of course, the emphasis on Western characters has its redeeming features for Western viewers: establishing empathy with the culturally familiar character, in culturally unfamiliar circumstances, may provide them "safe" grounding from which they can withstand challenges to their own perspectives. *Good Morning, Vietnam* and *Forbidden Nights* (1990) broker empathy with Asian cultures to Western audiences, but do so through the medium of unusually sympathetic, homegrown Western central characters. *Havana* (1990) surely means to bring us closer to the Cuba of the revolution, but does so through a recognizable American type connecting with a beautiful European who in turn has married into local culture. The very fact that only a familiar protagonist can adequately engage the viewer speaks volumes—perhaps about our need to interpret new experiences through old acquaintances, perhaps about our ambivalence when faced with a different frame of mind, a different world view. It seems the more complex human dilemmas can be most comfortably confronted one step removed.

In the end sober analysis will compete not only with gut reactions but with the sense of delicious complexity that modern society itself exudes. The best films rise as not only critical human stories but fascinating visual and sonoric experiences; no one set of interpretations can encircle their artistic boundaries. They stand on their own not as "representations" but, at some level, as necessarily "real." Full of sound, image, and fury, but signifying what? What are we to make of Wayne Wang's strained, painful, yet ultimately engaging *Chinese Box* (1997)? With melancholy and tension, it celebrates the end of a famous marriage, that of China and England in a fabled land called Hong Kong, yet seems to turn away from politics to focus on the troubled, scarred lives of English and Chinese. It gives poignant focus to John's impending death from leukemia, yet suggests the parallel collapse of the old Hong Kong, doomed to its inevitable history, almost reducing John's fate to metaphor. Of three central characters, the male is British and the women Chinese, perhaps consistent with the colonial dynamic: the women, as less powerful, are necessarily receptive to offers of "business" and "romance." In fact both have had stints in prostitution. Is Hong Kong's relation with the West one of pimp and prostitute? Young Jean's face bears the self-inflicted scars born of frustrations and self-loathing. She moves through the city enigmatically, open to crowds and contact yet loath to reveal herself, all the while craving a genuine affection. One young Chinese woman, or the soul of a city-culture? The City takes on the aggregate personality of the residents, and they in turn become The City; everything is deeply personal, yet everything is deeply political as well. John engages his surroundings through journalism, almost an impassioned voyeurism, but in the end he proves sentimental about life and love in Hong Kong. His great unfulfilled longing, for the moody, complex and beautiful Vivian, whom he first met in Bejing, has a human resonance, but also geographical and political ones. As Vivian finally rejects the role of concubine for a wealthy, corrupt Chinese and seeks a new life after John's death, we develop an eerie yet exciting sense of Hong Kong on the verge.

These unpredictable yet patterned recipes of the best human stories on film have long provided both immediate pleasure and a slower, more intellectual digestion. Add the wild spice of the crossing of cultures and the product is even richer. The film critic, the university film course, and books of film analysis all have a useful place at the banquet.

Chapter One

"Poor Relations": North and South of the Border

"This isn't the real Mexico, you know that. All border towns bring out the worst in a country."

Touch of Evil

"Last time we visited the States you couldn't wait to get away. You hated the crassness, the complacency, the pace."

Sweet Country

"I don't know what this bullshit is about Parador and its sovereignty, but if it wasn't for the U.S.A. handing it over to your forebears back in 1890, there wouldn't be any goddamn Parador."

Moon Over Parador

The meeting of the North of the Border and South of the Border worlds clearly carries enormous implications, yet that meeting proves relatively invisible at least North of the Border in film, in other media, and in popular knowledge. Not only do the Americas share a hemisphere, but they share an intermeshed existence along economic and political, environmental and scientific axes. Immigration into North America has most steadily come from the South since the 1930s, North American foreign investment, technical expertise, and expatriates have flowed in the opposite direction. In many ways, the North American Free Trade Agreement (NAFTA) only codified a process well underway: the very gradual but very steady dissolving of national borders for the movement of goods, services, and people.

Many North Americans, excepting the select group who concentrate

15

on Latin American studies, know much less about the nations and peoples South of the Border than they do of, say, France, or Italy. Most striking is the U.S. American ignorance specifically of Mexico and things Mexican considering the shared history and 2,000 mile border, considering the more than significant numbers of "Mexican-Americans," considering the size and potential of a Mexican economy and a growing population, the third largest in the hemisphere. In the mid–1990s the NAFTA agreement, continuing concerns about immigration, a stunning currency devaluation in Mexico and unprecedented economic "aid" by the U.S., political change and ferment in both nations and especially turbulence in Mexico, including civil war and sensational political assassinations, all these factors should have placed Mexico at the center of attention and study North of the Border. In March 1994, presidential heir-apparent Luis Donaldo Colosio was shot down—an assassination virtually as charged with significance as that of John Kennedy in the U.S., yet one that received virtually no U.S. media coverage. Why the relative invisibility of Mexico North of the Border? The answer is at once as simple and as complex as the driving forces of cultural life on both sides of the divide.

The metaphor of "Poor Relations" represents the story of North meeting South of the Border: this triple entendre embodies all the aspects of the faulty connections between the neighbors. Not only have relations often been "poor" in terms of understanding, cooperation, and respect, but they have tended consistently to focus on the "poor," in economic, educational, and scientific terms, that is on "underdevelopment" South of the Border. The relations have rested on assumptions that rich and poor are not only quantifiable criteria, but are clearly the important criteria. And in a third, related meaning which borrows from colloquial American parlance, the North/South connection has too often been tinged by the mutual awkwardness, subtle guilt, patronizing, and unequal influence that characterize rich and "successful" family members interacting with what are called their "poor relations," their less successful cousins.

The tale of North and South as told in film and popular culture is thus the tale of these many-faceted "poor relations." One common reaction to poor cousins is to ignore their existence, or at least to think as little as possible about their way of life; another just as common reaction to rich cousins is to view them with a mixture of admiration and resentment.

Film mirrors and informs about the cultural relations of North and South of the Border on several levels: the Hollywood products are broadly consumed throughout Latin America (e.g., most films shown in Mexican theaters are U.S. American, in English, with subtitles), the relatively few Latin products are rarely shown in the U.S. and Canada, and films whose stories are located at the intersection of the two cultures are relatively few and far between. Elucidating North/South intercultural films, in fact, "brillan por su ausencia" in the Spanish phrase—they are surprisingly rare.

The absence of film stories at the intersection of North and South is all the more remarkable when compared to the black/white presence in films produced in the North. Notwithstanding the obvious problems of almost exclusively white control of multicultural stories (discussed in the chapter on multicultural film in the U.S.) literally hundreds of films at least *feature* blacks, most often as representatives of a world apart within a world, and in other instances as simply "black versions of whites," as with Denzel Washington's portrayal of the gratuitously black journalist in *The Pelican Brief* (1993) or his role as an officer in *Courage Under Fire* (1996). In an easily recognizable story line, virtually a genre of film, unlikely whites and blacks are fused by circumstances, such as the prisoner-bonding of *The Defiant Ones* (1958) and *The Shawshank Redemption* (1994) or the crime-solving of *In the Heat of the Night* (1967) or *48 Hours* (1982). Where are the parallel films featuring Hispanics? Films with black actors of comedic genius such as Whoopi Goldberg and Eddie Murphy manage to simultaneously poke fun at both the "whites" and "blacks," while giving intelligence and a certain wry dignity to their characters. Where are the parallel films featuring Hispanics? "Objectively," for a host of obvious reasons, a large group of equivalent films at the cusp of Anglo and Hispanic cultures should figure in the prolific trove of North American films. Both demographics and history suggest as substantial a place for Hispanic culture in North American film as for Afro-Americans.

The relative dearth of films is punctuated by at least a handful worth attention. In many instances, certain facets of quality have been as disappointing as the quantity of films. Even serious efforts to serve up "real" film stories of the North/South connection, such as *The Old Gringo* (1989) with Gregory Peck and Jane Fonda, suffer from that ever present corollary of ethnocentrism: one's own culture rates much more attention, much greater depth and clarity of portrayal than other cultures. Even here, the Mexican characters are much less developed than the Anglo ones, in spite of the absorbing story based on the Carlos Fuentes novel. In other cases, sensitive and mimetically accurate films such as *The Ballad of Gregorio Cortez* (1982) offer quite limited dialogue and range within their general plot. Not until the appearance of *El Norte* in 1983 would a truly sensitive, far-reaching U.S.-made film give polyvalent treatment to the cultural chasm between North and South of the Border, and as the 21st century begins only one other film of similar breadth, *My Family: Mi Familia* (1995), has emerged.

The pleasant problem in analysis of, for example, the Native and the New Americans in film, is the embarrassment of riches—the list of films discussed must be pared. North and South of the Border film suffers from a dearth of material, but locatable films do represent several historical as well as contemporary epochs, as well as diversity in geographical and human settings. The existing body of films can therefore elicit much worth discussing about the North and South cultures, the mind-sets, spirits, and gaps in communication behind the "poor relations."

While looking at the films themselves, a basic question may be posed and constantly reassessed: how truly different are the North and South of the Border worlds? Are Latins simply suntanned and soulful Anglos, and is the contrast really so "soft" as we may sometimes imagine? In the widest view, the two cultures have evolved from not entirely dissimilar Old World roots, are informed largely by Christian belief systems; the languages though distinct are mutually approachable with much shared vocabulary. The elites of both cultures (and along accessible borderlands the not so elite) have long ventured into each other's territory, have sent their children to the same colleges, and have seen them intermarry. As commerce, in the broadest sense, between the groups increases some observers project that the gap between cultural perceptions will further diminish. Yet all of these observations, while to some extent valid, fail to account for both the wide continuum of "Hispanic" individuals in this hemisphere and the apparent "otherness" that virtually all Hispanics experience vis-à-vis the mainstream U.S. and Canadian, essentially Anglo world, and their consequently heightened sense of pan–Hispanic identity.[1]

The social structure in Latin America appears to some casual observers a simple divide of classes—hordes of relatively dark, often indigenous-featured Latin Americans subsisting in lands ruled economically and politically by much smaller groups of relatively white, European-featured Latins. In fact stark differences between rich and poor, a chasm between elites and the powerless persists—Mexico for example has one of the largest economic gaps between rich and poor in the world. However, when the sheer variety of Latin persons, their background, education, sophistication, and role in society are considered, the crude image of an upper-crust versus teeming masses gives way to a more complex *continuum* of stratification. Intermarriage has rendered much of the population in most of the Latin societies "mestizo," or mixed blood, and it is not that unusual to see darker Latins in responsible positions, or light skinned Latins of modest means. Brazil, Mexico, and many of the other Latin countries conduct their own internal soul-searching and ongoing public debate, debates which themselves reflect diversity and plumb the ideal of a just multicultural society. For my purposes it is also noteworthy that the culturally Latin vary significantly in their conceptions of the "gringo" world: it is for some the unattainable land where (economic) life is surely an improvement; for Puerto Ricans and Border Mexicans, a place they may visit with relative ease and frequency; for others, the place where family members have worked at times and returned with mixed reviews; for certain elites, a place to educate the next generation while continuing to regard Anglo world values with some reservations. Astute observers of film will note not only this diversity, but a gamut of perceptions and customs both within Latin cultures themselves and between the North and South of the Border worlds.

The Myth of the Alamo

Poor relations tend to make for writing conspicuously poor history, and nothing in the popular film history of the North/South of the Border struggle would suggest otherwise. Even the mythologized Native American stories have carried more realism onto center stage, as the white filmmakers have begun to invite voices from the other side to speak, in their own languages. More rarely has anything so refreshing appeared in portrayals of Mexico or Latin America in old Westerns or tales of the Border.

In the film based on James Michener's *Texas* (1994), however, the principal Mexican character, Benito, gives at least some measure of dignified and authentic voice to the "original" Texans, the Mexicans of Spanish descent. Leaving aside the issue of the preexisting indigenous peoples, the portrayal gives body to the rootedness of Hispanics in what was clearly Mexican territory before the English-speaking settlers began an armed rebellion, the war for "Texas independence." The clash of cultures is inevitable, because as Mattie tells her lover, Benito, "we are so different. We are two different peoples," and because "there's something in (the Anglo people) that won't rest, won't lay still, that just has to keep pushing." The film also suggests the reasons why the cultures intermingled and inter-married—the proximity and availability of frontier spouses—and the prag-matic reasons why English-speaking men took Mexican wives to ease their legal immigration into the Texas territory. In spite of the interconnected-ness, the way of prejudice, mistrust, and hatred prevails. Typically, after a casual street clash with white ruffians, Benito is threatened with lynching, for nothing more than for being a non-submissive Mexican; he fends off the mob only with the help, of course, of the legendary Jim Bowie. Still, when we consider the legendary tendency of Texans to present their history in starkly heroic terms, in spite of real Western histories presenting a much more complex and equivocal picture, the film deserves both a measure of respect and a reviewing.[2]

Alamo (1960) with John Wayne likewise spins the tale of the emergence of Texas. As with *Texas*, *Alamo* gives a measure of flavor to Mexico. "I thought it was all sun-burnt," exclaims Jim Bowie, "but there's beautiful little valleys ringed by mountains, as pretty as you please." And the people "have, well, have a spirit for life." However, in *Alamo* the only starring role played by a "Mexican" is the romantic interest of Davy Crockett, although she does lend dignity to the Spanish roots and Mexican character of Texas territory. Predominantly, not only the stars but also the dialogue and cultural presumptions are "Anglo," in the tradition of Westerns and their U.S. American audiences. Indeed, historians have noted that Alamo movies in general and John Wayne's effort in particular develop story line and character with a liberty utterly unfettered by worries over fact. The names of the chief combatants are accurate, but virtually nothing else is. The Alamo as known in popular history, encouraged by film, is both myth and mystification: was there less dignity and valor in Mexican soldiers, marching hundreds of miles under difficult conditions, fighting insurgents in territory that indisputably belonged to Mexico? Significantly, such films represent history written by the ultimate victors, disguised as fact but largely displaying, as usual, the collective wish, fantasy, and self-serving legends of the dominant culture.[3]

The Ballad of Gregorio Cortez, based on a real story-turned-legend of enduring importance to Mexican-Americans in the region, also testifies to the power of the dominant culture to define. Set in Texas at the turn of the century, the plot turns on a crisis sparked by a simple linguistic misunderstanding: an Hispanic is guilty only of speaking Spanish more competently than the sheriff's "interpreter" before matters go sour. The tragic events and manhunt that ensue are simultaneously viewed through Anglo-culture eyes, with a massive, coordinated pursuit and the flame of public interest fanned by the "white" press, and through the elemental Hispanic perspective—a lone man on the run, afraid, without resources, with only the aid of other Hispanics who empathize with his plight. Especially key are scenes in which both parties to the conflict recall their version of the critical moments gone awry, scenes illustrating that ignorance of language and cultural detail can, and does, trigger the misunderstandings that escalate into warfare. This film may achieve greater resonance than either *Texas* or *The Alamo* for anyone trying to re-enter the day-to-day realities of historical relations between North and South, distanced as it is from names enshrined in household myth and from the style of "epic" drama.

The Turn of the Century and the Mexican Revolution

At the time of the Mexican Revolution, in *The Old Gringo*, a frustrated spinster and a disillusioned writer find themselves in the middle of the conflict in Northern Mexico. From a different world in every sense, the gringa searches for fresh experience as governess of the children of wealthy Mexicans. The experience becomes more novel than she might have imagined when the hacienda becomes a revolutionary target, and the insurgents, representing an indigent culture in ferment, become the persons with whom she must communicate and cope. In the middle even of a civil war, she fascinates many of the Mexicans. They wonder why she is there, away from the comfort and privilege of her home—they surely would not go to her country if it were poorer, less comfortable, alien, and unsafe.

The old gringo himself elicits the same questions, as forays without apparent reason into other cultures almost always do. If nothing could be more intracultural than a revolution, more steeped in meaning and emotion that only natives could comprehend, then nothing may seem more out of place than outsiders. "Why are you here?" asks the gringa when first meeting the old man. "Well, why not?," replies the man, a writer based on the career and character of Ambrose Bierce. He has turned away from a lifetime defined by literary meaning in search of a meaning not easily defined by his previous experience. The gringos and the Mexicans talk past one another throughout, attempting to communicate across vast spaces of unshared formative experiences.

The world of revolutionary Mexico vibrates with shifting symbols; charged with significance for example is the hacienda captured by the rebels, who stage what can only be described as a "revolutionary ball," an actual while also metaphorical party at the site of vanquished privilege. The new revolutionary "general," distracted by the spinster's presence, pursues her romantically, perhaps in part out of intercultural curiosity, perhaps as an expression of his fresh sense of power, of social place: he now can look eyeball to eyeball with persons of privilege, including North Americans.

Also spanning the years of the revolution is the Mexican—not Hollywood—*Like Water for Chocolate* (1992), an expressive, artfully magical journey through the history of a Northern Mexico family as told by a granddaughter. Just like *The Ballad of Gregorio Cortez*, it offers greater insight into indigenous character because its central narrative (despite wild and surreal subplots) follows personal and family upheavals rather than historically driven crises.

Within the almost exclusively intracultural Mexican story, the portrayal of an Anglo physician gives the film a spark of intercultural interest. Significantly, the kind and intelligent Anglo doctor qualifies as "almost" or "nearly" in every aspect: almost but not fully fluent in Spanish, nearly but not quite able to blend into local life, almost but not ultimately attractive to his Mexican love, sensitive enough to nearly, but not fully, understand the Mexican soul. He may well epitomize one special facet of the "poor relations": that even those persons who cross the cultural line with sincerity, who communicate without patronizing, are still "others," still apart from the mindset and spirit, from full assimilation into another culture.

Transplanted Roots: Hispanics Live the American Dream

Pleasantly difficult to categorize, *A Walk in The Clouds* (1995), set deep in California wine country at the end of World War II, features the highly acculturated Aragón family of Mexican ancestry. The arrival of a "gringo," however, underlines the Hispanic identity of the family patriarch and energizes intercultural tensions. A young Victoria Aragón, pregnant, alone, and terrified of telling her father, encounters traveling salesman Paul Sutton, just discharged from the Army. To help her avoid her father's wrath, Paul agrees to go home with her while playacting the role of husband; the interplay of cultures and contrasts begins. Not only gringo but orphan, a young man with no ancestral moorings encounters a family anchored in tradition; an itinerant, he meets a family literally rooted in their vineyards. In the Mexican perception to be an orphan is to be symbolically more gringo than gringo, that is, to be entirely without roots and from a society that has forgotten the importance of family. To be a salesman is to drift as gringos drift, always without purpose except that of earning money. Gringos are not just outsiders, they are a people who have always missed the point, who have never quite understood the core of Hispanic values, and soul. Although an outsider not only to family but to tradition as well, Paul is accepted by many in the family for the very reasons that define *la familia*: the one chosen as husband by the only daughter.

In contrast to those stock situations where the Hispanic must adjust to the dominant influence of Anglo culture, the Anglo here must adjust to the Hispanic. Unlike the cliché in which a poor Hispanic feels outclassed among wealthier Anglos, here a young Anglo without resources enters a financially established family. In contrast to the myth of indolence in Hispanics, here the family is industrious and success-oriented, with the new

Young Paul Sutton begins to share genuine rapport with Don Pedro, the patriarch of an Hispanic family deeply rooted in California wine country, in *A Walk in the Clouds* (1995).

generation attending first-rate universities; the young Anglo appears shiftless by comparison. The questions in the minds of family members center on the core values of their culture: will this young gringo make his commitment for a lifetime, recognizing the importance of *la familia*, and will he accept the importance of the roots, the traditions, the quality of what transpires here in this vineyard, here in this home? Fortunately, the gringo himself defies stereotypes, for while lacking antecedents, seemingly adrift, he speaks sincerely, from the heart.

Although at first *A Walk in the Clouds* appears to suffer from Hollywood-style departures from reality, it is made, as is *Like Water for Chocolate*, from the magical—a type of surreal license with which many a Mexican legend is forged. Viewed as a tale from the 1940s handed down within the family to the 1990s, the account becomes family history as morality play, the emotionally authentic if embroidered story of the family's transition and survival. A sense of fate, and of fall and redemption, is crucial to the core of the family, and only the Anglo who can intuit that sense can fully understand the underlying culture, and the emotions of those within it.

Roots, tradition, identity, and family are all powerfully invoked in the film aptly named *My Family, Mi Familia*. Although considered in the chapter on the Multicultural United States it is equally relevant to North and South of the Border film; its patriarch and matriarch carry the essence of their native Mexico with them into California. Just as the vineyards of the Aragón family are still Mexican territory culturally, the small, proud East Los Angeles home of José and Maria Sanchez resonates with the values of central Mexico. Much of California in fact *was* Mexico until a few decades before young Jose walked across a border that was merely "a line in the sand." It was less a matter of Mexicans crossing a border than of the Anglo culture creating a new border, with Mexicans expected to readjust to the new economy and values. Still, in a time when the political borders were still loose the ethnic borders were more sharply defined—few in José and Maria's generation intermarried with whites, for example. The barrios of each culture were self-contained, and Mexican-American homes placed a great importance on the family, Mexican and Catholic style, that did not invite mixing with the broader society. A later time, when two of the Sanchez offspring marry outside "La Raza," one to a white female law student and the other to—of all things—a former priest, signifies both a merging of the subculture into the American mainstream and a concomitant dilution of traditional values.

Across the Border in Contemporary Times

A handful of pure action and adventure films have chosen to illuminate the Border as a nexus for corruption and conflict: for example, the nakedly violent *American Justice* (1986), a primal tale of evil with Mexican prostitutes as chattel, and *The Border* (1981) with a similarly sordid theme but more depth and at least the outlines of an intercultural story. In focus are Anglo characters on the American side, at El Paso, and even though we don't come to know Mexicans as individuals, the poverty on the other side and the waves of misery and migration it produces constitute a presence throughout *The Border*. The white protagonist, a border guard, is played by Jack Nicholson, significantly in perhaps the least recognized role of his career. Although the film has cops, thieves, mystery, murder, earthy language and other ingredients of broad appeal we may wonder if the stark portrayals of Mexican poverty and the callused psychology of borderguard life played poorly at the box office. Depressing characters and bleakly serious issues have seldom paved the road to film profits.

El Norte (1983) may achieve as fine a portrayal of the complexities and pathos of several different worlds in contact as film has ever expressed. Without pretense or seeming effort, gracefully, it cuts through layers of culture, socio-economic strata, language and perceptual issues, and fundamental crises in values. It begins in the poorest backwater in which poor cousins exist, the near-servitude of campesino life in Guatemala. Crushing repression and the murders of their parents impel a young brother and sister on a journey north to the promised land, the United States. As they pass through Mexico we again see the relative nature of social status among Hispanics: the youths seek to conceal their identity as Guatemalans of indigenous descent, apparently one of the lowest levels of status in the Americas. To even the Mexican-American coyote who extracts money, both from the youths and from their future employers, for spiriting them across the border, they are "poor relations" seen more in economic than human terms. Their first attempt at crossing, unsuccessful, brought them into contact with the "migra," the immigration authorities, who typify the absence of empathy and of trust between peoples. The different cultures war with their wits, conditioned by their backgrounds: the migra's good training in Spanish proves useless in one telling scene when Enrique and Rosi, under the assault of close questioning, confer on strategy in their indigenous language. "They're speaking some Indian language, I can't pin them down," grumbles one officer. Suspecting that they should be deported to Guatemala but lacking hard evidence, he finally shrugs off the matter, deciding to simply toss them back across the border. "Who cares?" he asks, encapsulating the essence of much of the sentiment towards the "poor relations." At the border itself, honest communication proves almost nonexistent as a tense game is played, under the rules of the powerful. As in most contests between unequals the stakes are also unequal, one "illegal" more or less amounts to a shrug of the shoulders for the authorities but may be a matter of economic, even physical life-and-death to the immigrant. While some migra officers are reasonably sympathetic, their comments underscore their mental and social distance from the poor from the South—the officers come from, and represent, a different world.

When the youths, Enrique and Rosi, begin to attempt to establish themselves in Los Angeles the worlds apart, and the dealings between them, become even more revealing. Rosi, more marketable, perhaps due to the assumed complaisance of female workers, is whisked into a sweatshop, run by an immigrant Oriental, as layer upon layer of the multicultural U.S. is revealed. Enrique has no prospect for employment until a desperate restaurant owner discovers him by chance. Both monolinguals, he and the businessman negotiate by charades, a fitting metaphor for the "conversation des sourdes," conversation of the deaf, that characterizes this level of

As Guatemalan siblings Enrique and Rosi have finally reached the Promised Land, Enrique proudly sports his busboy attire for an upscale Los Angeles restaurant, in *El Norte* **(1983).**

"poor relations." Enrique realizes he is being offered a paying job only when the Anglo, needing an effective prop, flashes a twenty-dollar bill, both a concrete offer and symbol of the relationship, always economic in nature. Bussing tables in the upscale restaurant, Enrique begins to learn the shades of difference among Hispanics working in the U.S.; for example, he encounters a "Chicano" who speaks no Spanish yet is an underclass citizen. His parents were of Hispanic origin, Enrique is told, so "that's why he does the same shitwork we do."

Rosi meanwhile has survived a migra raid and met a kindly woman, Nacha, to show her the ropes in L.A. Nacha, suggesting that Rosi study English, stresses that the public classes are free, with no questions asked. In response to Rosi's quizzical look, Nacha expounds: "If you try to figure out gringos, you'll end up with a giant headache. They're nuts." Rosi's first experience of El Norte was the war zone created at the border to keep out immigrants; after running the gauntlet of the border and of migra raids she hears that the government itself provides free classes in English to help immigrants adjust, with no paperwork required to attend. What is she to think? In those classes an Asian-American leads the group through the paces of superficial daily phrases, the logical starting point but also a metaphor for the superficial contact common between immigrants and their new culture.

Beginning to clean homes with Nacha in a rich Anglo neighborhood, Rosi encounters the same polite but superficial interaction from a matron. "Oh, you speak English. That's wonderful." "Just a little, I am learning." As the working of high-tech home appliances is detailed, Nacha interjects from time to time, "No problem, Mrs. Rogers." "Please, call me Helen," is always the reply, well-intentioned but hardly bridging the gulf, as perceived by her Hispanic laborers, of hierarchy and privilege. Such scenes from *El Norte* suggest that while polite kindness is always welcome, it has minimal efficacy either for resolving fundamental strains in the socio-economic fabric or for deepening intercultural empathy. [4] The "poor relations" are only different in tone, but not in substance.

In contrast to the serious *El Norte* and *The Border, Born in East L.A.* with Cheech Marin (1987) follows the highly comedic, almost loony trail of a "Chicano" accidentally deported to Mexico, his adventures in Tijuana, and his struggles to return to the United States. While lighthearted, even mindless, the film actually achieves a compelling depiction of the seedy world of "The Border." In a U.S. immigration facility Rudy, the L.A.-born central character, attempts to explain the mistake to an arrogant, non-listening clerk. "I don't know where you learned to speak English so well," snarls the clerk, "and I don't really care," concluding that Rudy is an illegal with a phony story, that his presence in detainment and his brown-skinned appearance must outweigh any evidence to the contrary. The film reminds us that circumstances—such as Rudy being caught without his wallet at the site of a migra raid in L.A.—and appearances—Rudy is clearly not, say, of Scottish descent—are in fact the variables to which Hispanics often fall victim. At The Border everyone is a type, falls into a category, whether migra or coyote or illegal or tourist, and no one sees reason to particularly trust anyone else. South of the Border, Rudy, who speaks virtually no Spanish, rates as something of a curiosity, a peculiar species of gringo, while North of the Border he will be considered Hispanic. Identity, it seems, is relative. [5]

So are identities relative in *A Million to Juan* (1993), also cut from the cloth of broad comedy, here modeled on a short story by Mark Twain. The hapless protagonist, a sentimental widower and single father, is an illegal under pressure to establish grounds for a green card. As he deals with the underbelly of the economy and sharp class divisions within his own "Hispanic community" the gringo world appears in several guises. There is the quintessential slumlord, steeped in a self-justifying, circular prejudice: his bigotry facilitates an utterly callous response to tenants' needs and rights, while at the same time he detests his tenants' lifestyles, their degradation, to which he actively contributes. There is the migra as institution, given to burdensome rules and red tape at best, to threats and surprise raids at worst. The migra does show a very human individual face, however, through a warmhearted woman, a caseworker who becomes emotionally involved with Juan. Finally, the woman's boyfriend portrays the "gringo from hell," the consummately materialistic, impatient, insensitive, and unsentimental Anglo. His heavy-handed behavior—he even chases a troup of serenading Mariachi players away from his dinner table because they are distracting—would be the stuff of badly exaggerated stereotypes, were it not for the fact that so many culturally Hispanic persons experience just such an Anglo world.

These films exemplify a basic problem in attempting to dramatize significant issues. *The Border* and *El Norte* provide unblinking, largely grim portraits of underclass life South of the Border and the economic realities of immigrants, and especially *El Norte* ends with substantial pessimism. Although the viewer may respect honest realism, such films do not afford light, relaxing entertainment, while *Born in East L.A.* and *A Million to Juan* are more likely to be recommended to friends. In entertainment, laughter is more popular than gloom, but what if authenticity demands a dark portrayal, if there's no truly comic side, if introducing humor only distorts the evils at play, devalues the misery of real people? Some theorists contend that humor serves as a mental anodyne, a clever path to passivity.[6] Whatever the legitimate role of humor in relieving tension and diffusing guilt, comedy inevitably will emerge as a tool in the portrayal of intercultural mishaps. In fact, several films discussed here and several in almost all of the other chapters use the comedic angle heavily, and often quite successfully.

Away from the Border:
North America and Latin America in Film

In contrast to the works considered this far, a handful of films choose settings away from The Border and Mexico, deep in Central or South America or the Latin Caribbean. They bear the content, messages, and symbolism of the North American relationship with the smaller nations of the Latin world: stereotypes of "banana" politics, of instability, of mismatched values and institutions between the Latin and the Anglo worlds. Perhaps no film better captures this essence emblematically than Woody

Allen's highly unlikely comedy aptly entitled *Bananas* (1971). Though zanier and more frivolous than even standard Woody Allen fare, it actually sets the stage quite nicely for the study of North American stereotypes of Latin America. Its farcical portrayal of a fictional republic named San Marcos touches every imaginable chord, from political change by assassination to specious and self-serving rebel factions, from callous disregard for human rights to empty third-world economies. "What's the primary export of San Marcos?" asks someone in a political meeting. "Dysentery," quips the American character played by Allen. Latin politics and life are farce, at least as seen through North American eyes, as seen for example in the opening gambit: a political assassination staged as entertainment, covered by live television. Sportscaster and media icon Howard Cosell calls the "play-by-play" of the shooting. As he next makes his way through the crowd for a last interview with the expiring president, he expects people to "Make way, please. This is American television, American television." In this show all Latin characters, even dying presidents or rising dictators, are nothing more than stock characters or bit players, and the real stars are North Americans, beaming fame and wit, conducting themselves with the superiority that accompanies membership in the "superior" culture. Indeed, the importance of being "American" in Latin America is emphasized in numerous ways, from the plan to assassinate an American for news coverage and political fallout, to the Allen line that it's "illegal to harm an American without written permission from the State Department."

Such heavy-handed comedy as *Bananas* may pass in one sense as harmless fun, especially in the Woody Allen theater of the neurotic and absurd in which all human posturing is quickly deflated by impish burlesque. However harmless the tacit intent may have been, the tacit messages received by the audience do nothing to grow respect for Latin America, or by implication for the Third World. If back stateside no U.S. institutions are taken seriously either by Allen, if official diplomacy and courts of justice are treated with the same disdain as "banana republics," there is still the sense that the irreverence is aimed at a more advanced, if pompous and pretentious society. The Latin republic, however, seems especially easy to ridicule, almost coming pre-packaged in satirical form. Two years earlier *Viva, Max!* (1969) had made unadulterated farce of a fictional attempt to recapture the Alamo, with real cultural wounds salted by pure satire. And merely to view *Moon Over Parador* (1989), an equally farcical quasi-imitation of *Bananas* filmed some eighteen years later, is to encounter the enduring North American caricature of Latin society as not only corrupt but trivially, entertainingly so. The disparaging message of such films, perhaps unintended, is that an entire set of cultures may be dismissed as "bananas,"

Woody Allen plays Fielding Mellish, improbably drafted as president of a Central American republic, in *Bananas* (1971). Farce reigns in the fictional land of San Marcos, as U.S. characters represent wit, and Latino characters represent corruption or pomposity, or both.

quite nearly "nuts" in all their political and social practices, in a region where nothing functions well except satire.

If no one is serious in *Bananas*, no one is smiling in the group of films that meet war, torture, and human rights in Latin America face to face. The issues so glibly satirized in *Bananas* form the serious stuff of life, death, and dignity in the real Latin America, as *Missing* (1982), *Under Fire* (1983), *Sweet Country* (1986), *Salvador* (1985), *Diplomatic Immunity* (1991), and *Alsino and the Condor* (1982) make clear. In showing elemental issues up close, each film illuminates fundamentals in the character of Latin and North Americans, in one sense distorted by mayhem, yet in another sense highlighted more clearly.

Missing with Jack Lemmon and Sissy Spacek constitutes a modern political morality tale based on authentic, recent history (the death of Charles Horman in Chile at the time of the anti–Allende coup). While the nation was originally left unnamed "to protect the innocent and also to protect the film," the implication that the same bloody dynamic could have played out in a number of Latin American nations is powerful in its own right.[7]

Arguably, the film focuses totally inward on U.S. American culture in its plot, characters, and themes. Everything turns on the search for the son of a New York businessman, who disappeared during the chaos of the coup, and virtually everything revolves around the interactions of the expatriates, the sub-rosa military "advisors" to the coup, the diplomatic corps, the expatriate journalists' community, and the worried father. The cliché that "Americans," almost by some divine right, should be immune to foreign danger even when on foreign soil is amply exercised. "Don't worry," assures Charles with heavy, conscious irony in his voice just before his disappearance, "they can't hurt us. We're Americans." More broadly the film provides an excellent look at crossing cultural gulfs. Charles's father arrives from New York with more than just his physical baggage, he carries also the baggage of U.S. American assumptions at every turn. Most of his dealings are with other Americans, long-term residents of the Latin country, and even as he attempts to understand he remains the archetypal North of the Border personality trying to comprehend the ways of Latins. In a brief but telling moment he scolds his daughter-in-law for choosing to live in the Third World, seeming unable to grasp that she and Charles found meaning in the lifestyle of the country, and felt not expatriate but at home there. He nicely illustrates the overwhelming tendency to "think one's home culture" everywhere in the world: he sees everything through "Anglo" eyes, housing and food and politics, and even "truth," the pillar of his Christian Science faith.

In *Sweet Country* a melange of U.S. Americans, Canadians, and Chileans take their genuine emotions and political beliefs underground in the face of the military regime which assassinated Salvador Allende and moved quickly to harsh dictatorship. Though the film renders a flat, disappointing portrait of a copious subject, if nothing else it retains illustrative value. For example, American actor Randy Quaid, portraying a member of the local military police, affects so awkward a Chilean accent in English that his performance could have been intended, à la *Bananas*, as farce. The intent, however, like the real-life historical setting, was deadly serious. Quaid underscores the pitfall, even irony, of gross miscasting in intercultural film. Pretending that anyone with a phony accent can pass as a Chilean may injure more than aid the cause of knowing another society, and may even tacitly convey that the foreign "other" is really us, just talking oddly, and by extension thinking and acting a bit odd as well. Clearly a good start in educating the audience to the authentic "feel" of another culture would be to use native actors whenever practicable.

A spicy romantic triangle of Anglos anchors the human interest of *Under Fire* as U.S. journalists "cover" the Nicaraguan civil war of 1979. As in many intercultural films the potential for a rich portrayal of another society and its people goes largely ignored while the scriptwriters develop the North American characters, even if everything surrounding the U.S. Americans in Nicaragua is more important than they are, even more interesting. As with *Sweet Country*, these deficiencies hold illustrative value. *Under Fire* serves as well as a study of the behavior of foreign correspondents, who often display a detachment verging on arrogance that parallels the insensitivity of the rich toward the poor. Foreign journalists gather in their own clique, removed from the stories that they are paid to report to editors who are still further removed. "[Where's Managua?!] Get a map, Charlie," yells an frustrated correspondent in a phone call back to New York. Professional "impartiality" may legitimize the emotional and moral distance—"I don't take sides, I take pictures," Russell Price proclaims when asked about his sympathies in the war. But photos and especially news reports are essentially constructs, or at least they arise, indisputably, out of culturally informed perceptions and choices. As photojournalist Price snaps a wealth of provocative photos, the question is joined: through which "lens" are we seeing this? Indeed, the theme of divergent perspectives, complicated by the craft of public relations, is woven into the entire saga. U.S.-backed dictator Somoza sports a slick North American public relations hireling, available day and night to adjust the "spin" on events; the rebels for their part prep their charismatic but dead leader to look alive for one last photo opportunity. Where does the "spin" end and reality begin? However, the imported journalists do finally show a humane and vulnerable side, are in fact shaken out of professional detachment to engage events on several levels. After a U.S. star anchorman is senselessly killed and the international spotlight suddenly shines on Nicaragua, a native nurse dourly comments that "Fifty thousand Nicaraguans have died, now one Yankee. Perhaps now Americans will be outraged at what is happening here."

The insightful *Alsino and the Condor* shows similar facets of the political and military relationships North and South of the Border, with the added dimension of a Honduran central character whose authentic-seeming world opens to us through his youthful eyes. Not surprisingly, the film is a left-wing, Honduran production; if U.S. films overwhelmingly have white American protagonists, Latin films are likely to have Latin ones, in this case "Manuel." The boy, growing up in a world of political repression backed by a strong U.S. military presence, dreams of flying, literally, of escaping the fetters of his existence. The head U.S. military advisor in his region takes him "under his wing" for fatherly advice. "Study hard, and you could be like me. Flying in helicopters, flying." Advice as arrogant as it is well-intentioned, assuming that this boy from a different world will want to emulate the invader from the North, it captures the essence of the dynamic: the locals are expected to listen when U.S. Americans talk. Even more fundamentally, scenes such as these encapsulate the Anglo-European faith in literacy and discipline ("Study hard") as the predestined path to social progress, as steppingstones within a social order intrinsically superior to one grounded in oral, informal learning.

Interestingly and significantly this indigenous production does not strikingly differ from North American film in the "factual" portrayal of the conflict—we see the same callous military dictatorship assisted by U.S. "advisors," the same extermination of troublesome campesinos, the same disregard for the "human rights" that North Americans take for granted. Still, the brooding emotions of a youth provide a fresh perspective and tone. Though not widely distributed in North America, the home-grown *Alsino and the Condor* can be located on video—it is worth the effort to see the same grim story through an authentically indigenous lens.

Director Oliver Stone's *Salvador* exhibits not only the brutally candid style of its director but the bald realities of a Central American nation in torment. El Salvador indisputably experienced *the* Central American holocaust, but what will forever be debated was the role the United States played in the carnage. In such highly political films the U.S. appears inevitably as a force which may almost be called a political personality: an overbearing presence in the cause of stemming the Communist tide. At a more individual level, then, interaction takes place within the relatively confining and awkward framework of economic dominance and military "aid": Americans are not simply individual humans but are also their tanks, guns, and powerful political pressures incarnate. Yet Stone casts other North Americans and Europeans who represent the spectrum of possibilities in relating to a Third World country in agony. In contrast to the diplomatic and military personnel, a dedicated core of medical and human aid workers, some of them nuns and clerics, represents foreigners with altruistic motives. And a third component of the foreign presence, journalists, represents a theoretically neutral, objective presence.

The primary U.S. American character in *Salvador* is nicely and perhaps realistically presented as driven by multiple motives: Richard Boyle is, at one and the same time, a "tourist" looking for cheap thrills, a damaged soul hoping to heal himself again on foreign soil, a working photographer trying to make a living on pictures of death, and a sensitive human deeply affected by the blindness, hypocrisy, and carnage that surround him. Most humans, as complex mixtures of emotions and motives, become different persons in varying situations, and perhaps nothing is more distinct than experience in an alien setting, surrounded by suffering, pathos, and death. Thus the film scores points for realism, but perhaps more importantly has avoided the stock portrayal of "good" or "bad" gringos, of persons painted black or white. When Boyle shows boorish insensitivity one moment and courageous outspokenness the next, duplicity in one breath and tenderness the next, displays self-indulgence followed by a concern for the safety of others, we may wonder if Stone is not consciously encapsulating the contradictions of the "American" character. Boyle, for his part, elicits from Salvadorans the same complexity and diversity of reactions that North Americans abroad so often engender: mixtures of resentment and envy, admiration and disdain, distrust by some and instinctive trust by others.

In the end, the balance of relations as portrayed in *Salvador* is one of political, military, and economic dominance, as power steamrolling a less developed culture and subordinating human relationships to this goal. While acts of altruism are offered by persons who seem sensitive and sincere, they remain only points of light in the darkness.

As absorbing as *Salvador* may be, the Canadian *Diplomatic Immunity* rates as the best of all the films showing North Americans in Central America. It creates a complexly genuine range of Salvadoran as well as North American personalities, bringing an authentic life as well to the dilemmas, the moral or philosophical gray areas, of relations between vastly different worlds. The storyline pivots on the visit of Canadian official Kim Dades to San Salvador to review the progress of her nation's aid program, stymied by the politics of the military dictatorship, and on her alliance with Sara Roldán, a local woman from a wealthy family now working for campesino rights under the aegis of the Archdiocese. Kim is the well-intentioned Anglo culture and its huge "aid" agencies made flesh; her flat, dry personality seems to be a walking bureaucracy. "At the moment the compound is not working," she crisply asserts in assessing a central aid project. "My job is to make it work. I don't have much time." Words that invite caricature of Anglo administrators by Latinos, although Kim's openness at times to self-reflection and even self-effacing humor proves refreshing. She dangles more cash in front of Sara, a bribe for a cosmetic facade before an official Canadian tour of her program, until Sara finally demurs, "Money is not everything, Señorita." "Where I come from it's pretty close," Kim wryly replies.

Later, when Kim's frustration mounts, Sara feels called upon to suggest that she take all her "energy and determination"—"and desperation," adds Kim, "don't forget desperation"—"desperation, si ... suppose you put it in something you actually believe in?" In fact, the question of what the Anglo soul genuinely wants, what Anglos really believe in emerges in myriad ways, both subtle and explicit, in this North American self-examination. By no means, however, does Salvadoran society shine in idealized contrast: from cold military strongmen to confused peasants to the enigmatic, privileged Sara Roldán, the local society is not immune to contradiction. Sara points out that soldiers may have equivocal relationships to rebel villages, may in fact have women and babies there. "Like everything," she stresses, "it is not so simple." While images of violent despotism clearly emerge from the film so does the sense of existential complexity, a refreshing reminder similar to that encountered in *Salvador* that uncertainty is more realistic than stock moral conclusions, that shades of gray often provide more authentic tones than Technicolor.

Also out of Canada, set in Montreal, the quietly intelligent and richly worthwhile *A Paper Wedding* (1992) adds fresh insight through an old plot, as a Latin American immigrant in danger of deportation encounters a French-Canadian woman willing to engage in a sham marriage arranged to save him. When pressure from the authorities requires that they actually live under the same roof, Pablo Torres and Claire Rocheleau must confront each other's lives. He represents a Latin unfamiliar to many North Americans: although from a desperately poor background he rose to lead an intellectually rich life until it again turned grim under political repression in his home country. He was witness to and victim of unspeakable brutality and torture. Yet he is adaptable, because of portable, polyvalent strengths, maturity, and multilingual skills; he survives with some measure of dignity as a dish-washing expatriate in Canada. Claire, a middle-aged professor of social history, is fighting a sense of emptiness in what should be a fulfilling life, seeing a married man in a dead-end relationship. Their divergent backgrounds serve as meditations upon deeply seated cultural values as well as the outcomes of modern lives—do wealth and comfort produce happiness, does poverty or abuse prevent it? Does a rigorous classical education produce wisdom? Around the edges of the central story we receive glimpses as well of a modern Canada with multi-ethnic dilemmas and at times purely racist tendencies.

The underrated *Havana* (1990) with Robert Redford takes us offshore to the Cuba of the Revolution, the casinos and American dominance, the sense that "here anything is possible" colliding with an uprising in Latin political consciousness. The abundant gringos wear easily identifiable motives: they are in Havana for pleasure and self-indulgence. Their only interest in local people or national politics springs from the narrowest self-interest, a concern that life on the playground not be disturbed by annoying distractions, especially revolutions. "We invented Havana, and we can god-damn move it some place else if (Batista) can't control it," grates the gambling kingpin as Cuba begins to slip from the control of North Americans. Gambling, along with prostitution a leading Havana enterprise at the time, supplies the metaphor for a rootless and aimless culture, for exclusively quantifiable ends. Artistic camera work depicts the cards through a glass table as suspended, floating in air, as perhaps disembodied from earthier meaning and values. Communication between the expatriates and locals is limited in frequency and extremely limited in scope: "another drink, bar-tender" represents its typical content and sensitivity.

The romantic and intercultural tension of the film springs from the chance encounter of gambler Jack Weil with an upscale woman of European descent, now married to a wealthy left-wing Cuban, who risks her life to support the revolution. Jack shows not disdain but essentially bewilderment: why would someone jeopardize a comfortable life for such an ethereal and "low odds" bet as the dicey revolution at hand? "You are arrogant, Mr. Weil," she protests. "What do you really know about Cuba?" "Who's in charge, how to stay out of trouble. The same as I know about any place." "That's not enough," she replies, thus contesting the essence of North of the Border arrogance, the belief that the bare pragmatic facts about a people and their country are sufficient. At the end Jack Weil's core values and lifestyle remain unchanged, but meanwhile he has grappled with a set of meanings alien to the expatriates in Havana. He never understands the gulf, though, between himself and his Cuban-European love, never understands that facts and probabilities are simply "not enough."

Havana does break from a mold in which historical events, especially violent ones, dominate the screen. While Batista's atrocities and Castro's takeover do occur as we watch, the gamblers' politically amoral, self-indulgent world ironically allows more one-at-a-time human perspective. The portrayal of self-involved individuals reminds us that below the field of vision of dramatic events, Cuban life and its own personal dramas continue, that even revolutionaries as well as expatriate gamblers must dine and sleep, each in their own fashion.

Toward Conclusions

A quietly submerged question that virtually haunts this chapter asks reasons for the dearth of Hispanic/Anglo culture films—of Hispanic characters as central players, or visible players at all, in films produced for North American entertainment. Hispanics have proved relatively scarce, all but invisible, and were it not for the telegenic carnage of civil wars in Latin America and the smuggling of drugs and humans, the "North of the Border" world would scarcely be reminded by mass media that "South of the Border" existed at all. Yet beyond these sources for drama there are numerous others: U.S. Americans meet and marry Mexicans and other Latins in significant numbers, share business relations in myriad settings, meet on long-term sojourns in a host of others. More significantly still, Anglos now occupy and rule what was once the territory of Hispanic culture (Texas and much of the Southwestern U.S.) while the Hispanic presence is keenly felt deep in Anglo territory (major cities such as New York and Chicago).

Logically, North and South of the Border characters should interact often on the Big Screen. So active is the Latin influence in numerous parts of the United States that Spanish is increasingly referred to as the nation's unofficial second language, and legions of service workers (police, firefighters, social workers, public utility employees, and the like) are trained in at least rudimentary Spanish if not in the rudimentary cultural realities of their Latino clients. The language is by far the most commonly studied foreign language by Anglos in U.S. schools, ostensibly signifying their interest and preparedness to engage with Latin culture. The more closely the lack of feature film (and other media attention to the South of the Border society) is examined, the deeper the conundrum. For this chapter numerous persons with extensive knowledge of the film arts or Hispanic cultural issues, or both, were asked to explain the scarcity, in North American film, of portrayals of Hispanics and Anglos interacting: the response has usually been somewhat perplexed, ending in agreement that the question, though important, may have no easy answers.

The introductory chapter postulated that relatively dramatic differences invite portrayal, whereas subtler aspects may not so tellingly engage filmmakers nor so easily resonate with film audiences. If the collision of nakedly distinct and opposed entities draws crowds to the box office, then the clash of white and black South Africans, of war-painted Indians and uniformed troopers, or even of Nepalese guru and Western ingenue are the stuff of which "interesting" films are made. Occasional films set in the heart of Amish country in the U.S. also attest to the fascination with stark contrasts, as do the films set on today's Native American reservations. The clash that animates the Big Screen may rest on sharp ideological or religious differences rather than ethnic or linguistic or overt physical differences; many German victims of the Holocaust, for example, could have passed for non–Jews. If direct violence makes a lively, marketable substitute for differences of ethnicity and culture, there should be no dearth of film treating the historical (and present day) collision of Anglos and

Hispanics on the Border. Hispanic lore still declares that the old Texas Rangers all had Mexican blood … on their boots! Though the equivalent crushing boot of the white Southern sheriff has figured in scores of U.S. feature films that pivot on black/white conflict, the parallel Southwestern film is noticeably rare. In addition to the grim realism of *The Border*, only *The Ballad of Gregorio Cortez*, slow moving and intelligent but virtually unknown, likewise engaged prejudice, until the impressive *Lone Star* (1996) (discussed in the chapter on multicultural U.S. film) finally stepped into the obvious vacuum with clear artistic, even commercial success. It should not have taken so long. The near end of the continuum of the Hispanic world may blend, without clear seams, into the main fabric of North American life, but instances of sharp conflict and raw prejudice remain easy to locate. The relatively "soft" contrast of the Latino with the predominately Anglo culture of North America can thus only partially explain the paucity of film portrayals.

Obviously opinions will differ on how easily the Latin cultural world can be projected within the framework of film. The sheer breadth and diversity of "South of the Border" regions, peoples, and nationalities in some ways belies the convenient, catch-all rubric of "Latin America." Yet film, uniquely, can bring fresh dialogue and fresh hues of Technicolor to each story, can give in other words individual contours to individual character. As such, the diversity of "*Latino*" characters and settings provides a wider array of targets for film, and should result in more, not fewer, story lines centered on North/South interactions.

What's more, for all its diversity, Latino consciousness shows consistency not only across certain fundamental attitudes, but as well in certain reactions to the "gringo" world. Much evidence indicates that in the South of the Border consciousness at least, sensitivities to cultural differences persist which are important to the Hispanic sense of identity, dignity, and self-worth.[8] In early 1996, for example, both of the hemisphere-wide Hispanic television networks reported very pointedly on the study, conducted by La Raza (an Hispanic rights organization), establishing that Hispanics capture few, and usually undignified roles, in U.S. American television drama. Sensitivity toward anti–Hispanic prejudice, in fact, seems to be one of the few issues on which the huge and diverse Hispanic world unites— there is a pride in the language and the underlying identity it encourages. The sense of alienation and even distrust intertwined with the Latino experience of the Anglo world may be the most significant unifying feature of this body of films.

From even the limited body of film which depicts direct contact between the cultures (and characterizations of one culture by members of

the other) it is clear that the people involved perceive fundamental
differences. Most often each side has perceived its own culture as superior,
the other as at least slightly odd. (Perceptions of "otherness" are almost by
definition unflattering, at all times and in all places.) "I was always afraid
of the unknown," says the gringa in the midst of her astounding experiences in Mexico in *The Old Gringo*. "Whenever my mother said someone
was "different" what she really meant to say was 'worse.'" Seldom are the
fundamental differences painted starkly, but hostile and perhaps accurate
perceptions become manifest in behavior or idiom. In *Mi Familia*, for example, we never hear directly from the "old Californian" how he perceives the
dominant culture, but his wish to be buried in his own backyard, his wanting nothing to do with the "pinche" Anglo system around him, speaks
clearly, with a message as eternal as his resting place. In *El Norte* the kindly
Nacha's remark that trying to think like gringos assures headache is meant
to bring a smile to the person who identifies as Hispanic, who will generally resonate to the slighting remark, even if examples of "nutty" Anglo
behavior would vary widely. In turn, the Anglo take on South of the Border may be openly derisive or may deal the subtlest snub of all—simply
ignoring ambient culture, treating Hispanics as if they were virtually invisible, of treating their territory as merely a place to escape boredom and
receive services through superficial tourism or expatriate life. The gamblers in *Havana* don't noticeably dislike Cuban culture, if only because
they have no interest in or experience of it; for example, they show no sense
of feeling that they are missing anything at all by not speaking Spanish.
The invisibility of the culture to them becomes their form of disparaging
comment about it.

In virtually all the films in this category, economic relationships drive
the interaction between North and South of the Border personalities and
conversations center on economic arrangements or other points of pragmatic contact: law enforcement or basic services such as medical care. Even
when the South had moved North, occupying large portions of American
cities, such as East Los Angeles, the relationship remained essentially
unchanged. The actual and symbolic bridge in *Mi Familia* was a conduit
for the Hispanics to meet economic needs in the Anglo's territory and on
the Anglo's terms, but the narrator pointedly reminds us that the Anglos
never came East, to visit the barrios. The Hispanic's journey into Anglo
territory might lead to a gradually deepening interaction, but always within
the context and parameters of the economic relationship. Only when Salvadoran Isabel disappears from work does her employer discover the truth
about her delicate immigrant status; later when Isabel, settled and married, becomes pregnant, her employer's friend observes that pregnancy

always follows an investment in a maid. "I'm happy for her!" is the reply. "She's been with us for three years. She's a member of the family." Perhaps. If so, as in many dysfunctional families, the deepest issues rarely surface into open dialogue while issues of co-dependence carry the relationship. The dependence may indeed become mutual—in many regions the dominant economy has grown dependent on the labor of the Hispanics—but the power, the center of the relationship gravitates clearly to the Anglo side. Few conversations occur which are not at least subtly based on the dominant society's terms, anchored in the Anglo sense of what is important, and conducted in the English language. In fact, almost no *intercultural* conversations in these films occur in Spanish: Hispanics are expected to master English well enough to sustain conversation, but not the other way around. A device of English language film, perhaps, but suggestive of real life dynamics as well.

Egregiously absent in these films is dialogue between North and South about issues at the core of their cultures, such as religion or family values, about the impact of music or poetry, or about dreams and aspirations. Both parties would find such probing, honest exchange awkward, because tacitly the understanding is clear: their relationship is not intended to be profound, or even sincere, nor will it ever really be permanent; it is a relationship of convenience.

Somewhat ironically, two films which may lack award-winning quality, or portrayals notable for verisimilitude, supply a prosaically effective level of interaction, interaction not driven by economic imperatives or police contact. In *A Walk in the Clouds* and *The Old Gringo* personal quandaries and what may even be called spiritual quests bring Anglos into contact with South of the Border characters. *A Walk in the Clouds* represents a striking departure in that issues of family, honor, and tradition are not only prominent but constitute the very brick and mortar with which the melodrama is built. A young gringo is morally on trial not as the patron with power over poor Hispanics, but as someone untried and unproven by the standards of the traditional Latino. Hispanics (especially the patriarch and other males) have more than authentic visibility here, they have the dignity and power derived from deep economic and spiritual roots.

Economic ties are as essentially absent between the characters in *The Old Gringo* as they are conspicuously present in most other North/South films. The old gringo and somewhat younger gringa come to Mexico by a sort of default: both have lost respect for their previous lives, and they have drifted, vaguely searching for something to live for, into the actual as well as symbolic deserts of northern Mexico. They arrive empty into the new culture as lost and eccentric representatives of their own; the old gringo, a disillusioned writer, sums up his presence by declaring that dying in the middle of the Revolution would not be a terrible end, and would in fact be better than the alternatives, such as disease or old age. The most fundamental, though unspoken, questions raised by the gringos' encounter with Mexicans are powerful: "Who are you, and what about your life and spirit brought you here?" on the one side, and "Who are you, so secure in your sense of place, when I have none?" on the other.[9] While the film may partially answer the first question through rich portrayal of its most expressive character, the most telling ways in which an artist might engage another culture are drowned by the nihilistic impulses of the writer and by the war. Regrettably, *The Old Gringo* never explores the Mexican character in sufficient depth to answer the second question, but the film, like life itself, may be forgiven some loss of focus in the face of the horrors of war.

Even as thoughtful sojourners, the gringa and old gringo manifestly search to fill needs, they imply unspoken desperation, and thus they may be seen to come for services, for the needs of self, little differently from the tourist, or the carpetbagger. The old gringo, especially, is drawn more to Mexico as a backdrop against which to reject his old life and chase the shadows of his soul than he is to an in-depth encounter with Mexican experience and thinking. Honest assessment of his motives at least helps to illuminate personal, even national character. His resulting experience, while certainly not superficial, is certainly not informed by a deliberate and genuine mutual respect—a reminder, again, that only a level playing field can elicit the interaction of equals.

The Future of North/South of the Border in Film

In *Clear and Present Danger* (1994) American star Harrison Ford is the honorable man in the middle as his government behaves both ignorantly and corruptly in a covert military campaign against Colombian drug smuggling. A well-oiled, closely crafted "action movie" in quintessential Hollywood style, it nicely serves to pose several questions about the political and social messages of our successfully commercial films. Here the CIA on the orders of its ultimate boss, the President, engages in illicit operations while lying to a duly elected body, the United States Congress. But do even the films that seem to impugn core American institutions imply, in their characters and imagery, that our systems are superior, if sometimes flawed, while the foreign systems are the truly dangerous and corrupt? Pitted against a headstrong President and a duplicitous CIA are

Latinos no less villainous than Ernesto Escobedo, a thinly veiled reincarnation of real-life drug kingpin Pablo Escobar, along with a Cuban whose "intelligence" services are for sale to the highest bidder. Which is the "clear and present danger," a superpower so strong, and self-assured, that even its covert military arm can change the political landscape of other sovereign nations, or Colombia, where the drug-smuggling economy is portrayed as out of control, a runaway social-political virus menacing the world at large? Is the real danger, ever present but clear only to analytical eyes, a depiction of Colombians who are either cornucopias of illicit wealth, ignorant tools of the rich, or cogs in a military machine? Where are the Colombians who work honestly at administrative jobs, provide medical services, sell fresh produce at corner stores, practice law ethically, or teach in colleges? The U.S. Americans are humanized by Jack Ryan's wife and children, by Admiral Greer's cancer, even by the President's horror at the murder of his friend by cartel thugs. Instead of equivalently rounded lives and emotions for the Colombians, they are cold, calculating "Orientals" of a different continent and ethnic appearance but with much the same unidimensionality (interestingly, even the U.S. Hispanic soldiers sent in the covert operation are not developed as humans, although depicted more sympathetically than the Colombians).

The tendency to use the culturally "other" for caricature or as props in popular stories and morality plays is perennial; undoubtedly it precedes recorded history. Even as sensitivity makes baby steps of progress we may fairly wonder if the future of North American film will offer many more such portrayals of South of The Border peoples. The film industry—with enormous investor capital at risk—functions of course as industry first, with art or social science a weak second. The temptation to slouch into successful formula for one more profitable venture will surely persist, and that formula generally casts the culturally familiar as "us," and the culturally different as "them," with all that dichotomy entails.

Yet there is reason to believe that other, more sensitive films will also reach the mass viewing audience. With hundreds of feature-length productions each year from North America alone, competing against myriad entertainment options for the jaded audience, commercial film needs fresh material—around the edges of predictable plots—to keep the sense of novelty keen. Between 1995 and 1997 film producers awoke, as if from Rip Van Winkle's sleep, and released the soap opera *Mi Familia*, the murder mystery *Lone Star*, the romantic comedy *Fools Rush In*, and the biographical *Selena*, all set squarely in Multicultural America and radiating implications for North and South of the Border film. Entertaining stories *can* be told while giving full-bodied character to Hispanics as they conduct their

daily lives. Not only do film directors need fresh, lively twists to old for-
mulas; issues characteristic of Latin life, both traditional and contemporary, hold the emotional and dramatic raw material from which arresting
film stories are made. To watch even a single episode of some "Telenov-
ela"—Latin-world soap opera—should make clear the potential of bringing Latin lives into predominantly Anglo-world entertainment. After the
appropriate translations of language and culture the Mexican, Venezuelan,
or Argentinian soap opera emerges as an animated first cousin of its North
American counterpart: romance and betrayal, pregnancy and childbirth,
wealth and intrigue, gossip and conspiracy, pride and hubris combine to
give constant emotional force to the immensely popular programs. And to
engage with classic Latin-world film and even literature is to encounter a
realm rich in legend, myth, martial conflict, "magic realism," and flights
of the fanciful, the surreal. American film achieved success with the melodramatic *Terms of Endearment* (1983) and the surreal *Back to the Future*
(1985), to name two deftly executed examples of their genres. It is easy to
envision North/South of the Border versions of these films, with Latino
characters sharing the stage with Anglos, bringing the extra sparks of
differing mind-sets and experiences to the Big Screen. Traditional Latin
culture carries its own brand of love/hate relationship with mortality, for
example, that might freshly sculpt the tragedy of a young mother's death
from cancer; likewise, that culture recognizes the past as a dynamic, tangible part of the present, giving Latin story lines a natural connection with
the phenomenon of time warp. The modern, Robin Hood-like tale of *Bonnie and Clyde* (1967), the domestic abuse of *The Burning Bed* (1984), even
the classic travel fantasy *Around the World in 80 Days* (1956) could all be
reminted with Latin emphasis, with Latino stars as central players. The
"popular outlaw" has his own meaning in the historical consciousness of
many Latin cultures, and the anguish of domestic violence is ripe for recasting within Latino values. The Mexican superstar Cantinflas did share the
spotlight in *Around the World in 80 Days*, but in a less than dignified, modern posture. Even apart from the issues of fairness and accuracy, the artistic imperative is clear—Latin characters have more to offer as norm-setting
stars than as wooden caricatures.

Often, the simplest social activities, such as informal conversation,
reveal differences that can play well upon the screen. For example, many
U.S. Americans have grown used to making "small talk" in their daily interplay, often peppered with clichés such as "how was your weekend?" or
"how's the family?" Before business meetings, for example, such casual talk
often serves as a prelude to the main event, the "important matters." Matters of family, to many Hispanic peoples, *are* the main event, the matters

of importance. These and other contrasts could clearly emerge from the screen to escapsulate North and South of the Border values and the emotional or perceptual differences which still often lead to "poor relations."

In the social sciences masterworks that examine differing cultural moorings, authorities such as Diaz-Guerrero have noted intriguing (if sometimes subtle) distinctions between Anglo and Latin norms for family, childrearing, love, sex, friendship, unity, trust, religion, morality, shame, education, work, accomplishment, community, society, government, politics, ethnicity, and national image.[10] What story lines could not be cleverly crafted around the seams of these contrasts, what story would not be leavened by Latino lives that have crossed with those of Anglos?

Filmography

Film (aka), year, country (language), director, producer/distributor, minutes

Alambrista!, 1975, USA, Robert M. Young, Filmhaus, 110
Alamo, 1960, USA, John Wayne, United Artists, 161
Alsino and the Condor, 1982, Nicaragua (sp.), Miguel Littin, Pacific Arts, 89
American Justice (*Jackals*), 1986, USA, Gary Grillo, TMS Pictures, 87
The Assignment, 1977, Sweden, Mats Arehn, SFA Film, 94
The Ballad of Gregorio Cortez, 1982, USA, Robert M. Young, Embassy Pictures, 104
Bananas, 1971, USA, Woody Allen, MGM, 82
The Border, 1981, USA, Tony Richardson, Universal Pictures, 109
Borderline, 1980, USA, Jerrald Freedman, Associated Film, 97
Born in East L.A., 1987, USA, Cheech Marin, Universal Pictures, 87
Clear and Present Danger, 1994, USA, Phillip Noyce, Paramount, 141
Cuba, 1979, USA, Richard Lester, United Artists, 122
Diplomatic Immunity, 1991, Canada, Sturla Gunnarsson, Metropolis MP, 96
Havana, 1990, USA, Sydney Pollack, Universal Pictures, 140
Latino, 1985, USA, Haskell Wexler, Lucasfilm, 108
Like Water for Chocolate, 1992, Mexico (sp.), Alfonso Arau, Miramax, 123
A Million to Juan, 1993, USA, Paul Rodriguez, Turner Home Entertainment, 97
Missing, 1982, USA, Costa-Gavras, Universal Pictures, 122
Moon Over Parador, 1989, USA, Paul Mazursky, Universal Pictures, 96
El Norte, 1983, USA, Gregory Nava, Artisan Entertainment, 139
The Old Gringo, 1989, USA, Luis Puenzo, Columbia Pictures, 119
A Paper Wedding, 1992, TV, Canada (fr.), Michel Brault, TV-Films Associés, 95
Salvador, 1985, Salvador/USA, Oliver Stone, Hemdale Film, 123
The Shrimp on the Barbie, 1990, USA, Alan Smithee, Unity Pictures, 90
Sweet Country, 1986, UK, Michael Cacoyannis, Cinema Group, 143
Texas, 1994, TV, USA, Richard Lang, ABC, 180
Three Amigos!, 1986, USA, John Landis, Orion Pictures, 115
Touch of Evil, 1958, USA, Orson Welles, Universal Pictures, 105

Traffic, 2000, USA, Steven Soderbergh, USA Films, 147
Under Fire, 1983, USA, Roger Spottiswoode, Orion Pictures, 135
Viva Max!, 1969, USA, Jerry Paris, Commonwealth United, 93
A Walk in the Clouds, 1995, USA, Alfonso Arau, 20th Century–Fox, 102
Walker, 1987, USA, Alex Cox, Northern Distribution Partners, 95

Chapter Two

Untranslatable Languages: Japan Meets the West

"Japanese way—shut up and take it."
"(American) way, me, me, me."

Mr. Baseball

"Wait a minute. Now there are some things here I don't understand."
"Yes."

Rising Sun

"Why do you have to be so Japanese about everything?"

Tokyo Pop

"He's got no right to that land.... That's American land, and it's gonna stay that way."

Samurai Cowboy

"Yes, I am a Christian. But first I am Japanese."

Shogun

The meeting of the Land of the Rising Sun with the Occident, over the last four and a half centuries, has touched deep chords of interest on both sides of the cultural gulf. It has been both like and unlike the meeting of China and the West. Japan, the Great Britain of the Orient, grew from small islands to world power, developing an organized, disciplined culture with a keen sense of particularity, superiority, and destiny. Japan connecting with the major Western nations represents the meeting of counterparts, the meeting of the "most successful" manifestation of Eastern culture contrasted with the parallel successes of the West. Its economic strength has made its interplay with the West inevitable. Yet, like the rest of the Orient, Japan is a world apart, at a huge distance from the West in geography, history, religion, language, mores, living conditions, even food. In a media, commercial, even retail age in which the season's clothing fashion may pass for culture, similarities are often seized upon and differences missed, as Edwin O. Reischauer stressed repeatedly in his magisterial work on Japan.[1] Japanese postwar enthusiasm for baseball, the game or the paraphernalia, by no means makes them less Japanese.

Among those who study the intersection of the Japanese with the world outside their island, it has become commonplace to observe their often extreme ambivalence about other cultures.[2] At once fascinated and leery, intrigued and repelled, they are often seen as torn between an accepting, outward looking and defensive, inward turning posture. It may be equally true that the West is ambivalent about Japan, that a love/hate relationship perhaps better characterized as respect/distrust or fascination/disdain also prevails in popular American or European thinking. Throughout Western popular culture, images of Japan as inviting while also alien abound in the novel, the mass media, humor and popular conversation.

The ambivalence is manifest not only in the wide assortment of Japan-West films, but within a number of the films themselves. In the last analysis, Westerners often don't know quite what to do with, quite what to make of Japan. Just as the Japanese appropriate attractive Western products, technologies, and even a handful of customs, while remaining resolutely, definitively "Japanese" in the process, U.S. Americans have tried repeatedly to dissect the Japanese industrial miracle and adapt Japanese wisdom to the U.S. economy, all the while remaining an almost infinite distance from the cultural essence of Japan. So different are the two cultures in their antecedents and moorings, social tones and meanings, that they may seem at times to speak in untranslatable, irreconcilable languages, making a true meeting of the minds extremely difficult. (Even the phrase "extremely difficult" has one "straightforward" meaning when used in the U.S. American world and quite another in English as spoken by Japanese in formal settings, where it is likely to be a diplomatic way of saying "completely impossible." The imperatives of one society require elaborate nuancing of unwelcome messages, while the other supposedly reveres the "candor" of literal meanings.)

Such nearly impenetrable differences are probably at the root of the predictable tendency to slump into the crudest of stereotypes. Popular Japanese images of Westerners are traditionally less than flattering or subtle while Western images of the Japanese have depicted inscrutable, perhaps treacherous beings well before and after the troubled period of World War II. In the particularly coarse genre of karate or "kung-fu" movies, Japanese have shared with other Oriental males the roles of cold, fighting creatures without names, or individual identities, reduced to their supposed core: tough, cal-culating, relentless. Even in slightly more elevated North American fiction and film, the Japanese have been not unlike a hi-tech and exotic version of war-painted Indians or a politically neutral version of scheming, Cold-War Russians. An authentic portrayal of Japanese *people* engaging life and inter-acting as individuals has been rare, until recently nonexistent in Western film, for a number of reasons. Japanese, like many other foreigners, have most often opposed Westerners in military, diplomatic, or economic arenas, and pointed conflict with representatives of another culture blunts the three-dimensionality of individuals. Additionally, the Western film is generally, by definition, made by Westerners, and even capable writers and directors have rarely been intimately acquainted with Japanese subtleties. The cul-tural consultant on a film site is a relatively new and, until recently, rare phe-nomenon. The common denominator audience, presumably, more easily relates to stock Japanese characters than the nuances of real ones.

In spite of or perhaps because of the great distance between the cul-tures, a surprising number of full-length feature films in recent years have been set squarely at the meeting of the two worlds. In fact, almost as many North American films focus upon Japan as focus upon the whole of the Latin American world (and outnumber those addressing the Arab world). If we immediately accept the economic explanation—Japanese "intrusion" into North American economic life—we must remember that Arab oil is central to Western economies and that Latin America is economically intertwined with North America. Clearly, other dimensions are at play. Beyond its worldwide importance as an economic dynamo, Japan has the power to fascinate and frighten, to simultaneously draw and repel, and to intrigue. Films centered on Japan or Japanese characters can not only make use of conflict but of the subtler forms of "inscrutability," of the complex-ity, quiet drama, and mystery of Japanese culture. "I've been living in this country for seven years and I still can't read the headlines," warns an expa-triate bartender in *Black Rain* (1988). "Yes means no, maybe means never...." Even relatively simple interchange may then resonate with fas-cination and tension, suggesting that the common film viewer does have a capacity for enjoying crossed perceptions, for at least vicariously explor-ing the distinct styles of differing cultures.

First Encounters and War

The interface of Japan and the West begins with the late sixteenth century "discovery" of Japan by Portuguese and English mariners. Based on James Clavell's novel, the *Shogun* (1980) epic about the first meeting of the cultures was not created as a feature film but rather a U.S. television miniseries, still available on video. It has informally but significantly influenced the education of U.S. Americans, as well as other Westerners, about pre-modern Japan.

To watch the complete *Shogun* story is not only to invest numerous hours in an absorbing historical "romance," but also to engage in intercultural observations through setting, color, context, language, and subtle comportment. Ironically, Westerners know so little about Japanese history that, unlike for *Texas* or *The Alamo*, they bring here no distracting loyalties about personages or factions supplying the dynamics of plot and are happy to accept *Shogun* as exotica. Its very glitzy, stardust surface serves an important purpose—to help hold attention in the midst of complexity, both in plot and multi-layered interactions; the tinsel of the inauthentic helps to command attention to the authentic. *Shogun* also serves as the most outstanding example of a notable phenomenon: in many Japanese-Western films the speech of Japanese characters is not translated, is not given subtitles. Is there an ethnocentrism that considers the precise words of Japanese characters as unimportant, or a sophistication that recognizes the difficulty of "precise" subtitled renderings for the communication of so different a culture? Or does the strong body and situational language in numerous scenes simply render a more powerful message without the distraction of printed words? Whatever the explanation, the incidence of such films is striking. Virtually all the films considered in this chapter use direct, unmediated Japanese speech in at least some contexts and some use it extensively.

Shogun begins where the first meetings of all cultures begin, with bewilderment and an inability to communicate. The shipwrecked English captain, John Blackthorne, must learn the world around him by observation, like a child, allowing the audience to do the same. The slow, deliberate pace and remarkably generous segments of spoken Japanese permit, in fact demand, that a Western observer focus closely on the core element in all communication: context.

One of Blackthorne's first lessons in his new environment demonstrates the importance of respect for authority, as a local official urinates on him for showing defiance. Absent are the modern give and take, the art of negotiation, because the concept of meeting the other culture part-way lay centuries in the future, especially for isolated Japan. *Shogun* features intercultural contact raw and unrehearsed, as Blackthorne attempts to comprehend and cope with his new surroundings. Naturally his Western socialization is his starting point; not surprisingly, through much of the story he is the forerunner of the textbook "gaijin" (a foreigner): too direct in his manner, insensitive to context, lacking in the proper deference and social graces. And perhaps predictably in a script written for Western consumption, Blackthorne's vices are dramatic virtues, as when he insists on his radically unconventional romance with Lady Toda. Bilingual informants, such as a Portuguese captain who observes that "everything in this bloody country's upside down," anticipate the Western take on the East across the coming centuries, even anticipate the myth of inscrutability. "You'll never tell with the Japos. They're all six-faced and three-hearted." The sensitive and soft-spoken Lady Toda insists that the visitor accept the utterly new environment as a given, immutable: "In Japan, there are only Japanese ways."

The structured formality of sixteenth-century Japanese culture is striking to Western eyes, while the surrounding social and political context is extremely rich. It is twice removed from current Western sensibilities, once by culture and equally by the distance of four centuries, leading to the question of the film's relevance to understanding contemporary Japan. Yet even across such time and space, echoes of the perennial intricacies of Japanese social forms may be heard. If nothing else, the initiate viewer should gain some sense of the dramatic weight of interactions within Japanese society as well as the difficulties in smoothly melding the Western and Eastern styles.[3]

Empire of the Sun (1987), perhaps one of the subtler, more sensitive films set in war time, amid the uncertainty and turbulence of Shanghai during World War Two, involves interaction and conflict among British, American, Chinese and Japanese. Again, powerful scenes in Japanese without subtitles convey meaning through dramatic context and body language. Far from patronizing its audience, the film expects and requires active, alert viewing, and numerous scenes are artfully ambiguous yet accurate snapshots of intercultural life as well.

The action is seen through the eyes of a young boy who had lived with his upper-class parents in the British enclave of Shanghai, with Chinese servants, until the Japanese invasion turned the city into chaos. An effective early scene depicts the family, attempting to escape the city in their chauffeured auto, looking out through their glass cocoon at the faces of fear, bewilderment, poverty, and resentment that epitomized occupied China. Then suddenly, in the chaos of the streets, their car is hit by a Japanese tank, representing a dramatic, military end to their lives as colonists. The boy, separated from his parents, ends up in a prisoner-of-war camp, where he increasingly displays the imagination, energy, and "pluck" that command the center of the film.

Given the enormous gulf not only of language but of victors and prisoners amid the culture of war, it is hardly surprising that virtually no literal "communication" takes place between the Japanese and the cohort of British-American prisoners, beyond that of menacing shouts with pointed rifle and bayonet as reminders of who dominates. Yet at other levels representatives of the several cultures notice one another, and most notably the spirit of the boy. His passion for aviation is boundless, and when he returns the stray model plane flown by a Japanese soldier, bonds of shared interests form that later save his life. The fast learning curve of youth for new languages and circumstances is also crucial: when the Japanese begin beating the camp physician presumably to assert their dominance, the boy confronts the violence, pleading the case in vehement Japanese, then immediately prostrates himself. The camp commander, apparently stunned at the mixture of courage and appropriate submission, quietly walks away after regaining his composure. Although such scenes may not delineate with academic precision the values of dominance, hierarchy, deference, and honor that permeate Japanese society and custom, their importance is powerfully evoked.

In one of the final scenes, the departing Japanese commander stops short to look at the boy and address a few curt words which are not translated, but which, we infer, essentially express respect for the young, foreign warrior.

A host of other Japanese-at-war-with-the-West films deserve acknowledgment: in *Merry Christmas, Mr. Lawrence* (1983), *Prisoners of the Sun* (1990), *Guests of the Emperor* (1992), and *Paradise Road* (1997) once again the Japanese rule prisoner-of-war camps where Westerners are interned. Reviews or synopses of these films commonly describe Japanese rule as "brutal," or deploy even stronger adjectives, though Western military behavior or for that matter the use of atomic weapons might be similarly described by the opposing side. In any event, the Japanese iron rule within such camps and the small, symbolic acts of Western defiance concisely reveal differing cultural outlooks. *Guests of the Emperor*, a sensitive and delicate as well as brutal chronicle of a Japanese camp in Malaysia holding Western women and children, offers the feminist dimension of a makeshift women's culture in confrontation with their rulers. A similar dynamic emerges from *Paradise Road*, as the male-dominated Japanese military culture set against a culture of Western women creates a tension well beyond the dire wartime realities.

The aftermath of war, for the Japanese, involved perhaps the most celebrated reconstruction in world economic history, with purposeful cultural adaptation taken to new heights, and with concomitant psychological fallout, even an intensified love/hate affair with the West. *MacArthur's Children* (1986), set in the immediate postwar, dedicates itself entirely to a panoramic treatment of Japanese society grappling with the inevitable social effects of the first and only foreign occupation of the islands. Individual Japanese nursed their scars, at all levels, while an entire society underwent rapid transition. Although American presence on screen is sparse in this Japanese production, the now dominant foreign culture represents both the cause and the pivotal point of the wrenching adjustment to a postwar national psychology. Not surprisingly, resentment drives much feeling and dialogue; perhaps less expected is Japanese fascination with American society, as represented by baseball. Also echoing memories of The Occupation, *The Yakuza* (1975) revolves around the flame that U.S. American Harry Kilmer carries for Eiko twenty years after their postwar romance, as he returns to Japan to assist a friend with a business matter. When he shows astonishment at the transformation he encounters, a Westerner living in Japan offers perspective. "The farmers in the countryside may watch TV from their tatami mats, and you can't see Fuji through the smog, but don't let it fool you, it's still Japan, and the Japanese are still Japanese." Japanese enough, it seems, that age-old values largely beyond the grasp of Westerners, such as "giri" or the code of debt and obligation, still dominate behavior and the course of events. Although foolishly unreal in numerous aspects, *The Yakuza* stands as the first serious attempt of Western filmmakers to depict code-driven, context-driven interactions between peoples in Japan. Surprisingly thoughtful, it offers the possibility of a soft, human face to Westerner and Easterner as well.

American Fantasies

In *Gung Ho* (1985) and *Black Rain*, we encounter absorbing yet flawed films that depict the contemporary Japan that exists only in shallow Western understanding, or even Western fantasy. Although both films make dramatic departures from realism, the offending story lines carry as much if not more potential for meaningful analysis as the better films. "Fantasy scripts" can offer not only perspective on the target culture but as well a measure of insight into the society with the need to fantasize. Both films are modern U.S. American morality plays with Japan, modern archenemy and sometime friend, as backdrop, as foil, or even alter ego.

The dreadful yet fascinating *Black Rain* rates as the worst of serious modern films set in Japan, engaging yet dangerously flawed in its preposterous central plot—American police outperforming Japanese law enforcement, on Japanese soil. The film gets its title from the bitter reminiscences of a Japanese underworld "godfather" who remembers the atomic bomb: "Then the heat brought rain, black rain. You made the rain black ... and shoved your values down our throat. We forgot who we were." In this film the victors of World War II win again, displaying a superior cunning, creativity, and resolve to capture a Japanese gangster who had committed murders in New York City. In the process, like storm waves on a rocky coast, they crash into traditional hierarchy, protocol, and law. During their first meeting with Japanese authorities, Detective Nick Conklin stages tantrums to get his way—"I'm just about an uptown minute from throwing you an international incident"—while the local chief of police observes to his men in (unsubtitled!) Japanese that Americans are sure like that—unkempt, uncouth, loud, unprofessional. "Just get us a cop that speaks English and can find his ass with two hands," snarls Nick. Judging from their behavior the Americans reserve the right to not only think but act "American" on foreign soil, as if there were nowhere on earth beyond the reach of their superior methods. Never do they entertain the thought of learning from the locals; rather they assume that the locals have much to learn from them about police work. Not having studied analyses of Japanese-Western interaction, not having seriously considered what behavior is most appropriate for "strangers," as a chapter in a highly respected analysis is entitled, they cannot realize how negatively their Japanese counterparts may view their intrusion.[4] In fact behavior such as shouting or losing self-control will likely produce the opposite of the desired perception, because the Japanese generally equate these behaviors with weakness, immaturity, and ignorance.

Interestingly, the film provides the raw materials for U.S. American lessons in humility: Americans acting naively in handing a prisoner over to gangsters masquerading as Japanese police (thereby providing derisive joy to local newspaper readers), Americans like fish out of water, completely dependent on bilingual Japanese for even the most fundamental of services or shreds of information, helpless and vulnerable on the streets of Tokyo. There are even the thinly veiled judgments on an America devoid of estimable values, as when the godfather refers to the code of his way of life. "I am bound by duty and honor. If you had time, I would explain what that means," he adds, clearly, condescendingly implying that there is more dignity in the Japanese underworld than in American law enforcement.

While the film leaves these rich and perhaps accurate images visible around the margins for the serious observer, center stage is dominated not only by a foreign detective hellbent on handling matters his way, but by a host of implications that the Japanese need both to loosen up and to do a better job of imitating Americans. Especially telling is the American

A U.S. American detective talks with an underworld chief and learns that even the Japanese criminal world considers itself driven by codes of honor and obligation, in _Black Rain_ (1988).

deafness and blindness toward their assigned police partner and interpreter—and the awkward positions they repeatedly push him into. After he is in fact suspended for tolerating Nick's interference in the case, Nick visits him at home and lectures, "We can fix it, Mas." "You cannot fix everything. I am not like you. For a moment I thought I could be ... Nick-san, I belong to a group. They will not have me anymore." "You're digging a hole for yourself, Mas. Sometimes, you've got to go for it."

In the end American drive, courage, and resourcefulness triumph as if an obviously superior system has had another successful field test, and as if representatives of the inferior system have finally caught on.

In _Gung Ho_, cut from a similar mold with heavy-handed, almost over-the-top character portrayals, dialogue is often reduced to wavelengths passing each other in space, and thus the cultures again speed toward an awkward collision. Again, in the end, U.S. American spirit shines with at least self-proclaimed success. In the average town of Hadleyville, Pennsylvania, a now defunct auto plant is taken over by the Japanese, who send a management team to develop higher productivity, at lower pay than under the union, from rehired workers. Though representatives from both sides prove quite unprepared to bridge the gap in understanding, the Americans have more conspicuously failed to do their homework, and shoot entirely from the hip in dealing with the new powers. Americans, especially, are unprepared for subtlety, the elements of protocol, glances and pregnant pauses, and the meanings between the lines. When the young, sensitive Japanese manager responds to the unsolicited suggestions of the American workers' liaison, Hunt, with the delicate hedge "I see what you are saying," Hunt believes this signifies agreement, not Japanese diplomacy.

Any viewer who begins to suspect that *Gung Ho*, for suspense or comedy, overstates the case, should consult the studies which demonstrate meticulously the predictable patterns of dysfunctional communication.[5] Consistent with complaints (worldwide and especially from Asians) about the "American style," the local representatives of the U.S. talk too much, listen too little, err with bluntness in their remarks, and put little stock in polite formalities—all alienating behaviors that cripple understanding. Also fundamental, from the beginning the differing meanings of work and of play contrast sharply, the Japanese as always cultivating a team approach to both, the Americans flaunting individualism and personal ego, because as Hunt counsels his bosses, "Americans like to feel special." While from the Japanese perspective Americans sorely lack a pride and drive for excellence in the auto plant, they approach softball with the resolve to win that the Japanese reserve for "zero defect" performance in industry. In the symbolically huge game played between the management, all–Japanese team and the Americans, one of the most disaffected workers smashes a plant manager to the ground while running the bases with lockjawed determination. The Japanese, while too polite to object directly, are clearly appalled at the unsportsmanlike behavior, because after all, this is only a game, played to relax and to forge group bonds, not a deadly, coldly serious task like running a production line. For Americans, sports represent a serious bottom line of ego and pride and perhaps also national identity, as evidenced by the numerous sports stories and analogies that pepper their discussions.

Enormously popular, *The Karate Kid* (1984) has spawned as of this writing not less than three sequels (of varying quality). In this simple yet engaging rendering of a timeless story, a young lad in search of his way in the world finds wisdom through an older Sensei; here the guru Miyagi also represents the wisdom of another culture: he is an Okinawan master of karate, and of life. While a youth audience, David and Goliath-style fantasy, the movie may be as close as many audiences ever come to considering the value of learning from another culture as Miyagi, laconically

When the Japanese take over a failed auto plant in Hadleyville, Pennsylvania, outright confrontation over management styles and expectations rapidly results, in *Gung Ho* (1985).

but gracefully, shares the core of his discipline. "You remember lesson about ... balance?" he asks young Daniel at a pivotal moment in his emotional life. "Now lesson not just karate only ... lesson for all life ... all life have balance ... everything be better. Understand?" *The Karate Kid II* (1986) even takes the action back to Okinawa, where rare moments illuminate the timeless traditions that grow and return seeds into the cultural soil. In one scene Miyagi, after several decades' absence, walks by a "Shinto Shrine" with Daniel; as they pause to watch an ancient figure playing traditional music to the delight of children, he comments simply "When I left he was same place, doing same thing, playing same tune...." The tale of the Karate Kid may be grounded in youthful and wishful thinking, but it also has roots in a respect for the time-worn disciplines of an ancient culture. North Americans may carry history and continuity lightly, but most other cultures experience its greater weight. Reischauer among others lucidly illustrate how doggedly the Japanese fasten to a detailed understanding of their past, carrying forward many rituals and practices with appreciative perspective.[6]

Americans Learning: Exposure to the Rising Sun

In *Tokyo Pop* (1988), *Mr. Baseball* (1992), and *Rising Sun* (1993), we encounter Westerners who experience the complexities of Japanese culture, learning and adapting in the process. Key characters achieve personal growth through broadened horizons; the clash of cultures is the anvil upon which hard decisions are forged and personal perspectives are hammered into new shapes; the clash yields visible results, if not always cultural compromise. In the "lightest" film, *Tokyo Pop*, a young rock 'n' roll singer flies to Tokyo on a whim, hoping to find work as a performer; she encounters the almost overwhelming frustrations of an unprepared "gaijin," before finally winning success as a pop singer, a platinum blond novelty from America. Although her specialized role allows her ephemeral viability in Japanese society, Wendy exhibits all the excesses of a more-than-American "American" style. At first glance just a light rock 'n' roll story with a foreign backdrop the film actually achieves more: a sensitive glimpse of Japanese culture and its different generations in transition, a lingering look at the migration of American pop culture worldwide, a case study of a singer digging into the raw surface of Tokyo life.

In *Mr. Baseball* "America's game" as adapted to Japanese life serves as the backdrop for an aging baseball star's abrupt encounter with difference and change: the ethic and practice surrounding his game, the only career he's ever known, differ in the Japanese context, where baseball predictably reflects the society itself. "Japan takes the best from all over the world," asserts the Japanese interior designer with whom he becomes intimate, "and makes it her own." Jack's challenge is thus to keep the core of his athlete's drive and personality intact while under assault from the leveling influence of a highly regimented, disciplined society, where "the nail that stands out gets hammered in." "Sometimes acceptance and cooperation are strengths, also," gently counsels Jack's girlfriend. To him the Japanese are uptight, rigid, completely without daring. To them he is another overbearing "gaijin," uncouth, unmannered, and self-centered—literally not a team player.

Jack begins where many Westerners begin in approaching Japanese culture: it is simply hard for him to grasp the profound currents of difference which run beneath apparent similarities in cities, buildings, sports, and lifestyles, and so he continues thinking and acting as he always has, but with drastically different results. He clashes with his team, manager, and native girlfriend, before eventually discovering his own capacity for humility.

Along the path of one man's collision with a foreign culture at a turning point in his own life, all the essential pitfalls in American expatriation to Japan are addressed. It becomes apparent the moment Jack steps off the plane that he is the American without protocol, who probably hasn't asked and certainly hasn't been told how he should behave at the level of fundamental courtesies. Thus the all-important ritual of greeting and exchange of business cards turns comical as Jack offers baseball cards, and the initial press interview reveals his insensitivity and detached arrogance. "My impressions of Japan? Lots of little people walking, talking very fast." He stumbles over the custom of removing shoes indoors as predictably as he does over Japanese names. As he begins to settle into Japan everything is subtly uncomfortable, unnerving, from fixtures in his apartment built for shorter people to the trappings of everyday life. He soon discovers he doesn't even know how to bathe, use the toilet, or find his way home without guidance.

Also authentic to the real-life expatriate experience is the role that "cultural informants" play in his education, the imported players for various Japanese teams who have preceded him. "Once you get used to sleeping in shoeboxes and chasing your food around the table, it's pretty much a … nightmare around here," joshes a jovial ballplayer as part of a verbal initiation ritual. His one American teammate plays a more serious and helpful role in interpreting the new culture, but not surprisingly the informants look through entirely American eyes, seeming to judge everything by its closeness to or distance from American practice. Theirs is factual, pragmatic information, intended to aid survival although perhaps not helpful toward deeper understanding. By contrast, his Japanese informant, soon his love interest, takes him to traditional temples and private homes, teaching a more reflective version of how to understand and approach what he encounters.

Beyond the level of protocol, there are the fundamentally different manners of viewing everyday events and responsibilities. Jack's truth is highly personal, egotistical, and pragmatic: when told the manager wants his mustache shaved, Jack replies, "Tell him this is the way he hired me, and if my mustache gets in the way of my swing, I'll shave it." Jack assumes his readiness for Japanese baseball by declaring that the game anywhere has "a stick, a ball, and a fence." The nuanced Japanese reply: The game has "many elements, all of which must work in harmony."

In *Rising Sun* U.S. Americans also squarely confront cultural difference, through the Japanese subculture of 1980s Los Angeles. The "Nakamoto" corporation and its steadily expanding empire have their American base in a downtown L.A. skyscraper, where, on the eve of a gala affair, a young woman's body is discovered, apparently strangled. Two detectives, one a returned expatriate with significant experience in Japan and

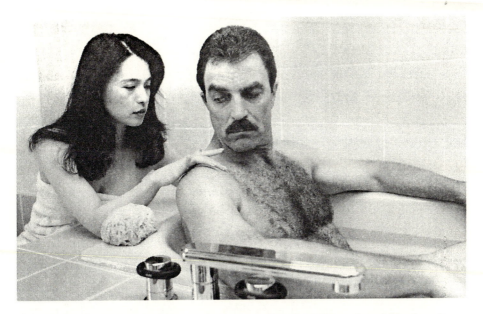

When Jack Elliot develops a love interest for the bilingual and bicultural Hiroko, he finds sensational romance and a cultural informant at the same time, in *Mr. Baseball* (1992).

the other a self-confident young African-American, tackle the complexities of the case, which soon becomes a matter as well of tackling the subtleties of a foreign culture. Although physically in Los Angeles, they find themselves transported to Japan.

Rising Sun is almost unique in the extent to which its Hollywood story line is also the spine of a veritable textbook for intercultural analysis. The opening frames in which Japanese play at being cowboys and an American cowboy's horse steps squarely on an anthill allude to broader issues: the supposed essence of American character itself as expressed in the myth of the cowboy, the Japanese attraction to the Old West as a telling aspect of the Japanese psyche, the anthill as metaphor for the frenetically productive Japanese, the crushing hoof as a metaphor for the continued dominance of the culture of the Open Range. Not only are such cinematographic references suggestive of far-reaching issues, but explicit instruction in protocol comes from the quietly eloquent yet specific teachings of the guru, Captain John Connor, based on his years in the foreigners' country. "Perhaps I can suggest a strategy," he counsels on the way to an encounter with the Japanese corporate officials. "When they bow you bow back, same depth, same duration ... and don't appear distracted. We may come from a fragmented, MTV rap video culture, but they do not."

The substance of Japanese culture is explored from the general to the specific, from roots to applications. Not only is the Oriental classic *The Art of War* invoked as the driving philosophy behind the surface of Japanese business—in another context it has been said that the Japanese "wage business"—but the complex interrelationships of groups, virtually disciplined armies, are revealed. To burrow to the roots of a particular economic crime is thus to dig through layers of interconnection and interdependence.

It should not be surprising that a murder mystery lends itself well to studying the interplay between cultures, because both rely on alertness to clues, to the subtly incongruent, the unspoken, the reasons behind the seemingly obvious. The detective's age-old search for opportunity, means, and motive need be altered only slightly to a search for motive and the meaning of cultural context. John Connor counsels the younger detective to take nothing at face value, to always ask why anything is done or said, in what context, to what purpose; in the process the unmistakable message becomes the deliberate, subtle, and highly contextualized nature of Japanese corporate behavior. Connor as informant-guru is so compelling as to partially upstage the sex, the murder, and the intrigue that energize the nerve endings of the viewer. Here cultural intrigue achieves the same level

Sharp Japanese–U.S. American conflict arises as Los Angeles police attempt to investigate a murder on Japanese corporate territory, in *Rising Sun* (1993).

of fascination. More generally, to the credit of the Hollywood scriptwriting teams, *Mr. Baseball* and *Rising Sun* present U.S. Americans learning, as finally aware that they must actually cultivate insight, and meet the other culture halfway.

Japanese Learning: A New Take on the American Dream

In *Picture Bride* (1994) and *Living on Tokyo Time* (1986), the Japanese central character comes to the West and attempts to make sense of immersion in a new culture.

Living on Tokyo Time takes a slow, pensive look at a Japanese girl, independent and adventurous by her culture's standards, as she tries long-term residence on the West Coast of the United States. Her expatriation springs not from professional or other necessity, but from the curiosity of youth mixed with a search for healing from a humiliating experience. Kyoko encounters a richly multicultural society relatively free from discrimination against Asians, yet finds no practical avenue through which a homesick and thoroughly Japanese young woman can feel at ease. Prejudice may be scarce in her new environment, but so are persons who can engage her at a vital level, a problem complicated by her halting English. In one particularly telling scene a frustrated Kyoko begins speaking in Japanese to the Japanese-American man whose apartment she shares, a man who wishes to deepen their relationship. "What are you doing?" Ken asks, "you know I don't speak Japanese." Even if he did, however, it might only open another avenue through which no genuine connection would take place.

Picture Bride chronicles the post–World War I journey of a young Japanese, Riyo, who lost her parents back home to tuberculosis, considered a quite shameful end within the culture of the time. Through photographs and matchmaking she finds her way to Hawaii, a plantation-based economy that was already polycultural, yet already run by Americans and other Westerners long before U.S. statehood. She came as the picture bride of a Japanese, of course, implying a Japanese insularity much too strong to contemplate arranged marriages with foreigners.

Picture Bride presents a delicate and charming story—although moored in the reality of stoop labor in the canefields of pre-modern Hawaii, it evokes indomitable immigrant will and spirit along with the Japanese sensitivity to beauty and the tenacious attachment to tradition. Polyvalent beyond any neat category, it could as easily demonstrate the multicultural United States as expressed in film, yet it rates mentioning in this context for several reasons. It hints at the Japanese place in the overlapping shades of ethnicity in the Pacific islands, as when native Hawaiian islanders mistake Riyo for one of them, but find they can converse with her only through the great unifying language, English. The film also serves as a reminder that the Japanese, too, have at times migrated to search for a better life and have changed as subsequent generations were born abroad. It marks the subtle degrees of separating from the "homeland," of becoming less Japanese and more Hawaiian with time, as has Riyo's husband Matsuji who preceded her by many years. Perhaps most importantly the film portrays, in a number of finely crafted scenes, the quiet intensity of Japanese tradition and its huge cultural distances from that of other peoples, as encapsulated in a scene when Riyo looks through a glass window at a well-intentioned Western woman, each pausing for a moment with a wish for further rapport, yet each unable to begin to cross the enormous gulf.

As the nineties unfolded, in filmmaking and in North American-Japanese relations, it may be significant that even the poor, essentially empty action-adventure film verged on meaningful content. Even the crude, almost wretched *Red Sun Rising* (1993), replete with stock scenes of martial combat, offers a few culturally suggestive moments, from opening camera work juxtaposing a high-tech urban Japan with the traditional tea ceremony to the spark of an intercultural romance between L.A. detective Karen Ryder and Kyoto detective Thomas Hoshino. They transcend a rough beginning to feel mutual attraction. "What is this? I don't read Martian," snaps Karen when first presented with Hoshino's native police credential. "Speak English? *Ingrish*?" "*Ingrish* is not one of my favorite languages," he counters, "but I speak it reasonably well." As he hitches a ride in her American car he remarks offhandedly "This car is huge." Her feisty rejoinder: "The way God meant cars to be until you guys came along and screwed it all up." "Low quality and lack of reinvestment ruined the American auto industry," he replies calmly. A martial arts back-and-forth dialogue continues throughout; at least the stereotypes that drive it have resonance for popular culture, at least we know that opposites simultaneously repel, and attract.

The more worthwhile *Samurai Cowboy* (1993) lays the need for friction squarely on the table. "What about ... all those people who won't work for you unless your name is Smith or Johnson?" asks a woman sympathetic to the new Japanese ranch owner. "We need those people." "Why?" "We gotta have bad guys," concludes the expatriate cowboy. At least, it seems, U.S. American film needs them, but the bad guys aren't who they used to be. The sympathetic characters in *Samurai Cowboy* are a burned out young Japanese businessman, Yutaka Sato, enacting the dream of the open West, and his motley ranch crew—a Native American mistreated by neighboring ranchers, a greenhorn rock musician, an old cowboy hanging on to a fading way of life. The new "bad guys" are all-American "Marlboro Men," often drunk on both booze and prejudice, living in the past. "Tell you what Jap, [we're] looking for a new cook, maybe you can fix [us] up some chopsuey." "Chop-suey is Chinese food," maintains Sato with poise and good humor. In both *Red Sun Rising* and *Samurai Cowboy* the Japanese "gets the girl" and the ignorant, parochial American their comeuppance, in films that, just a few years ago, would likely have chosen someone other than Japanese to be "the good guys."

Toward Conclusions

"Just because you speak English doesn't mean we speak the same language," protests a frustrated Jack Elliot in *Mr. Baseball* to his assigned interpreter, nicely encapsulating the essence of the relations between the cultures, traditionally separated by enormous philosophical gulfs, by almost unreconcilable dissonances in societal and world views, customs, and modes of expression. While Westerners have only rarely learned an Asian language many Japanese have learned English and other Western languages, and thus at least the outward veneer of exchange has become increasingly common in an internationalizing world. Yet at virtually all levels, from the most superficial elements of protocol to the deepest values, the cultures remain much estranged. But largely pragmatic reasons have brought the cultures together in real life, and film fairly reflects this: in North American films the Westerner in Japan (or the Japanese expatriate) always has a Western-style mission to accomplish, such as business or police work. Essentially absent is the Westerner in untainted pursuit of intellectual or esthetic enrichment, choosing to interact with Japanese as part of a spiritual or personal quest.

Social science analysis gives many a hint of the depth of Japanese subtlety and the continuing distance of their culture from others. To take but one example, there is some evidence that expatriates who learn more than rudimentary Japanese actually suffer worse, not improved relations for their effort, whether because their honeymoon as guests is considered over, because they begin to show depths of themselves that are glaringly at odds with the surrounding society, or simply because at some level the Japanese resent sharing the closely held currency of their language with outsiders.[7] Whatever the specific contour of the reasons, the counter-intuitive fact should give us pause: these are not simply a people just like us who make smaller, better cars and play a different style of baseball. Whatever the reasons for the fascination-fear relationship, popular film helps delineate its shape in both directions. The U.S. especially seems to fear economic invasion or foreign ownership (*Samurai Cowboy, Rising Sun* and *Gung Ho*) while the Japanese seem to fear or at least resent cultural invasion (*Black Rain, Mr. Baseball,* and *Tokyo Pop*) as a threat to centuries old, unique traditions and values.

In *Black Rain, Gung Ho,* and *Mr. Baseball,* key American and Japanese characters find a meeting of the minds in almost storybook endings of the triumph of friendship—American style. Notwithstanding the America-centric notion of friendship, how realistic are these Japanese-American bondings? In *Black Rain,* at least, quite egregiously Hollywood instead. Mas, who "belongs to a group," would likely never go "cowboy cop" in defiance of the established rules, and if he did, the mere practical success of capturing the crook would never lead to his full professional and social restoration. Yet the frontier, defiant American spirit is incorrigible: at the airport, Nick makes Mas a going-away present of the still missing prize of their police work: state-of-the-art, counterfeit plates worth millions in cash ... or a lifetime of disgrace. Japanese or for that matter informed Western observers have every right to exclaim in the vernacular, "These Americans just don't get it, do they? Mas doesn't want to live by these outlaw rules." Indeed, Nick from the first is as much outlaw as law enforcer, with contempt for his own legal system and a lone cowboy's code of self-defined justice. The myths of America's Old West are said to appeal enormously to Japanese tourists, whether as novelty or forbidden fruit. But in practical terms the Old West only echoes nostalgically in the culture of urban America (detective Nick Conklin), and to the Japanese it amounts to no more than fantasy, the appealing opposite of their everyday, closely structured realities. The outcomes of *Black Rain* are not only unrealistic but devalue the essence of one of the world's oldest cultures.

In *Mr. Baseball* the outcome of the game proves a degree more plausible, and also more dignified for both cultures. True, we are asked to believe that an American lone cowboy in a baseball uniform finally persuades his Japanese manager to take risks, to allow athletic spontaneity, to entertain the potential value of the "American style." Unlikely, perhaps. But the transformations are at least complementary. In a touching scene Elliot apologizes to his teammates, in carefully rehearsed Japanese, for his past arrogance and promises to honor Japanese-style team spirit in the future. Quietly, the players circle around Jack in a show of acceptance and solidarity. Sincere apology, with a show of respect for ambient values, may be almost universal in its effectiveness. Additionally the meeting of cultures includes romance, as Jack engages with Hiroko, who has become significantly Westernized through study in New York City, and both are forced to bend inward toward the other culture if they wish to pursue their mutual attraction.

Their love affair constitutes the most outrageous concession to Western sentimentality in the movie, with the specter of a Japanese father actually *encouraging* his daughter toward romance with a "gaijin." Although Japanese parental approval for such a love affair is simply not part of the cultural landscape, the phenomenon of intercultural romance and marriage itself is strikingly real. In fact, such unions have spawned their own field of study: they represent not only special problems but special links across cultures, the chemistry which has the potential to span differences, and intercultural film shows this interplay up close, as can no other medium.[8]

In the end Jack and Hiroko continue to love but back in the States, in English, ultimately more on American than on Japanese terms. Hiroko, however, welcomed an opportunity for more exposure to the States, and was functionally bilingual and bicultural. At least as portrayed by Hollywood, representatives of virtually every non–Western culture prove more willing and more competent to live in the West than vice-versa. Is this a compliment to the North American and Western worlds, their strong economies, their open borders, multicultural societies, the melting-pot history of the U.S. and Canada? Or is it a tart, unintended commentary on not only our monolingualism but also monoculturalism, on a regrettable arrogance and parochialism in spite of our multicultural roots? The question is left to give us pause. Why must the meeting of cultures be on essentially Western terms, and why must even a foreign spouse come here, to our culture?

It is hard to assess the cultural balance of trade in *Gung Ho*. In many ways it is cut from the same ethnocentric cloth, for while the Americans show that they can "work Japanese" the Japanese eventually come around to an American spirit, to the ability to "lighten up" and consider broader values than merely productivity. Indeed, the Japanese manager, first portrayed back in Japan in a retraining program based on humiliation and loud recrimination, experiences a partial Americanization, going so far as to suggest in front of his boss that "there are some things we might learn from these Americans." He even suggests that a subordinate might be excused from work to assist at the birth of his child, a human touch that the filmmakers represent as unusual within such a production-oriented ethic. The flavor, the tone of the film remains decidedly pro–American throughout as it pokes fun at the stilted nature of Japanese society, at an excessive rigidity, no matter how productive, which fails to fully appreciate human spirit—meaning, of course, American spirit. More than any other film in the genre, *Gung Ho* illustrates the problem of granting the culturally other a full range of emotions and virtues. Japanese society may exhibit what to North Americans appears a stilted side, formal, unbending, and seemingly unfriendly. But let Japanese interact with those they know and trust, in less formal settings, and a sensitive, warm, and gregarious side emerges which may far outdo Anglo barroom camaraderie. Even when Japanese interact with strangers or foreigners, under appropriate, non-threatening circumstances, a thoughtful and generous side often emerges which is not well captured by any of these films.

In *Gung Ho* the Americans never seem to consider, much less come to understand, the spirit of Japanese society, as if it offered little beyond an antlike intensity for making a factory hum. The workers also miss the irony of so freely criticizing the Japanese approach after their homegrown management had failed, leaving their town economically depressed. In the end do the Americans "win," that is, work at restored wage-levels under a Japanese ownership that is beginning to see the American light? Or do the Japanese win, successfully imposing their non-union regime, high production quotas, and quality standards on a bankrupt plant? It would be revealing to know if American audiences overwhelmingly perceive the former while Japanese audiences perceive the latter.

There are intriguing exceptions to even the rule of Western ethnocentrism, however, that tease out further perspectives. In *Rising Sun* John Connor and his lover indeed reside in the U.S., but not necessarily by preference. We learn that Jingo's biracial parentage, her physical deformity, and her open love for a "gaijin" combined to make her role in Japanese society untenable and that their escape was away from prejudice toward greater acceptance, that American terms were, relatively, the more flexible. As bicultural Japanese-Americans, though, they provide the exception in the film, surrounded not only by Japanese who remain an alien culture while living in and attempting to conquer Los Angeles economically, but also by thoroughly narrow Americans. "The guy's trouble" an L.A. police veteran warns, referring to Connor as the department's Japan expert. He's "too good a friend of Japan." In fact, this attitude mirrors what we know about the acceptance of returned expatriates to the U.S.: their fresh insight may be as much suspect as admired, their international perspective sometimes unwelcome, under the vague suspicion that they may have suffered some manner of contamination. Echos, indeed, of the ambivalent feelings that, reportedly, the Japanese have long held toward their insidiously Westernized, returned expatriates.[9]

Other dimensions of these films besides the happily-ever-after endings arise when testing for "realism." Does "real" mean a documentary-like anthropological accuracy, or does it mean an artistic brokering of understanding, impact with integrity, as it were? If the splash of brightly lit images upon the screen creates in one sense its own "language," it must obviously match a language that its audience speaks in order for understanding and resultant impact to occur. It is easily conceivable that painstaking "mimetic accuracy" and lovingly crafted "verisimilitude" might actually interfere with audience comprehension of the issues at play. Given that a film's storyline and details must necessarily follow some set of constructed expectations, no film can totally speak to or for a truly international audience.

In this sense it may be no major flaw in the films considered here that not one fully captures the differences in Western and Japanese body language. For instance, during the filming of *Shogun* a dilemma was faced: allow soldiers to raise fists and roar in approval at their new leader, or pay silent reverence, as would have been authentic. The director finally chose the explosive display that would fit Western audience expectations.[10] Filmmakers will always be constrained by the level of audience familiarity with the foreign culture portrayed, especially considering that within some cultures, notably including Japan, interactions are extremely contextualized. Only those familiar with the Japanese will perceive and correctly interpret the subtleties of behaviors, behaviors that often convey more significance than could any dialogue. For flavor, these films capture gestures like bowing and rituals like the exchange of professional cards. Yet experienced Westerners know that a host of the simplest expressions and gestures, from smiling to crossing legs when sitting, dramatically differ between the two societies and convey diverging significance. Japanese smiles and even laughter as signifying embarrassment, for example, are not reflected in these films—Mas in *Black Rain* or Ishihara in *Rising Sun* would have quite possibly exhibited moments of humiliated laughter in the more "mimetically" accurate of films.[11] But would the largely Western audience have understood, or would it have been distracted? Unless the script allows for explanatory asides, such as when John Connor plays the ever helpful cultural informant in *Rising Sun*, the audience is likely to grow confused, and the device of "body language subtitling" has not yet been invented. The filmmakers thus did what was less real in one sense and more real in another: they opted for familiar, comprehensible behavior to convey the emotions in play. In other instances it may be noted that body language and comportment were quite deftly portrayed; for example, the commuter-train scene from *Mr. Baseball* with the giggling Japanese girls, hand covering mouth, was "mimetically" correct. Given that the behavior did not too sharply diverge from audience expectations, and was therefore not easily subject to misreading, the filmmaker was free to quite accurately capture the gestures in authentic form.

Tokyo Pop and *Living on Tokyo Time* are cut from slightly different cloth, as both tell stories almost exclusively focused on personality, on average Japanese and U.S. Americans, rather than on action. Both films in this sense function as good tests of audience interest in cultural crosstalk. Just as the late nineteenth-century Western novel once focused on the everyday occurrence, these films exploit the fascination of ordinary persons coping with the eternally extraordinary—the settings, persons, and realities of unfamiliar cultures.

General audiences will prefer *Tokyo Pop*, its happy if bittersweet ending, its livelier action and humor. *Tokyo Pop* may appear "Hollywood" enough to portray the glitz of Tokyo's equivalent fame industry, and one American's success in it. But the film is really about a garden variety U.S. American pop-culture girl, Wendy, nose-to-nose with an utterly unfamiliar environment; more grandly it is about the search for maturity and personal identity as leavened by international encounter. Her experiences in Tokyo sow seeds of growth, though in the short run Wendy chomps through them quickly, consuming them, like fast food, with little reflection. Shades of the U.S. Americans in *Black Rain* and *Mr. Baseball*: Wendy's approach to her goals is the shortest line between points in Western logic. "Nothing is impossible" she trumpets in response to her new band's frustrations in achieving recognition, and she barges into the offices of a successful promoter, audition tape in hand. She is consistently a fullback lunging for a goal line in a culture with gentler, indirect routes to desired ends. When rapport with her fellow musician and love interest founders, she prescribes the classic remedy of her homeland. "In America we talk about our feelings...." "This isn't America," he reminds her, in the process emphasizing that this sympathetically candid, ingenuous figure in the eyes of the North American audience may seem boorish to the Japanese.

Tokyo, for Wendy, appears to be an exotic but flawed, deficient version of Manhattan. In the world of her artistic identity, as well, Tokyo can never be the real thing. "If I stay here I'll never know if I can make it" she remarks, referring to the American world of rock 'n' roll and revealing that her points of reference, her standards of "success" and "excellence," have really not changed. As the brassy, white-haired sensation from the alluring West, Wendy holds center stage in Japan for a time much as she commands the film's center. But around the periphery of her high visibility emerge Tokyo lives as they are lived daily, by the rank and file. From the group mores of the Japanese band to Hiro's work-ethic father and traditionalist grandfather, we see conventional lives relatively untouched by Western fashion, as well as other Japanese unhappy with the pull of the West. When Hiro, wishing to play tour guide, asks his mother which is "the most beautiful shrine in Tokyo," she exclaims "I'm so happy! You're finally interested in Japanese instead of American things." A society of the traditional contrasts with a society of the seductive, as Japan uneasily entertains the foreign influence, much like taking in an unruly foster child. Even Wendy's band-partners, worshipers of American rock 'n' roll and superficially Westernized, are still Japanese to the core: quiet and reserved, respectful of (or at least resigned to) hierarchy, sensitive to group feeling and process, cautious with strangers and foreigners. Western influence, while real and attractive to them, is but one variable in their complexly Japanese lives. Hiro lives with his family, unusual for his rock 'n' roll counterparts from the U.S.; Wendy, after all, has ridden rock vibrations all the way to Japan. The youth cultures, East and West, meet over what is a way of life and reflection of the culture for Americans but a variation on a way of life and a measured, contained aspect of the culture for young Japanese.

Living on Tokyo Time goes further still with a story line based on the ordinary actions of ordinary people, and may not hold the interest of the average viewer, especially the Hollywood-grown film viewer. Virtually nothing "happens" in the usual sense; the vital line of "action" between Ken and Kyoko is internal, sometimes quite unspoken, sometimes untranslatable . The patient viewer, however, can see representatives of quite different societies: Japanese exhibiting more reserved, less talkative behavior, more concern for family and tradition, more respect for marriage. Japanese-American, enigmatic Ken, significantly, is atypical of U.S. youth in some ways: taciturn, deeply serious about his music, and relatively unmoved by ephemeral pleasures. No explanation is given for the crucifix on his bedroom wall. Were Ken's ancestors among the few Japanese Christians, or is he simply attracted to showing icons in the style of American pop culture? Kyoko, meanwhile, has left her homeland for a very foreign experience, yet her reason for leaving—the humiliation of the code-breaking infidelity of her fiancé—drips of tradition. In *Living on Tokyo Time* characters and events are often hard to pigeonhole, as in the most artful stories, as in most of real life. The second tier of characters includes Ken's (also Japanese "looking") sister; though married to a "white," she is the dominant, brash figure, while her husband exhibits an almost "Japanese" quietness, restraint, and diplomacy. Ethnic complexity is a recurring if incidental theme: "How weird! Some Japanese woman answered Ken's phone," his sister exclaims when first hearing Kyoko's voice and accent. The delicate subtleties and ironies of culture as character are gracefully woven through the film, providing fresh hints of surprise at almost very turn.

At the end of the day Ken, whatever else defines him, is American, or at least most definitely not Japanese in the sense of the culture still on the islands. His New Age friend Lana counsels him on simple truths: that he and Kyoko come from "completely different cultures" and that "mixed" relationships need extra time to work out the inevitable challenges to understanding. In the end he knows how to be himself, not how to expand his emotional and mental horizons significantly. When Kyoko, unable to deepen a relationship with Ken, returns to Japan, he smashes his cherished guitar in frustration. Yet in a final scene he is pricing a new guitar, not a trip to Japan where Kyoko has invited him to visit. Clearly Ken has not broadened his horizons significantly in the process of knowing a truly Japanese girl. Kyoko has experienced the U.S. but not changed fundamentally either, and chooses re-immersion in the society she knows over a longer, more profound expatriate experience.

In many ways this body of film, taken as a whole, constitutes a regrettable picture of polarization between Japanese and Western, especially North American culture. Given the future interdependence of major world cultures, given the potential for warmth and empathetic exchange between the peoples involved, the message of insuperable difference seems unfortunately dark, pessimistic. However, we must realize that the "mind-sets" of Japanese and Westerners are commonly believed to be more similar than they really are, rather than mistakenly believed to be sharply dissimilar. Anyone from either culture, preparing for contact with representatives of the other, should find these films helpful. Sojourners are more likely to report the film differences as not exaggerated after their real-world experience, even perhaps as still understated, not quite dramatic enough to prepare them for daily life in so different an environment. These films, significantly, are almost all products of the United States, the culture most opposite Japan along key axes of social thinking such as individual versus group loyalties. Perhaps globalization does signal a slowly homogenizing world, but even so Japan and the United States will remain unusually distinctive societies, "outliers" in the scheme of one analyst.[12]

What are we to make of the fact that few Japanese films, at least very few of those exported to the West, feature foreign characters? One exception, *Rhapsody in August* (1991), presents the Western viewer with a provocative experience. Essentially a meditation upon the troubled, postwar Japanese soul its tension emerges through a grandmother, warmhearted but confused, reliving what for her is the unresolved trauma of the Second World War. In the same sense that she represents a society still coping with a defining moment in its history, the American actor Richard Gere represents the West. A relative by marriage, he comes on both family business and a vacation, passing pleasant days with his hosts until recalled to the states by a health emergency. Then he is suddenly gone almost as if his presence had never been real. He was at once one of them, family, a sympathetic relative who speaks reasonably good conversational Japanese, and a "gaijin," an outsider who shows only superficial understanding of the culture. His delicate status as a character, an object of fascination, so close and yet so far, epitomizes the complex, eternally absorbing relations between Japan and the West.

Filmography

Film (aka), year, country (language), director, producer/distributor, minutes

The Berlin Affair, 1985, Italy, Liliana Cavani, Cannon Film Distributors, 118
Black Rain, 1988, USA, Ridley Scott, Paramount Pictures, 125
Captive Hearts, 1987, Canada, Paul Almond, MGM Metro, 97
Collision Course, 1989, USA, Lewis Teague, CBS Fox Video, 100
Empire of the Sun, 1987, USA, Steven Spielberg, Warner Brothers, 154
Gaijin, 1979, Brazil (port.), Tizuka Yamasaki, Brazilian Culture Society, 105
Guests of the Emperor, 1992, UK, Anthony Page, Yorkshire Television, 120
Gung Ho, 1985, USA, Ron Howard, Paramount Pictures, 112
Hiroshima, Mon Amour, 1959, France (fr.), Alain Resnais, Zenith International, 88
The Karate Kid, 1984, USA, John G. Avildsen, Columbia Pictures, 126
The Karate Kid, Part II, USA, 1986, John G. Avildsen, Columbia Pictures, 113
Living on Tokyo Time, 1986, USA, Steven Okazaki, Farallon Films, 83
MacArthur's Children, 1986, Japan/USA, Masahiro Shinada, Orion Classics, 115
Merry Christmas, Mr. Lawrence, 1983, New Zealand, Agisa Oshima, Universal, 124
Mr. Baseball, 1992, USA, Fred Schepisi, Universal, 108
Paradise Road, 1997, Australia/USA, Bruce Beresford, 20th Century–Fox, 115
Picture Bride, 1994, Japan/USA, Kayo Hatta, Miramax, 95
Prisoners of the Sun, 1990, Australia, Steven Wallace, Sovereign Pictures, 108
Red Sun, 1971, USA, Terence Young, National General Pictures, 130
Red Sun Rising, 1993, USA, Francis Megahy, Imperial Entertainment, 99
Rhapsody in August, 1991, Japan (jp.), Akira Kurosawa, Orion Classics, 98
Rising Sun, 1993, USA, Philip Kaufman, 20th Century–Fox, 125
Samurai Cowboy, 1993, TV, Canada, Michael Keusch, Saban Entertainment, 96
Shogun, 1980, TV, USA, Jerry London, Paramount Television, 549
Tokyo Pop, 1988, Japan/USA, Fran Rubel Kuzui, Warner Brothers, 99
The Trout, 1982, France (fr.), Joseph Losey, Gaumont, 116
The Yakuza, 1975, USA, Sydney Pollack, Warner Brothers, 112

Chapter Three

NEVER THE TWAIN
SHALL MEET: CHINA,
INDIA, AND ASIA
MEET THE WEST

"You Westerners know nothing of sacrifice."
                                                    Turtle Beach

"It takes time for prejudice to die a natural death."
                                                    Which Way Home

"Oh, those magnificent Americans, so much power and so little under-standing what to do with it."
                                                    The Golden Child

"This place was different than what I'd expected ... it wasn't at all like what I'd seen in the Kung Fu movies."
                                                    Iron and Silk

Introduction

The physical distances between East and West have effectively dimin-ished, with even London to Bombay, or Los Angeles to Manila crossed in less than a day. But have cultural distances shrunk commensurately, pulled inward by international media, fast food, and science? To view the overall record of East meets the West in film, the differences run more deeply than jet travel or the satellite dish can easily bridge. Even "experts," like the ambassador in *The Ugly American* (1963) or the American scholar of Mandarin in *Iron and Silk* (1990), make frequent, almost inevitable

72

miscalculations. Long-term expatriates, such as Eliane in *Indochine* (1992) or René Gallimard in *M. Butterfly* (1993), may grossly overestimate their sophistication. Other expatriates may abandon, or never engage, the search for commonality. The Major and Mrs. Callendar in *A Passage to India* admit that they have, simply, no Indian friends. "East is East," she explains superciliously. "It's a question of culture." "Whenever I see one of them blowing his nose onto the pavement," says the French diplomat's wife in Peking in *M. Butterfly*, "I always remember what my father said: 'East is East and West is West and never the twain shall meet.' Then I feel much better." Such Western perceptions of insuperable difference are often echoed by Orientals. When Ming insists to her illicit Western admirer in *Iron and Silk* that "I live in a very different world from yours" she also implies that bridging the chasm between East and West is nearly impossible. From the separation of India from Great Britain in *Gandhi* (1982), to the discordant tones of Westerner meeting Filipino in *Perfumed Nightmare* (1977), to the Himalayan meeting of cultures in *Seven Years in Tibet* (1997) it is clear that different inherited mind-sets present thorny challenges to all interaction.

China and the West in Film

Professional careers in diplomacy involve by definition some engagement with foreign cultures and international issues; nevertheless, they do not guarantee awareness, sensitivity, or quality skills in human relations. In films set variously in Africa (*A Good Man in Africa*), Central America (*Missing, Diplomatic Immunity, Clear and Present Danger*), Russia (*The Russia House*) or Asia (*The Ugly American, The Year of Living Dangerously, Turtle Beach, M. Butterfly*)—we see "diplomats" most notably lacking the skills of diplomacy, of understanding people and events from a broad enough perspective to be tolerant, respectful, flexible, and ultimately effective. In *M. Butterfly* diplomat René Gallimard lectures a roomful of subordinates on the past deficiencies of French foreign policy in the Orient: "...we failed to learn about the people we sought to lead. It's natural, therefore, correct even, that they should resent us. How could they do otherwise when we refuse to treat them like fellow human beings?" His clarion call for sensitivity plays to expressionless, unimpressed faces; moreover his words bear the lead-weighted irony of his own arrogant, ill-considered, ultimately quite ignorant behavior during his sojourn in Communist China.

M. Butterfly offers a host of ingredients in action: the delicate diplomatic role of a Western embassy in a very non–Western country, the highly ambivalent reactions of the Communist Chinese to Westerners, the internal conflict within China, and perhaps the internal conflicts within the emotions and intellects of many individual Chinese. The film (based loosely on real events) pivots around the love story of a French diplomat and a Chinese "diva," a singer with the Peking Opera, and around the manifest inability of Gallimard to "think Chinese," to realize that in every dimension he is in over his head, in a world apart. "Deep down ... they find our ways ... exciting," he declares by way of reading the minds of the "inscrutable" Oriental. Upon his first meeting Song Liling, the warning signs abound, as he expounds upon the emotional poignancy of *Madame Butterfly*, "She loves him, but what can she do? It's pure sacrifice." His ultimate conclusion: "It's so beautiful." The Chinese reply: "Well, yes, to a Westerner."

The irony in the theme of a West and Westerner as quite "exciting" and finally irresistible to the Chinese is the allure pulling in the opposite direction, embodied in Gallimard who in his "libidinous cross-cultural leap" sacrifices a marriage, a career, and finally his life to an idealized attraction.[1] His infatuation with Song suggests not only his personal but also a Western restlessness, suggests cultural and romantic empty places that call out to be filled. Beyond that, his particularly Western ignorance of "an ancient culture" of great subtlety and complexity stands starkly highlighted, an implicit indictment of Western pseudo-sophistication and gullibility.

Gallimard's ill-conceived infatuation surely symbolizes a larger truth: that little is as it seems when dealing across a huge cultural distance, that the *illusion* of personal connection may be dangerously more common than genuine rapport. The core of the plot explores this illusion through the diplomat's ultimate touch of ignorance: Song Liling, in fact, is a transvestite whom Gallimard continues to love as a woman throughout a liaison of almost two decades. All female roles in Chinese opera are performed by males, and so with Song (as Gallimard should have known). Anderson concludes in reviewing for *Newsday*, "The real point is René's Western fantasies, so overripe he'll believe anything, including Song Liling."[2]

Professional film critics were, in fact, more attuned to the importance of cross-cultural insights in *M. Butterfly* than in almost any other intercultural film. While Corliss sees the parallels between "a man preposterously blinded by love" and "a European culture blinkered by imperialist prejudice in its view of the mystic East,"[3] Hoberman reflects on sexuality itself as a cultural construct.[4] Anderson highlights the suggestive, understated dialogue in which a highly "modern" culture has met a China "whose soul is rooted firmly two thousand years in the past," according to the cryptic observation of Song Liling.[5] The extraordinary personal events form a striking foreground, behind and beyond which the multi-layered background gives this film significant weight in illustrating the attraction, repulsion, and interplay of cultural polarities.

Bethune (1977) and *Dr. Bethune* (1990) provide two similar takes on the career in China of the eccentric Canadian physician, Norman Bethune, during the 1930s of The Revolution, as he helps Mao Tse-tung's forces maintain hospitals under wartime conditions. Undoubtedly the reputation of Westerners in the Orient was strongly influenced by the atypical, select group who ventured there—Bethune proves "Western" to extreme degrees: sure of the world, his role in it, his power to influence events, and the correctness of Western science and Western logic. "He wanted the world to conform to his own vision," remembered a friend. In one striking scene he humiliates a Chinese medical worker in public, ranting about the lack of competence, though he later apologizes publicly after having seen local realities. Bethune as friend of China remains distinctly Western, as in a subtly telling scene in which he and a Chinese exchange readings of their own culture's poetry, and Bethune reveals a strongly chauvinistic bias toward Western thought and expression. Despite all his "sacrifices" for the Maoist cause, he ultimately, in fact, takes little interest in Chinese people. When he has told his friend much about his Western life and the Chinese comments that he, too, was once married, Bethune proffers no warmer response than a barely sincere, "Oh, really?" He appears interested in China only through his own lens, in his own egocentric terms, intensified by his abstract, political certainties. The Dr. Bethune films among others raise fair questions of attitude and motive regarding medical and development workers overseas. Do these expatriates assume that the "superior" technology they bring obviates the need to mesh with the indigenous peoples, do too many have inflated egos or stroke an inner need by achieving high status within another culture, or are most guided by a selflessness hard for a cynic to comprehend?

In *Forbidden Nights* (1990) and *Iron and Silk* young U.S. Americans of the postwar era directly confront post–Cultural Revolution China, and in a promising role for cultural crosstalk—that of teaching English language and literature. As the first American teacher in Hunan Province, Judy Shapiro's role in *Forbidden Nights* is laced with delicacy, and subject to the predictable faux pas lurking beneath myriad details of behavior. Just arrived and completely exhausted, Judy finds an auditorium full of students waiting to greet her, yet when she introduces herself American-style, including her credentials and credits, an icy look from the audience signals a problem: Chinese would never present themselves in a way which seems to tout individual accomplishment. Judy's first days on campus are full of further revealing moments, if often subtle and unspoken, in intercultural adjustment. After her first night of sleep, she opens her window to see the campus square filled with students in choreographed exercise drill, emblematic of an ancient people in which individuals march collectively to the beat of their culture's drummer. In her first cafeteria experience she cannot get down food repugnant to Western tastes, and in her first bathing experience she learns that standards of cleanliness in water are, like most aspects of life, culturally defined. As Judy gradually learns to eat, dress, and even think Chinese, she begins to have romantic feelings for one of the most expressive students, Ma Soong. Though the journey of any such romance may be predictably bumpy, a roller-coaster effect is added by Ma's dubious political status, by the questionable legality of intercultural marriage, by the inevitable sensitivities on both sides. Furthermore, their relationship is simply dangerous, as he risks expulsion from the university or even imprisonment and she risks immediate expulsion from China. Ultimately, it is clouded by questions of motive—is he interested in a Western spouse as a ticket to a more attractive world, is she only interested in an Oriental love "experience"? Each sees the "contradictions" of the other's culture— the Chinese world so straitlaced after millennia of authoritarian tradition yet susceptible both to bribes and to political swings which can change rules overnight; the Western world so full of "freedom" that it becomes ill-defined license. Ma is concerned that he not end up just another romantic experiment for an American woman, that they should make a commitment like the ducks on Chinese ponds which have mated "forever." The road to their marriage is blocked, however, by still another very Chinese event, a sudden, local insurgence which turns Ma into an outspoken rebel, again risking prison within the rigid system.

Romance aside, *Forbidden Nights* serves as an effective portrait of a contemporary-culture Westerner adjusting to a remote province, Mao's birthplace, as the Chinese cultural flower opens ever so slightly towards the West. What's more, the sympathetic presence of "all–American girl" Melissa Gilbert, along with sympathetic Chinese stars, provides a very "human" flavor from a Western perspective to a story with broader implications. Young and single, Judy is a doctoral student from Berkeley "with all that that implies." Culturally her new host university is rooted not only in millennia of tradition but shaped by more than three decades of ferment since the Revolution, perhaps less ferment than turbulence, in which political winds have shifted every season. Cast as a sprightly gull gliding above a troubled sea, she embodies a sharp counterpoint to repressed Chinese ideas and emotions. Her archetypically American, outgoing personality creates friendship for her with various Chinese—with mixed results. Her assigned guide never fully understands or trusts Judy, and the warm-hearted regional head of foreign exchange contemplates her warily, much as aging cats watch young dogs. Throughout, the tenor of the East-West connections are tentative, muted, sometimes painfully humorous at once. To widen the horizons of Chinese students the authorities allow a Western-style social dance, but the distance between dancers is so rigidly monitored as to keep them looking awkward, a compelling metaphor for the distance that persists between East and West.

"I think a lot of Americans hope they'll find something in China they can't find at home. That was my idea, anyway," confesses young Mark Franklin in *Iron and Silk*, also a textbook of the direct encounter of cultures, starring Mark Salzman, who taught adult Chinese teachers of English in real life in 1982. "I hate to admit it but when I graduated from college I thought I was ready for anything, that is until I stepped off the train in Hung Jo. Here I was in a country of a billion people, and I didn't know a single one." Communicating with his students across a multifaceted divide, he is reminded that even the simplest, most basic perceptions are culturally defined, as when to his astonishment his class finds the actress Natasha Kinski unattractive, with lips that are "too big." "They're not too big, they're full." "Then they're too full. A woman's lips should be like a bud, small and delicate." And in response to an assignment to write about their "happiest moment," one student pleads that "I'm a sad person, and cannot remember happy moment," while some classmates choose to remember, vicariously, the happiest moments of others. "I had wanted to start the class off with something simple, but I was learning that nothing in China was simple, especially something like happiness.... I was teaching them the rules of grammar, but they were teaching me about their lives."

Mark's background of study in Mandarin distinguishes him from so many Western expatriates—it is he who is willing to stretch to communicate, to attempt the words and by extension the thinking of another culture. But much as in *Forbidden Nights*, the "Great Wall" of Chinese rigidity and perennial unease with Western ways proves too tall for American free spirits to scale. For example, as predictably as clockwork, Mark is attracted to a young Chinese woman, Ming, a serious student of English literature, but their already illicit relationship grows more dangerous still when renewed anti–Westernism suddenly signals the end of a brief détente. When in the manner of brash Western youth Mark describes their attraction as "our business" Ming demurs that "In China, it's everybody's business.... It's not as free as it seems.... I can't, I just can't do what I want, like you."

Scenes in which his Chinese tutor, Teacher Hei, coaches him on local folkways are concisely illuminating: "In China, when someone visits you in your home you always offer them tea and something to eat first," she explains, and proceeds to demonstrate the mock refusals, the obligatory insistence that are part of the protocol. This need for tutoring in even the most rudimentary social graces does raise the question, though, of the quality of Mark's training in the Chinese language: What kind of program instructed Mark in conversational Mandarin without also introducing him to the culture interwoven with it? Teacher Hei, however, gently guides Mark as his elder. "How can you think you understand everything?" she asks. "You're so young … so far away from home. I'm your teacher, if I don't care for you, won't you be lonely?" Revealing more than a teacher's instincts, her comments suggest the characteristic Chinese attitude that wisdom and method are carried in the vessel of elders and must be poured into their protégés in systematic, even ritualistic fashion. "You're too impatient," she admonishes Mark as he studies the written characters of the language. "You must know them by heart. Next time no using the book."

The most unusual and interesting facet of Mark's encounter with China is his devotion to martial arts, born in his youth through his love of Kung Fu movies. In asking the best teacher in the province to coach him he attempts to cross a long, arduous bridge, because many Easterners assume that Westerners lack the rigor to master these arts, lack the patience and self-denial to "eat bitter." Teacher Pan proves as exacting as the art itself, the culture itself; he incarnates the perception from the West, at least, that the Oriental masters squeeze carbon into diamonds. From his first day with Pan, when the lesson consists entirely of taking a ready stance and staring intently—after which the master recommends four to six hours daily practice—Mark learns the difference between mere training and discipline, or total devotion to an art.

In a revealing conversation with his student Sinbad, Mark learns that good food and regular sleep are what he most covets in life. Mark pursues significantly different desires, such as excellence in the martial arts and popularity with girls, prompting Sinbad to disagree: "But these things are so easy, all you have to do is work hard and be nice, but eating and sleeping, that's difficult, because we cannot control these things." In such terse dialogue fundamental differences become clear: a society in which freedom and luxury are commonplace but self-discipline is a rare trait as opposed to a society of constraint, in which self-discipline is virtually a requirement. In China, the sense of responsibility to a larger community, coupled with a narrower set of individual choices, accompanies a resignation to the inevitable power of authority. But Mark, generally quite upbeat and easygoing, commits small acts of rebellion when he feels his wings clipped by official policy. Ironically, in so doing he displays the very attitude of defiance that makes the Chinese regime wary of Westerners and that leads to campaigns to reduce exposure to foreign influence.

Forbidden Nights and *Iron and Silk* vividly remind us that "routine intercultural experience" is an oxymoron, that the most ordinary activities can afford surprise and fresh insight. Several films in which Chinese cross the Pacific to encounter the West reinforce that fact. In *Pushing Hands* (1992) an elderly Chinese comes to live with his son's family in contemporary New York City, while in *A Thousand Pieces of Gold* (1991) a young Chinese woman, Lalu, strives for dignity in the difficult environment of a small, gold-rush town in Idaho. The well-documented racism of the nineteenth-century U.S. combined with the unabashed sexism of the era to make her challenge substantial. In China, her desperately poor father had sold her to traders who in turn auctioned off wives in San Francisco, but Lalu, soon nicknamed Polly, anticipates feminist resoluteness by steadfastly refusing life as a man's property, or as a prostitute (almost the only occupation open to uneducated women at the time). Advertising for the video trumpets "a testament to the strength of the human spirit"—indeed true—as Lalu negotiates a delicate path through a maze of expectations based on culture, class, and gender. Traditional Chinese men expect subservience from women ("Come here ... Wash my feet...") that ultimately seems more alien to Lalu than the strange ways of the new culture. Significantly, she backs away from Chinese men in favor of independence and finally marriage to a white, suggesting that the gap between national cultures was easier for her to cross than the gap between the Chinese genders.

Apart from Lalu's enthusiasm for Chinese festivals and the consistent echoes of white racism, the Western viewer receives only a limited sense of Lalu as "Chinese": a leveling influence arises from frontier demands. Early in the film her awkward struggle with an alien language and ambiance does evoke an extremely realistic sense of sudden immersion. But when subtitled conversations soon disappear in favor of English spoken between Lalu and other Chinese, and she next conducts even sensitive, subtle conversations with whites, Hollywood's sacrifice of authenticity for viewer comfort clearly dominates again. The subtlest questions of how a Chinese woman could establish a sense of self in a white world, with a white husband, are never fully asked nor answered. The story would have cut deeper had it included more of the detail and self-reflection characteristic of "frontier diaries," but nonetheless stands as instructive for the viewer willing to listen between the lines.

Pushing Hands features a Chinese of the modern era transplanted to the West in the form of a much older man as typical issues of late expatriation arise. Chu is not interested in reminting himself in a Western image but rather in maintaining a Chinese dignity. While his son Alex works, he remains at home with his daughter-in-law Martha, a writer from the mainstream culture who harbors increasing resentment at having him under foot as she stares into her word processor, driven by very U.S. American personal, creative goals. While the primacy of respect for and obligation to parents is assumed by the elder and his son, the issue plays differently with Martha; in turn her mother's offer to assist in buying a capacious home offends Chinese-American Alex, an impasse the couple finds hard to resolve across differing ingrained expectations. Martha and her father-in-law, neither speaking the other's language, also suggest the awkwardness of sharing quarters without a cultural (or linguistic) basis for mutual understanding. Already in the middle between a spouse and a parent, Alex is doubly squeezed by the need to translate words and cultural meanings, thus amplifying the frustration of the interpreter's role.

In a refreshing departure from most intercultural film produced in North America, the cultural and artistic weight of *Pushing Hands* does not prove U.S. America-centric. It could have been named "*Writer's Block*"—a triple entendre playing upon the constipated emotions, stalled intercultural understanding, and stifled work of an Anglo character under stress. Instead *Pushing Hands* borrows its name and meaning from old Chu's version of the Tai Chi discipline, which emphasizes emotional as well as physical control, balance, and serenity. The film's moral core stays true to his Chinese discipline, as he seeks calm and coherence in what for him is a largely incoherent ambiance. Careful viewers will note intra-Chinese issues, such as the sometimes hostile feelings between mainlanders and Taiwanese, and will delight at a chance to eavesdrop on elderly Chinese adjusting, with both complaints and dignity, to New York City. From a grandson growing up with dual languages and acculturation to Chu's flirtations with a Chinese widow, fundamental family and social dimensions of culture are emphasized. Chu, who lost his wife to a beating by the Red Guards during the Cultural Revolution, makes clear the importance of human relationships. "Let me tell you something ... compared to loneliness, persecution is nothing."

In *A Great Wall* (1986) and *Eat a Bowl of Tea* (1989), China encounters the West in the form of Americans of Chinese descent. Set in New York's Chinatown of the '40s and '50s, *Eat of Bowl of Tea* reveals an aging, male community (the Exclusion Laws, until changed after World War II, had kept Chinese women out of the country) still quite Chinese but Americanized as well. Young war veteran Ben Loy journeys to China to visit his mother and returns with a Chinese bride. In the old country Ben stands out as an attractive novelty, a young Chinese-American who understands the language, is still one of them, Chinese, yet so clearly represents a universe they can scarcely imagine. Ben's mother, in effect a lonely widow for decades after her husband's emigration, opens a cupboard to reveal a host of electric kitchen gadgets, all sent over the years by Ben's father, all useless in a village without electricity. The seductive trappings of a culture often travel without the transfer of the power, the structure underneath; American cinema too has reached China, but needs more than linguistic translation. Ben meets and soon loves Mei Oi and, in one of the film's most artful moments, he proclaims his devotion while in the background a movie screen oozes U.S. American love-fantasy. Thus Ben and Mei Oi stand ready to embark in search of the American Dream in the New Land, Chinese enclave style. One young woman sets out for America while the old wives stay behind, as discounted as pre-technological China itself.

Though most of *Eat a Bowl of Tea* features Mei Oi on American soil in search of happiness amid a subculture of Chinese-American males, enduring solitude in her new environment, most of the camera time of *A Great Wall* occurs back in the old country, as Chinese-born Leo Fang takes his American-born wife Grace and son Paul to visit family in Peking. "How much do you earn a month over there?" inquires Leo's sister before her husband admonishes that "It's not polite to ask Americans that." "He's my brother. I can ask him anything." "In the States no matter how much you earn, it's never enough," replies Leo. "Over there the person who owes the most gets the most respect." The Great Wall then, beyond a natural wonder, is insuperable difference laid in stone, as the film offers the point and counterpoint of a traditional China and a culture diluted by Western influence. Interesting yet still alien, the West arouses the curiosity of even Leo's aging brother-in-law. "I hear that almost everyone in America has V.D. Is that true?" Seductive, yet still distant, the West more than tickles the curiosity of the youths who study English and wear American-style T-shirts; but in countless ways a Great Wall remains, even in basic contacts with North Americans. When Paul attempts rudimentary conversation with his cousin Lili—"What ... do ... you ... do ... for ... fun?"—she clouds with confusion and asks in Chinese, "Uncle, I've studied English for years. How come I still don't understand him?" When the linguistic hurdle is jumped, the next layer of difference appears: "We don't play, we study," she replies simply, although Western perspective tugs at her throughout the visit. When her mother monitors her personal mail Lili even confronts her with a Western word "Privacy.... You can't translate privacy," to which her mother shoots back "You've grown wings ... trying to fool me with foreign words." The Great Wall, the earth's most visible landmark, was intended to arrest invaders from the North, but as Fang cryptically tells his wife, "the invaders are from the South."

So ubiquitous in fact is the theme of the invasion of corrupting Western influences that it drives even such a crime-and-intrigue film as *Red Cor-
ner* (1997), in most ways a stock triumph-over-evil fable pitting an
American businessman against shadowy, nefarious Chinese interests.
Although the American, Jack Moore, does stand falsely accused of a murder, one vein of analysis holds that he is truly "innocent" only in U.S.
American thinking: he has been drinking heavily and entertaining a Chinese woman, about whom he knows almost nothing, in his room and bed.
Such behavior, perhaps foolhardy in any context, does not resonate with
Chinese morals and certainly does not qualify as "innocent" there. The
North American take on the film however (and the slant constructed by
the filmmakers) spotlights not Jack Moore's very Western, brash behavior but the "outrage" of an innocent man tried under an alien judicial system, strikingly depicted as draconian. Not only the judicial system but the
larger society proves rigid, secretive, and corrupt, without the stone of a
single cliché unturned. Jack Moore's high volume defiance of "injustice"
rings as understandable—at least to North American audiences—although
it also rings with the same loud, non-conforming self-absorption that partially spawns Eastern distrust of Westerners. Defense attorney Shen Yuelin
embodies the Western sense of heroism, determined to fight selflessly for
the "right" and the "truth." Yet her character, cast as admirable and sympathetic, provides a basis for sharply different interpretations. Shen may
be viewed as humanizing, as exclaiming the distinction between an evil
system controlled by elites and the nascent, American-like heart of the Chinese people; her character equally could patronize the world's most popu-
lous culture, discounting profound differences in perspective.

Although the sharp indictment of Chinese bureaucracy may ring true,
the film leaves the impression of over-played characters from "central casting"—Jack's young Chinese business counterpart, for example, shines as bright,
personable, and ultimately quite duplicitous. All too commonly, in film depicting cultures quite different from their own, filmmakers regress into wooden,
if not unrealistic, portrayals.[6] Somewhat paradoxically, for Orientals in Western film the more egregious stereotypes manage to hint at utter inscrutability yet clear, evil intent at one and the same time. At least the absorbing *Seven
Years in Tibet* largely avoids this trap. A young, self-centered and arrogant
German mountain-climber, Heinrich Harrer, finds himself stranded, literally, at the top of the world, in Tibet during and after World War II. Some
viewers will find the transformation of a Nazi into a thoughtful counselor and
advocate of the Dalai Lama less then plausible, but the shaping influence of
long experience in a highly different ambiance has often proven, more than
plausible, even genuine and inevitable. The why of foreign exposure may be

An American of Chinese heritage plays football with his Chinese cousins at The Great Wall, theme and symbol for the continuing barrier between Eastern cultures and Western, in *A Great Wall* **(1986).**

less important than the length and depth of the immersion, because Heinrich must settle into Tibetan life on all levels, in respect to all needs, without the privileges of the colonist or the protective enclave of an expatriate group. Not only does Heinrich's persona undergo transformation, but traditional Tibetan personalities gradually change shape with surrounding forms. The upheavals of the epoch included the invasion of Tibet by the Communist Chinese—the same dark spirits that haunt *Red Corner* lead pan–Asian repression here—and Tibetans act with realistic stress and bewilderment in the face of assault on all they hold dear. The sympathetic character of the very young Dalai Lama implies the freshest message of all on the meeting of peoples: openness to other customs and practices may indeed co-exist with deep commitment to inherited values.

Southeast Asia in Film

Heaven and Earth (1993) may represent the archetypal film of Southeast Asian-Western interaction in this century, eliciting as it does at one and the same time the grisly history of Southeast Asia, the roots of ancient peoples, and Western society in myth and in flesh; in the end it offers a subtle and complexly human face for the meeting of persons from distant backgrounds. Bearing the stamp of its director Oliver Stone for emotion-pounding realism, it evokes not only the lunacy and tragedy of military aggression in Vietnam through decades of Japanese and French and finally U.S. American invasions, but also the dignity and fortitude of a people not well understood beyond their own borders. Buddhism is portrayed, unpretentiously, as a spiritual sea of meaning and depth, moving quietly beneath the troubled waves crashing through the invaded country.

The direct interactions of Westerners and Vietnamese are confined to the exploitive attitudes of GI's looking for prostitutes until Marine Sergeant Steve Butler meets and soon loves Le Ly, whose young life has survived all the tragedy and abuse that a tormented country can offer. In her, he sees the myth of the Oriental woman embodied, petite and beautiful, calm and complacent, a means to soothing his soldier's soul, a center for a centerless life. In him, she sees American opportunity and know-how, a path to a better life, a chance for ties to a new society when so much of her old one has become a nightmare made flesh. Not until they are back in the U.S., coping with life in San Diego, do their different backgrounds, religious practices, and belief systems strain their ability to weather hard emotional times. Relatively few films portray, as does *Heaven and Earth*, an intercultural couple for years first in the home ambiance of one, and then coping, long-term, with the other's sharply different environment. Viewers may perceive that Le Ly operates in both cultures with greater serenity, dignity, and flexibility, whether because of the complacency expected of women, of the wisdom taught by adversity, or of her Buddhist moorings. But when, at the end, she revisits Vietnam, Westernized edges show around her serene Buddhist center, a reminder that even inner Eastern qualities consistently evolve in shape.

Such generally thought-provoking films about Vietnam as *The Hanoi Hilton* (1987) or *Casualties of War* (1989) offer deep texture through which to experience the culture of war, but little insight beyond that of aggressors and victims. At least there is food for thought within the drama of war, the interplay of powerful and powerless: though reprehensible, the sadistic treatment of Americans in the North Vietnamese prisoner-of-war camps is better judged in the context of Vietnam's long history of foreign invasions. For the typical film-goer *The Hanoi Hilton* will probably reinforce stereotypes of the Oriental warrior as ruthless, even perverse: certainly brutalities made vivid for the screen are more immediate than historical and social contexts. *Casualties of War* may reinforce contrasting stereotypes as young GI's ooze an utter lack of understanding or caring about Vietnamese people, and when a young Sergeant even compares the rape of a local girl to the sport of using rifles, one of the least flattering images of American culture is hammered into the sensibilities of viewers. Of course, tarring U.S. culture with the brush of sadistic soldiers may be unfair in that occupying armies, in all times and places, have carried along the crude ethnocentrism with which most of us grow up. Because combat soldiers are most distinctly not social workers or cultural anthropologists, their attitudes all the more may suggest the most common patterns of interaction. Whatever the political prejudgments of viewers or their pre-set emotions, such films add graphically to the already huge volume of history, fiction, reportage, and autobiography about Vietnam.

In *Good Morning, Vietnam* (1988) army-radio humorist Adrian Cronauer does attempt friendly relations with a lovely young Vietnamese and her brother, underestimating as do so many Westerners the cultural gap. In one delightfully instructive scene he invites Trinh on a date and is soon buying movie tickets for twelve, so well-chaperoned are unwed Vietnamese girls. Behind a surface of innocent, well-intentioned interactions, the film revisits troubling questions about the dynamic between the wealthy invader and the poor native, the occupying army and the occupied. As even the sympathetically drawn Cronauer arrives in Saigon noticing attractive women and commenting that he feels like "a fox in a chicken-coop," the theme of exploitation, not the interplay of equals, is engaged. "You phony, like Americans and French before you," charges Trinh's brother Tuan. "I know Americans. They see a girl ... they bribe her money ... and they try to take her into a bed." "What's wrong with that?" asks Cronauer. "It's more devout here," Tuan replies simply. The theme of American wealth also appears, as when the humorist deals out local currency like playing cards to Trinh's relatives, jovially asking "what's one-thirteenth of a dollar between friends?"

Although on one level sympathetic throughout to Vietnamese the film's action and dialogue patronize them consistently. When Cronauer tries his hand at teaching English classes with down-to-earth, street slang, the burlesque may reinforce, whether intentionally or not, the tendency to see non–Americans as essentially comic, inept imitations of Americans. Fortunately some turnabout represents fair play, as when the Vietnamese delight at Cronauer attempting to eat local food, and American military, political, and popular culture, as spoofed by the professional radio satirist, is to be taken any way but seriously. Nonetheless, even the sympathetic Americans take Vietnamese culture less seriously still. "My village not too far from here," Tuan informs a depressed Cronauer. "You could come see how we live." "Listen, Sparky, I don't think seeing your little production of 'Our Town' is gonna cheer me up." In the end, Cronauer has misread his closest Vietnamese acquaintance, much as his entire society may have misjudged the Vietnamese people. "You not understand, you not," insists Thrinh as she attempts to explain once again the gulf between them. "No, no friends…. Vietnamese ladies, not friends." When Cronauer admits that she is right, that their lives from divergent cultures could not easily fuse, and quips that "I say tomato, you say xioh phoung," he finally acknowledges deep divisions that go far beyond mutually unintelligible words for the same commodity.

The consummate French cinematic rendering of Vietnam in anguish, *Indochine*, also explores the very heaven and earth of the human capacities for suffering, cruelty, compassion, and ignorance making George Santayana's point—whole societies that flunk courses in history have simply failed, like individual students, to examine the text closely. A tour of the French years in Indochina gives the later U.S. American experience a grisly quality of déja vu. The portrayal of the ruling French as arrogant, decadent, and out of touch is lucid and compelling. In one scene a French pair make love impulsively, in the backseat of a car, after ordering the Asian driver to get out and wait in a pouring rain; in another, their navy sets fire to Vietnamese boats, at sea and with children on board, because the boats are running drugs—consumed chiefly by the French themselves. As the life of young Asian orphan Camille unfolds from her beginnings as the adopted child of white owners of a rubber plantation to her revolutionary fire at film's end, the imperialist French culture, the independent Vietnamese spirit, and the interplay between them emerge vividly.

Tanh, the son of wealthy Vietnamese, conducts a double life, pretending cooperation with the ruling partnership of Vietnamese aristocracy and French imperialists while committed to an independent Vietnam. Revolted by imperialist brutality, Camille sheds her quasi–French identity for a nationalistic one as totally as a snake sheds its skin. Both have been brought up to appreciate the fruits of European culture, but neither can reconcile the French aspects of their experience with dignity and independence for Vietnamese people. Eliane, for her part, drenched in decadence and privilege, is searching vainly for meaning through opium and trysts with men, yet she considers herself no longer culturally French. "The difference between people isn't skin color, it's the taste, the fruit," she counsels Camille. "A child who only crunches apples can't be like me. I'm an Asian. A mango." Yet less Asian than she can imagine, unable to fully comprehend the experience from the other side. "I'll never understand French people's love stories," sighs her Vietnamese contemporary Minh Tam, a

Humorist Adrian Cronauer yearns to share a relationship with the lovely Trinh, but learns that the distance between East and West is often insuperable, in *Good Morning, Vietnam* (1988).

wealthy peer. "There's nothing but folly, fury, and suffering. Just like our war stories." Speaking from equal social rank but from a culture apart, when a marriage between their children is contemplated, Minh says, "Two boys ... they'll give us two boys. We'll be happy in our old age. And when our time comes, we'll die contentedly, surrounded by our children and grandchildren." This summary of life's essence distinguishes her Asian society's soul, and behaviors, from those of a French élite who ruled, but never understood.

In *The Killing Fields* (1984) and *Which Way Home* (1990), the horrors of Cambodia under the Khmer Rouge assault the screen with more grim realism than all but a stone-hearted viewer can stand. Yet candle-lit moments in all this darkness suggest the natures of the peoples involved. In *Which Way Home*, Karen Parsons, an American nurse in a camp for refugees, attempts to flee ravaged Cambodia with orphans after the violent deaths of their parents, and the resulting adventure-drama provides insight into inter–Asian as well as East-West tensions. Cambodians, Vietnamese, Indonesians and other peoples that appear physically and culturally similar to Western eyes harbor their own deep sense of differences, and their abiding prejudices. The plot centers on the rescue of Parsons and her youngsters by Australian loner Steve Hannah and his small cargo ship, which is like a good woman to him, he says, in that "she's never let me down, she doesn't nag, and she likes me just the way I am." This characterization of the perfect companion is as Western, that is to say oriented to individual fates and "freedom," as the mind-set of the young refugees is Eastern, demanding patience, solidarity, resignation, and faith. In an ironic twist a Vietnamese orphan who has joined Parsons and the Cambodians steals a gold Buddha from a temple, and the icon's pricelessness in both monetary and spiritual terms becomes a pivotal point in the drama. The intimacy of life aboard a boat magnifies both human difference and commonality, as Steve and Karen become surrogate parents for the makeshift family; and while the youngsters quickly improve their English and their understanding of Australian and American character, they remain devoutly Buddhist, quietly Cambodian and Vietnamese in their outlook. Survival and health, security and serenity as Eastern drives stand sharply opposed to Steve's extreme Western character, especially in the era of the Killing Fields.

Sometimes the adults, more than the children, grapple with the meaning of a multicultural world in turmoil. When Karen comments that she always thought "America and Australia must be a lot alike ... a kind of melting pot of all races and nationalities," Steve replies that "it can be a problem." Fearing misinterpretation he quickly adds, "I'm not a racist." "No one ever is," rejoins Karen. As the small vessel of "boat people" seeks safe haven for the children in several Asian ports, however, the film serves as a sad reminder of the failure of governments to help those in need, especially those from elsewhere.

The Killing Fields, while essentially a portrayal of the darkest, most violent side of the human race, does offer a portrait of the dignity and strength of its Cambodian star, and of an Asian outlook on life, grounded in fatalism, sharply contrasted with the Western manner of going hands-on with the universe itself, like Melville's Captain Ahab. Similar themes are invoked in the Malaysian setting of *Turtle Beach* (1991). Though less known, (and sometimes confused with *The Killing Fields* due to its alternative title *The Killing Beach*) *Turtle Beach* offers a wider meditation upon the human condition as expressed though differing cultures. Its remarkable central character, Minou Hobday, is a multilingual, multifaceted Vietnamese, a crusader for refugee's rights, married to the Australian ambassador to Malaysia. Though living in luxury bordering on decadence, at times complexly cynical about the human condition, Minou ultimately reveals "culturally Vietnamese" characteristics: she is dedicated to her people, her refugee cause, and her own three children (stranded in Vietnam) above all else; and her pursuit of her goals is spirited and relentless. Viewers should also perceive nicely crafted variations on well-worn stereotypes of Westerners in Asia who bring with them casual wealth, Anglo-European sensibility, career needs, enlarged egos, and the rest of their cultural baggage.

The Western tourist, much like the expatriate, often proves to be retreating from or searching for something, and the quest takes them East. In *Beyond Rangoon* (1995) young Dr. Laura Bowman, fleeing the pain of the murders of her husband and child, recalls that a trip to the Orient was prescribed by her sister, also a physician. "A touch of the exotic ... would get me away from all the things that reminded me of what had happened." In the brutal Burma (now Myanmar) of military dictators opposed by heroine Aung San Suu Kyi, she meets in gentle professor U Aung Ko a believable incarnation of Eastern philosophy at the opposite pole from her experience. "I was brought up to believe that if I worked hard, if I was good, I had a right to happiness," remembers a grieving Laura. "We are taught that suffering is the one promise life always keeps, so that if happiness comes we know it is a precious gift, which is ours only for a brief time," U Aung Ko gently replies. If not happiness, Laura has at least rediscovered purpose by film's end, ministering as physician to the battered Burmese refugees. In spite of the high melodrama a reasonably authentic feel emerges from *Beyond Rangoon*. Yet a closer analysis may reveal somewhat dim cross-cultural enlightenment. Despite an engaging story, the lasting impression for the Western viewer may fall into limiting categories: Eastern countries as backward and in need of Western assistance, Eastern societies as composed of either effete monks or malicious strongmen with nobody in between, Western professionals as offering salvation to a ravaged East on the one hand, or on the other as virtually assured spiritual renewal there.

"You ... grow addicted to risk," concludes the Australian photographer Billy Kwan in his diary, describing young, very masculine and very Western journalist Guy Hamilton in *The Year of Living Dangerously* (1982). "You attempt to rule neat lines around yourself, making a fetish of your career and making all relationships temporary, lest they disturb that career. Why can't you give yourself? Why can't you learn to love?" These are central, haunting questions about the ambitious, self-contained "Western character." All too easily lost in a slick, engaging yarn of action, exotic scenery, and raw Western beauties (Sigourney Weaver, Mel Gibson) are the subtleties of one culture meeting another, although at times the overwhelming difference of Indonesia, from a Western perspective, is palpable upon the screen. "Most of us become children again when we enter the slums of

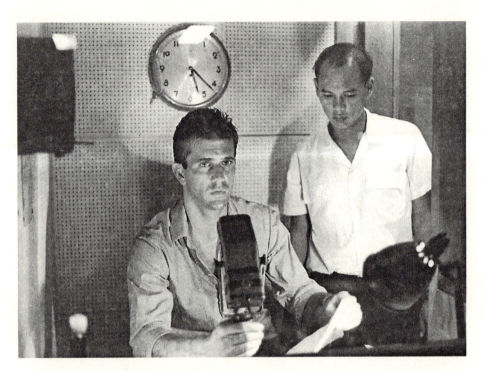

Australian journalist Guy Hamilton, shown here with his local assistant Bembol Roco, is thrown into a world beyond his understanding in *The Year of Living Dangerously* (1982). Across the distance between cultures, even the feelings of close working associates are sometimes a mystery.

Asia, and last night I watched you walk back into childhood," writes Billy of a Guy overwhelmed by fresh, intense sensory experience in his first exploration of Jakarta's streets. The enigmatic Billy, born of a Chinese father and himself "not quite at home in the world," stresses that, beyond the striking differences in physical circumstances, different belief systems are in contact. "In the West we want constants for everything, everything is right or wrong, or good or bad, but in the Wyang no such final conclusions exist," warns our informant describing the sacred shadow play in which opposites are constantly in conflict, yet in balance.

Another intriguing polarity appears in the form of the Filipino love-hate toward the Western world and especially the United States. While *The Madonna and the Dragon* (1986), a distinctly low-budget chronicle (with commensurate cinematic quality) of Western journalists amid Filipino civil war only teases issues of the Filipino psyche engaging the West, of the moth and flame fascination, *Perfumed Nightmare* works similar veins with unexpected depth and riches. In spite of its quasi-documentary style it not only elicits the interwoven histories but as well consistently evokes artistic tensions matching its title. "You cannot build rocket ships from bamboo," concludes protagonist-narrator Kidlat Tahimik, said by elders to be "fascinated with the white man's mind," as was his father. Despite a love of things Western and especially technological—incredibly, he is president of a rural chapter of the Werner von Braun fan club—Kidlat engages with the West with the same ambivalence that he holds toward his native Philippines. "Did you know Paris has twenty-six bridges?" he writes home to his mother while visiting Europe. "Why can't we have progress like this?" he asks, perhaps partly tongue in cheek. His fascination with the outward trappings of modernity is matched only by his regret over fading, traditional Filipino ways of life.

The special gift of the film lies, in fact, in its artful rendering of opposing cultural forces, even within one lone, searching individual. If Kidlat dreams of a moon landing one moment he displays equal reverence for traditional symbols the next, such as rural bridges that link villages or religious icons that ward off danger from a vulnerable people. And the "jitney," a species of colorful, homegrown minibus that conveys indigenous culture as it conveys people, is admiringly cast as central to the flavor of local life—the film beams upon its construction from recycled jeeps as a proud, symbolic craft. If Kidlat really believes that the bamboo culture "is doomed to extinction," as he claims, his camera often disagrees, capturing a dignity and even cheer in rural Filipinos, a dourness in the faces of the technologically advanced. How consciously, or accidentally, has Kidlat slipped irony into his tale? Did he know, for example, that Werner von Braun was forgiven his clear Nazi credentials by the United States because his scientific expertise was in demand?

The exploration of the West meeting Southeast Asia has come a long way since 1963 when the film version of *The Ugly American* brought awareness of Third World struggles closer to popular consciousness and the concept of "ugly American" behaviors into the common discourse. While heavy-handed, lopsided political relations may dominate events in the film, individual Easterners and Westerners are engaged in refining personal values and learning about self and others. For the Westerner the plot suggests the surprising turns and surprising intensity of emotions hidden below the Asian surface. The fictional location of Sarkhan conveys the broader, illustrative suggestion that these dramas can be, and are, played out in myriad settings. A story line that pivots on a worldly, thoughtful U.S. American egregiously misreading his close Asian friend, and his friend misreading him as well, surely can be extrapolated to the still rickety bridge of understanding between East and West.

The worldly pessimism of films like *The Ugly American* stands as important counterpoint to the cheery, "getting to know you" messages conveyed by one genre of classic tale such as the musical *The King and I* (1956). Yet the most recent incarnation of this British-Thai nineteenth century encounter, *Anna and the King* (1999) deftly adds suggestively intelligent moments (and well-written cross-cultural dialogue loosely based on the real-life governess's diaries) to the rich visual pageantry of the fable. Across such a cultural distance, even (or especially) the well-intentioned action may bring unexpected consequences—Anna's clumsy meddling in Royal Family affairs costs a concubine her life. Ultimately, trial and error proves just that, and ignorance is far from bliss, when negotiating the expectations of a culture highly different from one's own.

India and the West

"A man's journey to the end of his obligations is a very long road," counsels Hasari's father in rural India in *City of Joy* (1992). "It might not be what you expect." Hasari and his family thus set out on a very Third World odyssey, beginning with a change from bucolic poverty to urban squalor, in search of a brighter life. Members of Hasari's family experience all the trials and indignities of an unforgiving Calcutta—including the intra-Indian disdain of lower castes—until their lives are transformed by their encounter with Westerners who run a free clinic. Roundly panned by critics as shallow, patronizing, virtually corny in its Western Savior theme, *City of Joy* nonetheless offers rich food for analysis along with memorable scenes and dialogue.

"Do you believe in anything?" a British nurse working with the poor asks the cynical young physician from Houston, a question that might be posed at the individual level or, equally, at the cultural. The reply: "I believe in the Dallas Cowboys, most consistent winners in modern sports history." Dr. Max Lowe, the wandering surgeon with a troubled, Western soul, stumbles by chance across misery and need, and ends up adopting the human family itself. In addition to medical skills he offers facile, paternalistic advice at every turn. If even the community of Western film reviewers disliked such ethnocentric arrogance, imagine the Indian reaction. "You are from a rich country, Doctor. For you money is a piece of paper with which you buy something you want. For me it's a wall, a beautiful wall, a protective wall, a wall that separates me from the degradation on the other side," explains an Indian slumlord, attempting to describe a wholly different world. "I'm proud of [that wall] … and those poor souls on the other side, they're proud of it too. Do you understand?" Others such as the slumlord's son mince fewer words, and simply confront Max with their hate of "interfering foreigners who think they're better than me." Even Hasari, of the dismal ghetto that Max's free clinic serves, blows up in exasperation from time to time: "You are a Gora, a white man. You're different. You think you can buy people's hearts by giving them things, building clinics, being a big man?" Lowe's personal epiphany, and the measured triumphs of First World–Third World partnership in the slums may ring as barely plausible, but the flares lit in the process highlight numerous vignettes of the search for common ground despite sharply different personal backgrounds and expectations.

Remarkably offbeat, *Bengali Night* (1986) may not offer the cinematic quality nor depth of *Heat and Dust* (1982) or *A Passage to India* (1984), but provides classic grist for the intercultural mill nonetheless. It turns on the most fundamental of misunderstandings between cultures, as a young British civil engineer accepts an invitation to recuperate from an illness in his Indian employer's home, falls in love with his host's nubile daughter, and assumes not only that the love is acceptable but that his host has subtly played matchmaker. Sen in turn assumed that his hospitality would be understood and accepted as intended—that Allen would conduct himself as a brother to other household members. Sen hoped also that in time the friendship might blossom into hospitality in England for his own family. "I invited you into my house because I thought that together we could build something between our two cultures," he writes after everything has gone sour. "Instead of that, you have destroyed my family, and above all the faith I had in the West." As in *A Passage to India*, a misreading of social contexts and especially sexual contexts leads to fatally serious consequences.

The history of Western influence in India is long, and the specifically British experience in India creates arresting stories in such films as *Heat and Dust* and in *A Passage to India*, based on the widely acclaimed E. M. Forster novel. *Heat and Dust* seemed low-key and coolly paced to some popular reviewers, even bordering on the "tedious." To any viewer fascinated by culture touching culture, however, that friction generates a constant, subtle heat (a quality for which director James Ivory is deservedly renowned). In an additional, unusual dimension the East-West relationship is explored both in a contemporary setting and one several decades old, as Anne's modern odyssey to Satipur is largely driven by the search for the story of her great-aunt, Olivia, who never returned from India. Through flashbacks the original, haunting story rearises.

"All that spicy food they eat, it heats the blood," a British matron warns young Olivia in the 1920s. "They only have one thought in their heads, and that's to ... you know what ... with a white woman." Perhaps not surprisingly, it is age-old Indian society that seems relatively impervious to change and Western culture and values that seem to have changed, superficially at least. The modern Westerner is plausibly made more subtle and deliberate, for example, in judgments voiced about Indians. Likewise, Anne is free, in large measure, to explore Indian culture openly without offending British mores; in fact, to the amazement of Indian women who keep wanting to find her a husband, she travels alone without direct responsibility to an expatriate community at all. Not so in Olivia's time, as a very complex set of mores within the British conclave mixed with the intricacies of the surrounding culture, and thus her daring spirit "outraged two conventions. Those of her people and of the Indians." Although Anne's era and thinking are "modern," "contemporary," one message between the frames of the film may well be that "plus ça change, plus c'est la même chose"—that ultimately very little changes.

Anne reincarnates Olivia's experience of two generations before in a surprising array of details, including an unwanted pregnancy and a brush with traditional Indian obstetrics. Her intentions, like Olivia's, are benign, but she floats across a world largely beyond her comprehension. When an Indian girl seems obviously in need of psychiatry, Anne cannot refrain from pushing the Western solution. A memorable portrayal of the expatriate pathetically "going native" appears in the form of Chid, an American who has shorn his hair and shed other trappings in an attempt to find a "spiritual rebirth," though a Western arrogance remains—he even lectures Indians on the subtleties of Hinduism! When Chid fails ultimately to achieve a more satisfying spiritual life, the viewer may choose from meaningful options: are we to believe that "enlightenment" itself is an illusion, only real to a superstitious East however seductive to the West, or should we understand that achieving such enlightenment involves a level of discipline rarely inculcated in the West? Such fruitful questions sprout freely in the multi-layered soil of the film.

A masterly study of India and the West attempting to connect, *A Passage to India* lays out its delicate story with unusual fidelity to Forster's original intent. Although Forster enjoyed more capacity—time and space—in the novel, the nearly three-hour film version itself leaves few ideas unexplored. To the viewer not accustomed to looking carefully at the seams between cultures the story may seem top-heavy with the now clichéd theme of interracial rape—the prosecuting attorney even fills all ears in the court with his "universal truth: The darker races are attracted to the fairer, but not vice-versa." Yet much more is at play: the British Raj insulated by their very condescension, some Indians pathetically infatuated with colonial culture,

In 1920s Satipur, Olivia accepts the attentions of an Indian aristocrat. Her unconventional tastes and behaviors "outraged two conventions, those of her people and of the Indians," in *Heat and Dust* (1982).

others in a perpetual state of emotional rebellion, and beyond all that a kaleidoscope of irony and conundrum. Is the Hindu fatalism which Professor Godbole infuses into every event a millennia-old reaction to "powerlessness" in a Western sense, or the missing link in Western intellectual growth? Are British "reserve" and "refinement" shown to be neither, measured against the sun and spice of India?

Beyond a sensitive study of Indian and English personalities and the sociology within which they meet, the film suggests the primal importance on who and what *defines* beliefs, justice, truth, and culture. The sensitive, open-minded Mrs. Moore and Adela Quested think quite differently from the stuffiest English, but they view even the friendly brotherhood of peoples with English hues and tones. "I do not see why you all behave so unpleasantly to these people," scolds Mrs. Moore as if good manners were primarily at stake. Young Adela toys with experiences just exotic enough to slightly warm the cool English temperament, until one adventure spins out of control to become the center of the story. How far, really, does either culture reach into the other, even after a shared experience of generations?

Adela Quested and Dr. Aziz attempt a friendship across different cultures, different religions, all complicated by their different genders. The inherent dangers rise as pivotal events in *A Passage to India* (1984).

The unflattering judgments of each group about the other—English arrive with different levels of arrogance but "they all (soon) become exactly the same" asserts an Indian—speak to the distance yet to be spanned.

The rendering of authentic Muslim and Hindu Indian perspectives bestows the dignity that so many Western films deny; what's more, some

viewers may sense a portrayal of Eastern life in which non-linear thinking is "less untrue" than Western systems, in which experience is genuinely
as enigmatic as the echoes rumbling through the Marabar caves. The centrifugal forces render authentic engagement difficult, however, as Dr. Aziz
and Professor Fielding struggle toward trust across years and frustrating
experiences. The film does highlight the virtues and limitations of cinema
as a medium through which to understand peoples. Some will predictably
judge from the novel's high perch: "Those unacquainted with the book will
be free to find it a marvelous film," condescends the *New Statesman*.[7] Yet
the consensus holds that the novel's sophisticated content was transmuted
nicely into sight and sound, that the effective visual imagery and dialogue
in authentic voices meaningfully, even powerfully convey Forster's vision.
The explorations of humanness are rich and deep, and even professional
anthropologists have accepted Forster into the brotherhood.[8]

Gandhi presents not only the end of the specifically British India and
the genesis of an independent nation but also a profound meditation on
East-West ways of being and believing. In many respects an intra–Indian
saga, the film takes its intercultural resonance through Gandhi's acquaintance with the West, as well as through the reactions of the Western mind
and spirit to Gandhi's presence. That an essentially "naked Indian" would
capture Western attention and become a household name speaks volumes
about the meeting of the cultures. However *Gandhi*, more broadly, highlights the pitfalls of films that center on major celebrities and historical
events. Viewers are likely to bring the baggage of previous exposure to the
historical "facts" along to the screening, dampening the possibilities of considering and learning anew. Yet the sincerity and depth of the film, like
the man, can introduce Westerners to an India beneath fakirs and hypno-
tized cobras, and pave the road to empathy with unfamiliar, average-sized
existence on the Mahatma's subcontinent.

If *Gandhi* provocatively explores political, social, and philosophical
issues, *Praying with Anger* (1992) represents the most unpretentious yet
penetrating treatment of the ordinary young Westerner meeting contemporary India. "Now I stood on unfamiliar ground, looking at unfamiliar
faces, wondering with one word, why? Why was I here?" Young David
Raman is Indian in skin only, it seems, having grown up in the U.S. to professional, Westernized Indian-born parents; his enrollment in an Indian
university brings also his first visit to ancestral soil. Living with the family of a classmate, he is exposed to several levels of the society and, quickly,
to numerous lines drawn in the cultural sand, as when a professor warns
him, the first day, "I don't know how American universities are run. I'm
sure they let you dance on the desks there. But here, it's different. I require

unconditional obedience, understand?" On his road to a subtler understanding of Indian and his own hidden roots, David spouts the superficial,
as when he enthralls the daughter of his host family with his version of
U.S. American life. "You can be whoever you want, go wherever you want,
be with whoever you want. Being different is accepted there, there you're
an individual. Here you have tradition ... and you just have to follow it."

Praying with Anger is a sensitive meditation upon what occurs when
"nurture"—a very "American" upbringing—interacts with "nature" in the
form of Indian ancestry and appearance. Ironically, young David meets
more hostility because he radiates at once sameness and difference to other
Indians. He is caught between the expectation that he behave as "Indian"
as he looks and the fact that he is known to be American: "So you think
you're better than us because you went to an American university?" some
classmates ask as part of a menacing, hazing ritual. In his bright expectations of life, love and the future David is hard pressed to do other than
think American, but ancestral chords resonate in his search for self as he
discovers an Indian identity, a feeling that India is also, culturally, his
home. However, as in other such intelligent screenplays as *Iron and Silk*
there is no illusion of successfully leaping every cultural chasm. As in *Iron
and Silk* the protagonist is smitten with a local girl, for example, but the
Western knight does not carry off the lovely maiden held captive by a conservative culture. The calm with which Sabika accepts her arranged marriage, an "appropriate" match, draws on centuries of inherited behavior. Her
serenity and security within the boundaries of her culture are neither psy-
chologically nor philosophically easy for Westerners to grasp, yet they stand
at the core of much of the difference between East and West.

The Orient and the Occident: Toward Conclusions

"I realize it's very hard for you to take in, but it's your destiny to find
the Golden Child," says Kee Nang in *The Golden Child* (1986) to the comic-
cynic persona Chandler Jarrell, played by Eddie Murphy. "And it's your
destiny," counters the U.S. American from Los Angeles, "to seek some serious psychiatric help." (The dialogue loosely refers to the belief that every
"ten thousand years" a perfect child is born, a perfect healer and spiritual
leader, and that "A Chosen One" also exists who can protect the child.)
Such a seemingly frivolous exchange neatly illustrates telling dimensions
in the nature of the relative mentalities characteristic of the East and West.
However Westernized the outward trappings of the Eastern culture, beliefs
and practices reaching back for millennia inform present behavior in ways

that are perennially hard for outsiders to grasp. The most archetypal Western response might variously be termed pseudo-sophistication or blasé disbelief, but in the end some ineffable pull from Eastern culture influences, often seduces, the same Westerners. Though the wildly surreal events of the comic-drama *The Golden Child* are not to be taken seriously by the Western audience, the metaphysical myths of the East touch a chord, and some measure of mutual attraction to the West for Easterners consummates the romance: Chandler and Kee may never reconcile world views entirely, yet they ultimately connect wonderfully. "I have ruined myself with the American," confides Kee to her father. "He is a fool." "But he is brave," counters her father. "He's irresponsible," she adds, but her father insists, "He's generous." "He thinks of nothing but protecting his own feelings," she persists. "But if you touch his heart, there's nothing he wouldn't do for you," he responds. "He believes in nothing," she continues, coming even closer to the core. "And still he does what is right," concludes her father, "...and when you want to marry him, you have my blessing." A U.S. American as an American might wish to see himself, as in the end doing what "is right." Such a sweet, happily-ever-after outcome may overly flatter the archetypal Western character, the yin and yang of East and West may be idealized in the dialectic, yet it lucidly reveals key points of intersecting mythology, as portrayed by popular film makers of the West.

The East represents at once indecipherable mystery (*M. Butterfly*, *A Passage to India*) and compelling wisdom (*Iron and Silk*, *Beyond Rangoon*, *Gandhi*), the snake charmer's skill and the cobra's danger, a haunting but often impractical past. The West represents a spiritual youth, as yet undeveloped, but also honesty, growth, and an optimistic future. The very Western, fanciful recreation of an ultimately Eastern search for spiritual continuity in *Little Buddha* (1993) elicits all of these impulses, and exercises all of these myths: lamas from Bhutan who establish a Dharma center in Seattle discover that a child living there may be the reincarnation of the deceased Lama Dorje, a greatly respected teacher. A traditional realm stands juxtaposed with Seattle, modern life stands far removed from asceticism, as Lisa and Dean Conrad, the boy's parents, display a liberal-minded befuddlement at the prospect of their son's special status. The powers of the film medium are apparent as color, mood, and tone convey towers, glass, grandeur, modernity and sterility in the New World, and ancient structures, primitive streets and supportive traditions in the Himalayas. As the birth of Buddhism is recounted the circle of ironies and complementarities becomes complete: a very non–Eastern U.S. American actor, Keanu Reeves, strains credibility as Siddhartha; the Buddhist legend enjoys perennial resonance in a culture that represents nearly its opposite; meditation allows triumph over vices that nonetheless consume modernity; a lama's wisdom and serenity reemerge in the vessel of exuberant children. Past, present, and future bend into a common vortex much as in Eastern mysticism.

If some primordial magnetism at times attracts East and West, enduring connections, much like marriages of opposites, may prove difficult in practice. It emerges clearly from the body of West-meets-the-Orient film that the East *is* culturally distinct in ways not likely to be eclipsed soon by globalization in economics or entertainment. Exaggeration is unnecessary to establish melodramatic contrast—the authentic, ordinary lives of Asians and Westerners provide indelible differences, the cultural geometry of peoples intersecting at unusual angles. Young David Raman in *Praying with Anger* may have a good friend and informant to guide his entry into Indian life, may know intellectually that culture is beneath the skin, but he finds himself speechless on encountering the different worldview face-to-face. Mark Salzman of *Iron and Silk* spent years preparing to function well in China, yet his mind-set and emotions were still unprepared to encounter a millennia-old, collectivist consciousness. Australian mariner Steve Hannah in *Which Way Home* never expected his boat to become the floating home for a motley crew of Asian orphans, youths at once desperately needy and yet more emotionally grounded than he, while Dr. Bethune, straight from the comfortable life of Canada, is a strange apparition in war-ravaged China; the Chinese had expected lectures only on medicine, not on life, from someone not based in their experience. Whether the central characters of a film are Westerners or Orientals they almost invariably, predictably continue to think in their native patterns long after confronting a new environment (*Forbidden Nights, A Thousand Pieces of Gold, Heaven and Earth, Red Corner*). Both Westerners and Orientals encounter realms whose physical design and social structures, and ambient psychology as well, differ so fundamentally from their experience as to be almost unfathomable (*M. Butterfly, Which Way Home, Seven Years in Tibet, Perfumed Nightmare*). The English women across the generations in *Heat and Dust* who confound Indian mores may be rebellious in nature, or may simply fail to understand the country below the surface. The constant "surprises" of Southeast Asian behavior in *Turtle Beach* may be surprises only to outsiders. The contradictions of the West as perceived by Kidlat in *Perfumed Nightmare* and Chu in *Pushing Hands* may only reflect the staying power of consciousness born of a wholly different society.

Which tradition adjusts better to the other is itself a culturally relative question. Perhaps the relatively shallow traditions of the West invite fulfillment with Eastern spirituality, or perhaps the very "openness" characteristic of Western culture suggests a willingness to explore substantially different lifestyles and the social and spiritual traditions behind them. Yet Westerners adjusting to Oriental cultures with both humility and comfort prove exceedingly rare: even English teachers Judy Shapiro (*Forbidden Nights*) and Mark Salzman (*Iron and Silk*) have to struggle against sliding from educator to missionary, preaching the evangel of open, free "American" ways. And both get into trouble, making waves in the intricate social waters around them, by merely following the social "instincts" so natural to North Americans. *The Ugly American* of course presents one classic pattern—the Westerner who apparently understands and adapts to an Eastern culture—but times of crisis elicit the reflexes of the dyed-in-the-wool Westerner underneath. From the colonialist characters in *Indochine* to the self-appointed medical messiah in *Dr. Bethune* it is easy to see an Asian truth, that foreigners may be *in* the East for a time, but they are not *of* the East. By contrast, Orientals blend more often into Western society with humility (*Pushing Hands, A Thousand Pieces of Gold*); the sinew of their Asian values sustains them in hard times—they gracefully adjust or adapt more than they change or assimilate. Do Westerners engage in deeper transformations upon the meeting of the cultures, or do Easterners?

If all the foibles of characters adjusting to a fresh milieu are forgiven, the essential *humanness* of both Eastern and Western characters shines through nicely in these films. A character's sheer desire for engaging the other culture is one clear path to audience sympathy: what Westerner does not delight at the young Dalai Lama, brimming with curiosity about the West, importuning Heinrich daily for tidbits about the forbidden realm? In fact, a range of other qualities will tug the strings of empathy as long as they resonate with the viewer's internalized values. Although from rural China of the nineteenth century, Lalu in *A Thousand Pieces of Gold* wins the sympathy of twenty-first century, North American, largely urban audiences through qualities that Western culture labels dignity, tenacity, and pride. (It would doubtless be edifying for Westerners to see the film with contemporary, rural Chinese audiences for their reaction to Lalu and the larger setting.) Judy Shapiro may commit many missteps in *Forbidden Nights*, but we infer that her essential decency and good intentions shine through to most Chinese almost as clearly as they do to us. Even the overbearing Max Lowe from *City of Joy* has vulnerable, caring qualities that partially offset an archetypical arrogance, though his high volume personality represents a common pattern. Almost by definition, Western individualism is a large pill to swallow (*Dr. Bethune, Praying with Anger, Seven Years in Tibet, The Year of Living Dangerously*), innately unpredictable and even threatening to Eastern consciousness, but Eastern constraints on individual "freedom" are especially problematic for free-spirited Westerners (*Heat and Dust, Praying with Anger, Forbidden Nights, Seven Years in Tibet, Turtle Beach*).

Easterners and Westerners in the end will continue being essentially who they are, playing out the vision of society inculcated from birth. Even though she has no knowledge whatever of the U.S. American workplace, Leo Fang's sister cannot refrain from giving her brother (Chinese) time-worn counsel about his problems back in the States (*A Great Wall*). "Get someone to smooth things out. Never disagree with your leader, you hear?" In *Bengali Night* Sen's outrage at his daughter's romance with a white man owes more to culturally ingrained reflex than Western-style logic, while Kidlat in *Perfumed Nightmare* may significantly worship modernity but continues in many ways to "think bamboo"—to long for the tone and texture, crafts and human relations of the traditional Philippines. In *Heaven and Earth* Steve Butler lives out the torment of a Western soul and psyche, never able to draw on the resources of a Buddhist wife who has suffered as deeply as he. Adrian Cronauer in *Good Morning, Vietnam* is trapped in a Western humorist's irreverence that defines his distance from the Vietnamese and their feelings, however benign his intentions, and "The Ugly American" displays a classic immodesty, unaware of when humility, on several cultural levels, is called for. East and West *do* meet and sometimes attract like polarities, but rarely shall the twain be comfortably alike, much less exactly the same, in the world at large or in East-West intercultural film.

Filmography

Film (aka), year, country (language), director, producer/distributor, minutes

China/The West

Bethune, 1977, TV, Canada, Eric Till, CBC, 88
Between the Devil and the Deep Blue Sea, 1995, France, Marion Hansel, DPS, 92
Chinese Box, 1997, France/USA, Wayne Wang, Trimark Pictures, 99
Dr. Bethune, 1990, Canada/China, Phillip Borsos, Fox Lorber, 115
Dragon Chow, 1987, Germany, Jan Schutte, Probst Film, 75
Eat a Bowl of Tea, 1989, USA, Wayne Wang, Columbia Pictures, 102
Forbidden Nights, 1990, USA, Waris Hussein, Warner Brothers, 96
The Golden Child, 1986, USA, Michael Ritchie, Paramount Pictures, 94
A Great Wall, 1986, USA, Peter Wang, W & S Productions, 103
Iron and Silk, 1990, China/USA, Shirley Sun, SUN-Productions, 94

M. Butterfly, 1993, USA, David Cronenberg, Warner Brothers, 101
Once Upon a Time in China, 1991, China (man.), Tsui Hark, Film Workshop, 112
Pushing Hands, 1992, Taiwan (man.), Ang Lee, Ang Lee Productions, 105
Red Corner, 1997, USA, Jon Avnet, MGM, 119
Seven Years in Tibet, 1997, USA, Jean-Jacques Annaud, TriStar, 139
Soursweet, 1988, UK, Mike Newell, Skouros Pictures, 110
Tai-Pan, 1986, USA, Daryl Duke, De Laurentiis Entertainment, 127
A Thousand Pieces of Gold, 1991, USA, Nancy Kelly, Hemdale Home Video, 105

Southeast Asia/The West

L'Amante, 1991, France/Vietnam, Jean-Jacques Annaud, MGM, 110
Anna and the King, 1999, USA, Andy Tennant, 20th Century–Fox, 147
Beyond Rangoon, 1995, USA, John Boorman, Castle Rock Entertainment, 100
Casualties of War, 1989, USA, Brian de Palma, Columbia Pictures, 120
Good Morning, Vietnam, 1988, USA, Barry Levinson, Touchstone Pictures, 121
The Hanoi Hilton, 1987, USA, Lionel Chetwynd, Cannon Group, 126
Heaven and Earth, 1993, USA, Oliver Stone, Warner Brothers, 140
Indochine, 1992, France (fr.), Regis Wargnier, Paradis Films, 155
The King and I, 1956, USA, Walter Lang, 20th Century–Fox, 133
The Killing Fields, 1984, UK, Roland Jaffe, Warner Brothers, 142
The Madonna and the Dragon, 1986, USA, Samuel Fuller, Ind., 109
90 Days, 1985, Canada, Giles Walker, NFB Canada, 100
Perfumed Nightmare, 1977, Philippines, Kidlat Tahimik, Flower Films, 93
South Pacific, 1958, USA, Joshua Logan, 20th Century–Fox, 167
Turtle Beach, 1991, Australia, Stephen Wallace, Regency Int., 88
The Ugly American, 1963, USA, George Englund, Universal Pictures, 120
Which Way Home, 1990, TV, Australia, Carl Schultz, Turner Pictures, 138
The Year of Living Dangerously, 1982, Australia, Peter Weir, MGM, 117

India/The West

Bengali Night, 1986, UK, Nicolas Klotz, F.P.C. Productions, 153
Bhaji on the Beach, 1993, UK, Gurinder Chadha, Channel Four Films, 100
Bombay Talkie, 1970, India, James Ivory, Merchant-Ivory Productions, 110
The Buddha of Suburbia, 1993, UK, Roger Mitchell, BBC, 220
City of Joy, 1992, UK, Roland Joffe, TriStar, 134
The Deceivers, 1988, UK, Nicholas Meyer, Merchant-Ivory Productions, 103
Gandhi, 1982, UK, Richard Attenborough, Columbia Pictures, 187
The Guru, 1968, UK, James Ivory, 20th Century–Fox, 112
Heat and Dust, 1982, UK, James Ivory, Merchant-Ivory Productions, 130
Little Buddha, 1993, UK/USA, Bernardo Bertolucci, Lauren Film, 140
My Beautiful Laundrette, 1985, UK, Stephen Frears, Orion Classics, 93
A Passage to India, 1984, UK, David Lean, Home Box Office, 163
Praying With Anger, 1992, USA, N. Night Shyamalan, Northern Arts Entertain., 107
Sammy and Rosie Get Laid, 1987, UK, Stephen Frears, Channel Four Films, 97
36 Chowringhee Lane, 1981, India, Aparna Sen, Film Valas, 122

Chapter Four

"BLACK AND WHITE IN COLOR": AFRICA AND THE WEST

"There's always war and poverty here, but I love these people and I cannot bear their suffering. Sometimes it seems so hopeless that I think I will leave. I never really decided to stay, but each time I came up for air it was springtime, and I was planting again. The truth is, I love it here. This is my home."

Gorillas in the Mist

"We're not owners here, we're just passing through."

Out of Africa

Introduction

Among the meetings of cultures that are absolutely tailor-made for the Big Screen, the meeting of African peoples with Westerners is the most conspicuous example. The reasons are easy to grasp, beginning with the stereotype of dark skin for Africans and light for visitors, and even the visually diminished pre–Technicolor films provided stark contrasts. In the old, predictable films with "traditional" African dress and a few "authentic" ritualistic behaviors, the meeting of whites with Africans might as well have been with Martians. The movie audience didn't need to keep antennae tuned for subtle differences; instead they would have been hard pressed to recall any similarities, to realize that members of the same species, after all, were interacting. From cannibalism to nudity to the "primitive" pulses of drums, often set beside an Englishman who would "dress for dinner" on safari, the two worlds generally offered a contrast as blunt, as black and white, as the ethnicities.

A more intelligent level of films dealing with Africa and the West has superseded the white-man-in-the-cannibal's-pot. They are set in virtually all corners of the African continent, with numerous Europeans and North Americans representing the outsiders. Yet with relatively few exceptions, the contrasts have re-emerged, albeit in more modern trappings, almost as starkly as before. The black cultures have remained "primitive," the white "modern"; the Africans uneducated, the Westerners the bearers of science and progress. The disfranchised culture still relies upon powerful Westerners, the black culture still depends upon the "generous" one.[1] To an African nationalist, the "exploited" people are usually still the pawns of the manipulative Westerners. And Africa often continues to be cast, simply and vaguely, as "Africa," almost as if any one village comprised the entire continent.

Obviously reality is more subtly shaded, involving all manner of cultures from "cradle of civilization" societies to "primitive" hunter-gatherers, and involving intra–African slavery, wars of conquest, and other exploitations. Though the peoples in and around the world's second largest continent are all rather loosely tagged "African," North Africa's natives may racially and culturally fit more nearly under the "Middle Eastern" rubric, and even the term "sub–Saharan Africa" can disguise enormous diversity. A present-day Africa with literally hundreds of languages and distinct cultures coexisting within some sixty sovereign nations, with intra–African wars and even genocide a bitter part of present realities, underscores the fallacy of treating the continent as a monolith (standing in solidarity against Western intrusion). Profound examination of these intra–African tensions goes beyond the reach of most Western film; analysis of them goes beyond the charge, and competence, of this work.[2]

Even if the modern Africa and The West films only suggested passing insight on topical African problems, they would provide grist for analysis. The best of these films hold more, however, from the suggestive clashes of *Master Harold and the Boys* (1985) and its evocation of values at the core of human existence, to *The Lion of Africa* (1986) and its surprising meditation upon the soul of a white African, from the humorous flights of *The Gods Must Be Crazy* (1980) to the serio-comic treatment of African societal intricacies of *The Air Up There* (1993) and *A Good Man in Africa* (1994). These films and numerous others shape a surprising variety of lenses through which to view numerous African groups encountering the Western world.

South Africa and Apartheid on Film

If Africa meeting The West has provided the most stark and black-versus-white of all portrayals in film, South African film has drawn the most distinct line in the sand. Recently, in the West and especially the English-speaking West, "apartheid" became infamous, and persons with little knowledge of the world outside their doors grew aware of the blatant divisions between the white and black humanity. While the crudest form of political repression, it seems, controlled the floodgates in the short run, it made the most blatant racism on earth more visible, adding to pressures for change. When Nelson Mandela strode out of a South African prison in 1990, a political cartoon showed him entering prison as dwarf-sized, but emerging as a Paul Bunyan giant almost three decades later, while the caption had South African officials boasting, "I guess now we've cut him down to size." The cartoon, drawn for the common reader in the English-speaking world, assumed knowledge of Mandela, of his significance. Indeed popular sentiment had forced bans against investment in South Africa, especially from the United States and Canada. Against this literally and figuratively black-and-white background, then, came a spate of films depicting the underbelly of South African racism. On both political and human levels the message was unmistakable: a Nazi-like minority are capable of whatever brutality necessary to maintain power over the black majority and prolong their comfortable status quo.

The practices of apartheid are too well known to need further recounting—they were so starkly extreme as to make most film depictions flat, unidimensional. Blacks are either simply submissive or defiant, and whites either sympathetic or repressive, and any interplay does little more than dramatize or verbalize those basic attitudes. There is, however, some room for the study of variety and intercultural exchange within the context of these quintessential roles, and therefore still much upon which to reflect. In *Bopha!* (1993), *Cry Freedom* (1987), *The Power of One* (1992), *A Dry White Season* (1989), *Master Harold and the Boys*, *Sarafina!* (1992), *A World Apart* (1988), and *Cry, The Beloved Country* (1995) we see South Africa in agony. *Cry Freedom* renders the authentic narrative of Steven Biko, murdered for opposing the repression of his people, and the white journalist who takes risks to support him. The story is well known to North American audiences partly because U.S. American stars, not South African actors, play the major roles in the film (as they do in several others), and judged by time on screen the white man, who sacrifices a privileged way of life, lays greater claim to heroism than Biko, who gave his life.

In the same vein *A Dry White Season* tells a basic tale of apartheid politics and of courage in the face of brutality. Ben du Toit begins as a complacent though decent South African, but after the murder of the son of a black friend, he becomes utterly disillusioned with apartheid. His growing courage in the face of long odds is matched by that of the blacks, those in real danger, who share center stage with him. However, in *A World Apart* the white protagonist family never held to the illusion that the reigning system contained a shred of decency, as journalist Diana Roth battles it incorrigibly and, as we learn in a postscript, is finally murdered.

Bopha! and *Sarafina!* look inside the natives' soul as interracial strife becomes visibly central and black characters finally stand as the protagonists, the stars. In *Bopha!* American star Danny Glover convincingly portrays a black policeman serving an apartheid regime which his own community, even his own son, have begun to energetically resist; his crisis as the man caught between career and ethnic loyalty provides the central tension around which an apartheid morality play unfolds. In *Sarafina!* the beatific presence of Whoopi Goldberg and other black stars gives brightness to the otherwise dark ambiance of apartheid.

Cry, The Beloved Country, based on the famous Alan Patton novel and set in 1950s Johannesburg, also goes beyond exclusively white characters as stars; in fact the clear emotional centerpiece of the film emerges in the commanding presence of the U.S. American star James Earl Jones, as the Reverend Stephen Kumalo. In perhaps the ultimate agony for a man of the cloth, he learns his son is guilty of the murder, or at least manslaughter, of a white man, for which South African "justice" of the epoch predictably demands the ultimate penalty. However, through broad irony and paradox, the story gives new breadth to the unequal meeting of these cultures; the white man killed was a champion of the cause of native peoples in South Africa and had even started a black Boys Club. The drama becomes the agony of two fathers who develop a mutual trust and respect, as the white father searches for the meaning of his son's life. He sadly recounts to his wife passages he had found in his son's journal, revealing that their son felt that he had been "taught nothing about the country in which he lived.... We called ourselves Christians but we were indifferent to the sufferings of Christians ... that when we say we are Christians what we mean is that we are white."

Beyond the agony of the fathers looms the agony of South African society itself, divided and morally in pain. Beyond the clear separations come the chance but inevitable encounters of lives sharing the same land— it is significant that the fathers were neighbors in the beautiful back country, many miles away from the fateful meeting of the sons, and that Stephen Kumalo knew James Jarvis "by sight and by name," but not personally. At their first meeting, a delicate and brilliant moment in filmmaking, their mutual grief manages to span, almost, the vast chasm between their lives. Scenes of earthy realism that rise into symbolism grace the film, as when Kumalo invites Jarvis to take refuge from rain in his valley church, a church with a decaying roof, as only a church of the poor side of South African society would be.

The Power of One, set in the South Africa of the 30s, 40s, and 50s, has the broadest cultural and philosophical reach of the apartheid films. A young English lad heads off to boarding school and his first exposure to another dimension of prejudice in South Africa—lingering hostilities between Afrikaners and the English. Afrikaner students mercilessly harass "P.K.," and he finds strength only back home when a native medicine man leads him through rites in the discovery of courage. Soon the orphaned boy comes under the tutelage of a kindly and cultured old German, estranged from his country during the war, who takes charge of his education as a surrogate grandfather. Although a man of music and letters, "Doc" makes the savanna their classroom, teaching P.K. that all wisdom can ultimately be learned from nature.

When Doc is sent to a prison camp for the duration of the war, P.K. visits him daily and observes apartheid cruelties up close; aiding the black prisoners where able, he learns to speak certain of the tribal languages. Although black and white alike experience tribal or clan antagonisms in highly multicultural South Africa, a black prisoner weaves around P.K. the myth of a "rainmaker" who will rise to cool the plains, and bring harmony among the people; P.K.'s gift for the word, in multiple tongues, enhances his effectiveness. In a telling climax to the prison years, when he leads a pan-tribal group in singing for the white audience, they express defiance in a dialect unknown to the ruling whites. After the war he studies at a clannish "English school," busy earning a scholarship to Oxford while surreptitiously romancing the daughter of an Afrikaner leader and illegally teaching English to blacks. But the tragic death of Maria, his forbidden love, and a bloodbath in one of the black townships leads P.K. finally to choose between an elitist education in England and the dangers of staying in the South Africa to battle apartheid. The film makes amply and starkly clear the brutality of the white supremacists; especially chilling are two incidents in which the almost recklessly courageous P.K. is reduced to watching silently as "kaffirs" are savagely beaten, because any intervention would have been futile, and perhaps would have exacerbated the sadism.

Whether because largely Western and largely white audiences might better identify with Anglo characters, or because the South Africa of the day afforded them a wider range of movement and expression, in this film as in *Cry Freedom* and *A Dry White Season*, white figures, if not the only sympathetic characters, remain central, are the principal heroes. Black characters display depth, dignity, and wisdom, however, in the roles that society did afford them. Quietly providing roots and nurturance for P.K. was his indigenous nanny, and in a common pattern with hired caregivers, she proved more meaningfully maternal than his mother, providing much of his original sense of home and security. Blacks offer many gracious, even nurturant moments, some so fleeting as to risk escaping notice, as when Maria of the dominant class nervously makes her first foray into a black ghetto, and is approached with smiles by Miriam of the community. "You look cold. Please take my blanket." "No, no, really I don't need it." "It's all right," Miriam insists. "I'll return it at the end of the (evening)." "Keep it, really." "I couldn't possibly." "My pleasure." In Miriam's community a blanket is clearly not so easily replaced: the film medium can best give such simple incidents significance and the full power to alter perceptions, simultaneously for Maria and an empathetic audience.

If the medicine man was the first black influence in P.K.'s coming of age, the aging convict Piet proves equally important, maintaining a steady and wise presence in the face of complete debasement by the dominant whites. He teaches P.K. to box, continuing the development of manhood and confidence fostered by the medicine man, but also teaches him about the meaning of myth, hope, and harmony African style, conveying the earthy philosophy that the oppressed have often relied upon for survival and a sense of self-worth. P.K.'s opponent in a clandestine boxing match in the black ghetto adds still another guiding voice in the wilderness of non-understanding, as he calls for freedom for his people, beginning with the forbidden tool of literacy. In fact, the learning of English by black South Africans takes on both practical and symbolic significance. Although obviously not the original tongue of any of the indigenous groups, English had potential to increase harmony among oppressed blacks as a lingua franca and as a means to wider education, and therefore employment, even to citizenship in the modern world. Beyond that lies the cultural-political importance of English as opposed to Afrikans as a language: when schooling was finally offered to blacks it was not unusual for them to resist schooling in Afrikans, demanding English instead. Perhaps the English dominance was never quite so immiserating as that of the Afrikaners, firmly in power by the 1950s. Thus the knowledge of English came to mean defiance of Afrikaner oppression, a both real and symbolic significance invoked also in *Bopha!* and other films.

Master Harold rises into a class by itself as a deft screenplay (from the play by Athol Fugard) comprising only one set and three characters—it allows a look beyond the surfaces of white and black personas to the souls beneath.[3] In his secondary-school years an English boy, "Master Harold," or "Hally" as the servants have always called him, gradually takes on the role of man of the family, replacing an ill and alcoholic father. As the story unfolds it becomes clear that "Sam," the elder of the servants, has in many ways functioned as his guide toward manhood, that Sam constructed and helped him fly his first kite, helped him through years of homework, and prodded his thinking about the nature of the world. So close has their relationship grown, in fact, that it verges on slipping across the sharply defined lines of apartheid, of becoming too "familiar," as Harold's parents have warned. When Hally at one point stiffens in irritation and snaps, "You're only a servant in here, and don't you forget it," the remark stings with the slap not only of devalued status, but of belittling shared times and experiences. Hally, entangled by emotions of appreciation for the lifelong, avuncular caring of Sam and Willie, is nonetheless wrapped in misgivings about needing the friendship of blacks—those of lowest status in his society. Sam, complexly combining dignity, wisdom, acceptance of the social system he has always lived in, still displays a quiet philosophical rebellion against it. His long-standing, nurturant feelings for Hally conflict with resentment of the apartheid context which surrounds them. Even when Hally tries to support the servants' interests, his thought and expression patronize them, as when he chooses to write a school assignment about the ballroom dance contest for local blacks. His professor "...doesn't like natives. But I will point out to him that in strict anthropological terms, the culture of a primitive black society includes its dancing and singing."

The climax, with increasing emotional intensity, suggests another difference between the cultures, between British concepts of emotional reserve and a more "African" confrontation with pain and truth. Sam, despite every reason to feel abused, continues to reach out to Hally with offers to renew dialogue, to renew their mutual experience. Philosopher and mentor to the end, Sam observes that "there was a hell of a lot of teaching going on here, one way or the other."

In addition to the settings of South Africa, other "apartheid" systems have been insightfully, productively treated in film, for example, the English-colonial sagas of *Mister Johnson* (1990), set in "West Africa" in the 1920s, and *The Kitchen Toto* (1987), set in Kenya at the time of the Mau Mau uprising in the 1950s. The painfully authentic dilemma of a young Kikuyu tribesman emerges starkly in the Kenyan story, as white political power, traditional culture, and black adaptation all occupy awkwardly different points on the moral compass.

Mister Johnson offers still more color to black on white, as several layers of cross-cultural paint are applied to the porous, rough-hewn surface of the colonial experience. In one of the best dramatized studies ever of the "development" process, The Road built by the English cuts through sixty miles of bush, and innumerable flashpoints in African-English relations. "With our road we civilize the people," chimes the African anglophile "Mr. Johnson." "But why should they be civilized?" pointedly inquires a tribal leader. "All men like to be civilized," replies Johnson, begging numerous questions in one stroke. The complex economic and moral inputs of the building project engender sometimes dubious, or unpredictable, but certainly always revealing outputs. The local "Emir," warily watching the English from a distance as the jackal watches the lion, suspects the road will bring, ultimately, not "wealth" or "progress" but an erosion of respect for traditional authority, such as his. Around the road building effort, countless metaphorical calluses are worn on old African feet wearing new English boots, and the camera penetrates deeper than the damned-or-damned dilemma to suggest myriad sore points. The seemingly blunt caricatures of traditionalists adjusting to modernity may be, on second look, caricatures of the awkwardness wrought by the English, if not of the English themselves. When Mr. Johnson, beaming pride with his white bureaucrat's suit and official post, mixes traditional urges with English tastes and pseudo-sophistication with hypocrisy we may wonder if an English filmmaker's framing of Africans or an African's image of the English is grinning across the screen. As well, the fragile and ephemeral nature of status, power, and dominance is evoked by the turn of events. If Mr. Johnson, representing African culture changing and adapting, experiences such highs and lows of fortune, perhaps English colonial society itself is only marking time.

Mister Johnson as intercultural drama proves well suited for film— illustrative of the power of the medium to reconsider the familiar while affording the unfamiliar a sympathetic face. While the camera cannot fully convey the heat, dust, or the sheer enormity of the African bush, it nicely captures the human response. Celia Rudbeck, wife of the ranking English authority, conveys a tolerance, forbearance, and kindness under difficult conditions that models graciousness in meeting other peoples, in all times and places. The cinematic immediacy of pride, pain, indignity, and dilemma show through multi-colored circumstances, and in fact the disparate characters power, status, and circumstances highlight the seemingly universal fragilitly of human pride. Hubris, not merely Western, is universal.

Not only the English speaking world but other societies as well have engaged the African continent for conquest and study. Most notably, in the French West Africa of pre-independence a similar racial and caste system reigned, and French filmmakers have meditated upon it with a mixture of guilt and fascination but insight as well. Today, France is more closely attuned to the African experience than is the U.S. or the United Kingdom: the ghosts of Africa's political history are geographically, socially, and philosophically more intimate to the experience of French intellectuals. The body of French films that treat the African-French experience express a reflective sensitivity and a consciousness of French colonial contradictions.

The films considered here are all embedded squarely in the experience of colonization in French West and North Africa. In the quietly meditative *Chocolat* (1988), a young white woman, returning to the Cameroon of her girlhood, relives and rethinks through flashbacks the life of ruling French colonists. In *Coup de Torchon* (1981), French at their least flattering run a small town in the French West Africa of the 1930s, in *Black and White in Color* (1976) French colonists vie with Germans at the onset of World War I, and in *Overseas* (1990) the French colonialists are blind to the heightening energy of the Algerian revolution, closing in on the tranquil privilege of their way of life. In a tone as stark as the black and white cinematography, the classic *The Battle of Algiers* (1966) presents the futility of the French clinging to their belief in cultural superiority and their colonial powers. Beyond the ugliness of colonialism as an institution, one almost inevitable take on these films is the surprising narrowness of "worldly" people—French culture as portrayed by French filmmakers emerges as self-contained, self-satisfied, and suited to only a limited, stunted species of world leadership. *Coup de Torchon* more than hints that the very dregs of French society gravitate toward the colonial life, and even more than the other films it mixes the affectation-puncturing farce of Molière with gray existential meditations worthy of Camus or Sartre, spiced with a dash of nihilism from the central character. In *Black and White in Color* lazy priests peddle Christian icons to a culture they only brush against, not really engage, while inept colonists organize, as if in children's make-believe, a supposedly disciplined arm of the French empire, now technically at war with neighboring German colonies. Black characters in these films, although victims, are not especially sympathetic either—the French have always been sparing in the allocation of sympathetic characters in film, and miserly in the allocation of heroic ones. In the more nuanced *Chocolat* the clearly intelligent Protee handles a house servant's role with dignity, composure, and restraint, while negotiating such pitfalls as the matron's clear sexual attraction to him. Such almost clichéd devices do represent a reminder of the lose-lose outcomes of the dialectic for the servant class: the matron, to avoid temptation, has Protee banished to harder duties away from the home. Small rebellions are the revenge of the colonized—in a noted, powerful moment Protee encourages the little daughter of the whites when she asks about touching a boiler pipe, knowing full well her hand will be burned. And although large rebellions are the ultimate outcomes of these relationships, the French in *Overseas* and *The Battle of Algiers* are in classic denial, declining to see the inevitability of a major shift in ethnic relations. In these films the mixture of pre-modern cultures with French officialdom produces low comedy, or painful abuse, but no real sharing of perspectives. Nothing about the encounter of cultures is uplifting for anyone, and no intercultural understanding emerges to stand the test of time.

Out of Africa: African-Western Film in Transition

When U.S. movie giants Robert Redford and Meryl Streep starred in the hugely successful *Out of Africa* (released in 1985) they may not have been conscious of making a film at the edge of old and new approaches, of beginning a move away from previous films set in Africa. Beyond a tale of aristocratic expatriation, coffee husbandry, safari and exploration, the film rendering of Isak Dinesen's (pen name for Karen Blixen-Finecke) autobiographical work attempts some meditation upon the Western personality amid alien cultures. Set in Kenya around 1913, epic in length and intent, it does feature countless scenes of black-white interaction, though for the most part still tuned to the perceptual frequency of whites. Black characters take realistic shape but are not fully developed enough to become the dominant, sympathetic characters; at times they are little more than the "foil" for whites like Karen, essentially the human furniture around which Europeans can be posed, postured, and defined. In background music (grandly, classically European), cinematography (stunning portraits of Africa for landscape lovers), and overall focus, it is less "Africa" than a Western filmmaker's fantasy cast upon Africa commanding the Big Screen. Nonetheless, a modern sensitivity to the meeting of peoples flickers around the edges of self-indulgent aristocrats enjoying Grand Adventure.

Although the film's point-of-view is most assuredly white, its pivotal characters begin the process of redefining relations with Africans—Denys with his hands-off respect for the centuries-old practices, Karen with her quiet and sincere, quasi-missionary wish to serve the "needs" of natives. The philosophical difference between them results in one superb exchange—"You don't think they should learn to read?" "I think you might have asked them." "How can stories possibly harm them?" "They have their own stories, they're just not written down." "And what stake do you have in keeping them ignorant?" "They're not ignorant. I just don't think they should be turned into little Englishmen...." The fundamental difference in viewpoint affords a look at two models of colonists vis-à-vis Africa and the Africans: for Denys the wide-open continent belongs to anyone and no one, and he leads safaris, sells elephant tusks, and leaves natives to their indigenous state, in both sickness and health. Karen unabashedly brings European ideas of education, medical care, justice, and behavior to her plantation. In a brief, telling scene she prods a young native to seek modern care for a festering leg. "If you take it to hospital, I will think that you are wise, and such a wise man as this I would want to work in my house, for wages...." A comment which reveals an alert, practical psychology mixed with genuine caring, packaged in colonial manipulation and patronizing, all at one and the same time.

Karen exemplifies the complexity of well-meaning colonialism. It is difficult to imagine Denys, for all his decency and sympathy for native peoples, prostrating himself to beg consideration for the Kikuyu, as does Karen

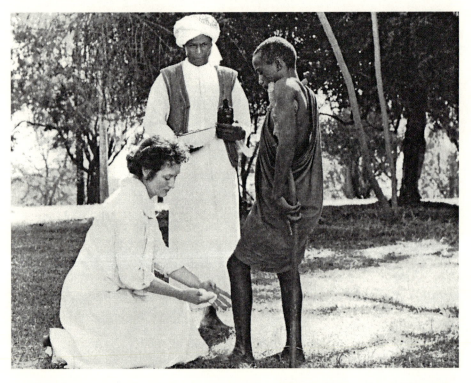

Karen represents the well-intentioned side of colonialism as she cajoles and patronizes, yet shows a sincere concern for the leg ailment of a Kikuyu youth, in *Out of Africa* (1985).

before her return to Denmark. Strikingly, the only time she demonstrates a willingness to beg in any fashion comes for "selfless" reasons, and the scene speaks loudly as a call for conscience, for the responsibilities of colonists. In final scenes, an aging Baroness back in Denmark recalls the magic of Africa, defined by adventure and her love of Denys's untamed spirit, but remembered in European shades and tones with little sense of the greater ambiance, of indigenous realities. To slide back into Euro-ethnocentricity proves insidious in African landscape film: more recently the indigenous was pushed even further to the periphery in *I Dreamed of Africa* (2000). This in spite of a title, as in *Out of Africa*, that implies a focus squarely on some core meaning of the Oldest Continent. The English film *White Mischief* (1987) does achieve truth-in-titling, as the icon of white beauty Greta Scacchi charms and dazzles, and as her race's soap opera presumes importance amid African lives.

Africa Lite: Comedy on the Savanna

The Gods Must Be Crazy and its sequel have met with enormous popular success as comedic, almost slapstick romps through the desert and savanna of Botswana. Central white characters are keyed to such common denominators of commercial film as the attractive blond and the woman-shy man who's handsome, well-intentioned, but hilariously clumsy around the opposite sex. The action is woven around such staples as shootouts with automatic weapons, the explosion of cars through checkpoints, the taking of innocent hostages. Although tamer moments, such as the comedies of breakdowns in transportation and missed appointments, suggest the perils of imposing modern expectations on "pre-modern" settings, almost nothing in these films justifies their inclusion in a serious cross-cultural analysis. Almost nothing, except the quasi-magical inclusion of the Bushmen of the Kalahari as co-stars.

Uniquely, the films present a white filmmakers' view of a Bushman's view of the modern, essentially Western-driven world and offer moments that are surprisingly challenging to Western perceptions, for even unsophisticated audiences. In the opening minutes of the original film, in fact, a narrated visit of the utterly pre-modern Bushman culture juxtaposed with scenes of the stilted complexities of contemporary urban Africa skewers the blithe assumption that the modern society is by definition more intelligent, advanced, or ultimately durable. The life of the Bushmen is portrayed as near-idyllic, free of modern stresses, while urban life is chock-full of ulcer-producing frustration, complexity, and inanity, for when "civilized

When a Coke bottle, the first they've ever seen, falls from the sky into the remote territory of the traditional Bushmen of the Kalihari desert, a farfetched yet illustrative cross-cultural romp ensues, in *The Gods Must Be Crazy* (1980).

man" decided to improve life "somehow he didn't know when to stop. The more he improved his surroundings to make his life easier, the more complicated he made it. So now his children are sentenced to ten to fifteen years of school just to learn how to survive in this complex and hazardous habitat they were born into, and civilized man who refused to adapt himself to his natural surroundings now finds that he has to adapt and readapt himself everyday and every hour of the day to his self-created environment."

The interplay involves peoples whose world views, not to mention practices, folkways, and customs, are so utterly different that each is hard pressed to even comprehend the other. Having strayed from his home territory and killed a domesticated goat for food, the Bushman cannot grasp that such a practice is ever proscribed, because tended herds, private property, laws to protect property, and a legal system to enforce those laws are all completely alien to his experience. His courtroom interpreter cannot meaningfully convey his plea to the judge because the concept of "not guilty" does not exist in the Bushman's world. When he receives a ninety-day term, his interpreter remarks that he has received a "death sentence."

With no concept of confinement, or of the duration of "a sentence," the Bushman will surely die of profound depression, so his friends employ him as convict labor, as an "ecological consultant." When Bushmen and modern African culture come into contact there is ample room for wondering whose culture is most "advanced" or "flexible" or "accommodating." Are the Bushmen a "primitive" people because they can scarcely imagine any reality beyond the physical environment of the Kalahari, or because they experience any language except their own as the chattering of monkeys? Or is the modern world going backward, forgetting human adaptation to nature and destroying its psychological equilibrium in the process?

Based on William Boyd's novel, *A Good Man in Africa*, whose title refers to the earthly dignified physician Alex Murray, could as easily have been named "Diplomats in the Mist" in reference to the roles played by Sean Connery's white co-stars. They are British diplomats, blissfully uncaring, it seems, that their understanding of Kinjajan values and custom is, to say the least, extremely foggy.

The black lover kept by Morgan Leafy is typical of the web of hypocrisies in the film, as is his superficial diplomatic liaison with Sam Adekunle. Hazel, an attractive indigenous woman, would like a public relationship with Leafy, who is only comfortable with the clandestine trysts he arranges at his second, unofficial flat. Like so many connections across cultures, theirs seems limited to mutual convenience. As for the official diplomatic relationship, its basis, worse than mutual convenience, is fairly described as mutual disdain. To the British the reigning powers are corrupt, devoid of civilized substance, and unpredictable, while to the indigenous officials the British function as little more than a disguised extension of the naked colonialism that had once taken land from Sam Adekunle's family in what was called a "compulsory purchase." While African statesmen give such evidence of preparing to cope with the larger world as English fluency and European educations, British diplomats as typified by Leafy are reduced to admiring a local political speech but then admitting, "No, [I don't speak Kinjaja], but ... the tone, the mood...." In fact Leafy, referring to the multifarious political parties of the country, confides "at least I made a big effort to learn as little as possible about them. Incredible to think that British government policy could be based on my report."

Arthur Fanshawe, the British High Commissioner, adds an almost "over-the-top" portrayal of Brits abroad, infinitely insensitive, obtuse in dealings with the natives, and so self-satisfied as to think that the sun never sets on his empire's superiority. "It's unbelievable. A pagan religion at the end of the twentieth century," he exclaims when exposed to indigenous practices. The rich supply of heavy-handed moments in the film do more than maintain a constant comedic tone, they underscore as well that something is much amiss in the connection between these cultures.

Reflections on the Value of Humans and Wealth

The protectors of wildlife versus the poachers in Africa create a natural spark to ignite popular film: the forces of good (often predominately white!) confronting the forces of evil (usually a mixture of black and white) through danger and intrigue while innocent, spectacular animal life hangs in the balance. Popular, suspenseful, violent, and sometimes given to storybook endings, the genre nevertheless offers thick material for analysis: clashes over short-term economic gains versus enduring treasures, bureaucratic and political ingredients, the confrontation of races and cultures, and even inter-species philosophical questions. To view these films is to see an Africa whose "soul" and "salvation" seem to hang upon the tusks of elephants, the hands of gorillas. Yet if this is so, what do such films say by omission about millions of malnourished children, death from myriad diseases, illiteracy in an information world?

The films considered here, *A Far Off Place* (1993), *Gorillas in the Mist* (1988), and *Ivory Hunters* (1990), all revolve around the fight to preserve wildlife; in the process, all explore the nature of human existence and values. *A Far Off Place*, a Walt Disney film in all senses, features three youthful stars—a white boy visiting Africa, a white girl born and raised there, and a young Bushman who has learned enough English on the edge of the Kalahari desert to bridge traditional and modern Africa. After the murder of their conservationist parents at the hands of poachers the youths, their own lives threatened, set off across the desert on an odyssey of survival. Despite the syrupy flavor of Doctor Dolittle and the stuff of childish fantasy, the film provides intercultural grist, with its real star, the Bushman, showing the wisdom of trusting our primordial senses and of experiencing life as a harmonious web, in contrast to a world of antagonism for the sake of profits. The African-born white girl provides a paradigmatic study in living at the cusp of cultures, as her Western parentage and education commingle with her manifest love of and trust in the wisdom of African culture. Predictably, the less experienced white boy learns the African desert in the accelerated fashion of emergencies, with predictable, often comic results.

A Far Off Place shares with *Gorillas in the Mist* and *Ivory Hunters* a refreshing message set amid the dismal specter of the poachers' slaughter: black and white, so to speak, are no longer so black and white. The poaching community has grown quite multicultural, comprising whites driven to add ill-gotten wealth to their already privileged lives and blacks of various backgrounds: not all educated whites appreciate the treasure of endangered species, nor do all blacks honor traditional patterns of coexistence with wildlife. Set beside the heavily armed black poachers and their sometimes white employers are black officials who devoutly press to save wildlife; set beside the corrupt, iniquitous whites stand the educated, privileged whites who take extreme risks to save vulnerable species. Thus, in several senses black and white fade into shades of gray. There is also the ambiguity in the fight, especially waged by non–Africans, to defend wildlife without concomitant attention to the local human and economic realities which may largely drive and sustain the poaching. For some analysts, the intense Western interest in wildlife provides the surest evidence of all of a neo-colonialist attitude—Africa appreciated for its pleasures and seen through the Western-privileged lens, and not Africa of, by, and for Africans. The same Westerners of leisure who once killed wildlife now wish to shoot it with cameras, but the Westerner, well apart from African realities, remains the same.

Such ambiguously cast Westerners appear in *Ivory Hunters* and *Gorillas in the Mist*. Sigourney Weaver stars in the freehanded, perhaps idealizing dramatization of real-life Dian Fossey, the protegée of paleontologist Louis Leakey, in this confluence of Westerners, Africans, and gorilla studies supported by the National Geographic Society, a saga ending in Fossey's death by murder.[4] As depicted in the film, her clash with the peoples, powers, mores, and values in the surrounding East Africa mountains could scarcely have been more profound, and her demise, unlike the demise of the magnificent gorillas, seems clouded in the misty moral picture sketched upon the complexity of modern Africa. Fossey becomes utterly enchanted with the gorillas, in fact she experiences with them variations of the reacculturation that often occurs upon close contact with human groups. She begins to act and think in the fashion of gorillas in order to gain closer proximity, empathizing profoundly with their physical and social presence. Yet notably, beyond a fondness for her principal guide, she shows no similar fascination, much less empathy, with the indigenous groups in her area. Indeed she is soon clashing with local culture, overruling timeless traditions, for example, by destroying the traps set to harvest animal food. "But they have done this for centuries, their fathers and their grandfathers before them," explains her guide. "And their sons and grandsons after them, unless we change it," she rejoins, with the arrogance of the colonist. In seeking to protect an ancient resource, the mountain gorilla, she becomes obsessed with the race against time and with surmounting barriers, Western style: folkways, beliefs, or bureaucracy become obstacles to be dynamited by a

Dian Fossey develops admirable inter-species sensitivity for the magnificent mountain gorilla of central Africa, but at the same time she sorely lacks inter-cultural sensitivity, in *Gorillas in the Mist* (1988).

Western will. She is soon wreathed in awe and legend by surrounding peoples, some considering her witchlike—perhaps a feminist resonance of the film, because her threatening presence comes packaged in that rarest of African creatures, a powerful, independent, and strong-willed woman.

Perhaps the ultimate arrogance occurs after Fossey and her assistants have captured a small band of indigenous poachers: she has them placed standing on chairs, bound and gagged, ropes around their necks. To the absolute horror of her aides she pushes the chair from under one poacher. As the victim falls safely to the ground it becomes clear that only a scare was intended. Nevertheless in saving another species' soul she has lost human, humane perspective. The skeptic about the Western presence in Africa could reasonably view her as merely a modernized colonialist, after a new kind of gold, but an interloper still, trespassing on others' sacred ground. The violent end to her life and her work represents a truth larger than Fossey—that cultures offer durable resistance to forced change, that the arrogant colonial may win battles, but lose wars.

Ivory Hunters (also released under the title *The Last Elephant*) is the jewel of wildlife lovers-versus-poachers films, featuring not only elephants you would wish to take home, but multi-dimensional humans of several cultures as well. Novelist Robert Carter arrives in Kenya to search for his assistant, whom he soon learns was murdered on the savanna while photographing poachers at work. Thus begins one Western man's journey into the maw of the ivory-trade underworld in the heart of East Africa and his discovery of the principled Africans that stand against it.

He arrives as most Westerners arrive, still back at home mentally with phones and faxes and dependable transportation, the trappings of an "efficient" society. Exemplifying the boorish side of whites, as imperious as he is impatient, Carter demands immediate attention and expects subservient responses. Quickly, the guide-pilot Jomo decides that he needs to be warned that "respect is a key word for the Masai. With it we'll give you the world. Without it you're on your own." Carter's ethnocentrism is so pronounced that the police inspector politely but firmly rebukes him: "What makes you think ... that our criminal justice system is less rigorous than yours? America has no monopoly on civil rights. Far from it, I'd say." Still, Carter's brashness is so overdone (or U.S. Americans can at least hope the character is exaggerated) that the inspector, unintimidated and unruffled, can smile, "I'm actually beginning to enjoy your impatience, Mr. Carter. It is so delightfully predictable." Contrary to the expectations of anyone who devours films of Americans defying foreign bureaucrats (à la *Black Rain*) Carter's impatience never contributes to solving the murder, much less to resolving the broader problem that emerges.

Whites are portrayed as ultimately not in tune with the realities of Africa. Elephant veterinarian and advocate Maria Di Conti cannot believe that a poacher's accomplice is in her employ, Carter is not able to grasp or predict the next turn of events, even when asked to work as a kind of undercover agent, whereas Inspector Nkuru (played not by an African, but by James Earl Jones) is the wisdom of the oldest continent incarnate, sage and imaginative, deliberate yet decisive. "We're excellent stalkers here in Kenya. We survive by not throwing our spears until we are within range." Another deeply African character, an aging Masai leader and Jomo's father, delivers the theme: "If man allows the beasts to die, man's spirit will die of loneliness," a theme repeated at the end by his grandson, emphasizing the continuity of generations as well as the continuity of African wisdom. Kenyans are rounded out with a sense of self, purpose, dignity, and integrity (except for the criminal element); the sympathetic whites, though endowed with helpful specialties from the West, need guidance and protection, like the elephants.

More Culture Than Meets the Eye: A New Africa in Film

For centuries Africa has attracted the white traders and hunters, the Western educators and missionaries, and the medical and development workers. All, it can be argued, have represented colonial societies and colonial thinking, all have pushed the African cultures they encountered toward alien Western social organization, all have made Africa less African. Yet few maintain that the presence of Albert Schweitzer carried the same meaning as a foreign official conscripting for a colonial army. As always and especially with interactions between cultures, God and the Devil lurk in the details, with the flavor of each relationship separately blended. In *The Lion of Africa* and *The Air Up There* we encounter another kind of Africa, and whether we label it post–colonial, neo-colonial, or something new altogether, clearly the intercultural chemistry has begun, at least, to change with the times. *The Lion of Africa* might seem an odd place to begin a serious search for the new dialogue. It renders an entertaining, light-action version of the contemporary savanna, and charms white audiences perhaps primarily through the interplay of its male and female white stars. Yet saving graces win it a place among Africa films that transcend old stereotypes. In the first place the operators, traders, leaders, and other players in this corner of Africa come from varied backgrounds, and white does not necessarily correlate with exploiter, nor black with victim. Western physician Grace Danet—she is even dubbed "Schweitzer"—aspires to improve medical care apparently on Kandinko tribal terms, not her own. Sam, a white, truck-driving hustler known by the nickname "trader," appears cynical about the Africa around him, surviving by his wits from day to day. Henry Piggot is an Oxford educated but corrupt black administrator whose response to a cholera epidemic is merely to offer more European cheese to his guests. Characters of still other stripes, such as a bald Arab, represent the underworld and fringeworld of this corner of Africa. Many of these characters are heavy-handed, almost stock, but the overall effect suggests a more nuanced and less predictable society. "That's Africa, all right," declares Piggot at one point, "too full of surprises."

One touching surprise reveals a cornerstone of the human story—Sam, we learn, had a black African wife and child, who both died in an accident, and he stays on in Africa through his memory of them. "Mara and the child, they have found peace with God a long time ago," his brother-in-law confides to Grace, "...it's Sam who worries me. Sam is a good man ... but he suffers in his soul." The power of the scene and of its implications reaches gently across the rest of the story, to suggest surprises in the heart of Africa.

The Air Up There also follows an unlikely path to explore afresh the meeting of continents, for here a white man arrives on a new form of business—headhunting in a sense, recruiting a native to play college basketball in the United States. Western-style "education," of course, is what he can offer in return, a commodity of more value in some cultural systems than others, and when his quarry turns out to be the heir to a chiefdom, the twists in perception become sharper still. The uneasy meeting of Africans with Anglo values is matched, however, by Jimmy Dolan's engagement with Africa. His classic Anglo impatience encounters the African timetable and he discovers, like so many sojourners across cultures before him, that the road to comprehension is not straight and narrow, but broad, unpredictable, and serendipitous. ("I'm afraid I have bad news for you. You have missed the last bus." "Oh! ... When was that?" "...Nineteen seventy-four.") It was just this experience he lacked, as a headstrong athlete-turned-coach who needs to grow up, calm down, and take a more inclusive view of being human. In achieving a personal end the coach becomes interpersonally a new man, mellowed, made wiser by his journey, taught a measure of humility by contact with values larger than his own career.

Warring black factions representing old and new values, as well as white missionaries with painfully pointed opinions, round out the cast of characters, but the stars are the athletes, white and black. Saleh, the chief's son, just as he is equally made of the "right stuff" as an athlete, furnishes a black presence to equal the impact of the white protagonist. His poise, sense of personal and cultural self, and dignity command attention; his qualities may even suggest, by contrast, that Western character lacks depth and grounding.

Toward Conclusions

As stressed in earlier chapters, the starkest contrasts and conflicts make the hardest-hitting stories for the screen and therefore drive Hollywood and other popular fare. Westerners in an awkward and sometimes violent collision with African societies supply the natural material, even if they represent but a slice of a broader picture. In real life the Westerners who have come to the continent, from a host of backgrounds, bring an array of substantially different agendas. But film entertainment narrows the range of Anglo characters and their actions, so that more similarities than differences emerge.

In *Mountains of the Moon* (1989), based on the nineteenth-century quest of Richard Francis Burton and Richard Speke to find the source of the Nile, Westerners blaze through East Africa on a voyage of "exploration" and "discovery," essentially wishing to map the continent, in Sir Edmund Hillary's phrase, "because it's there." No attitude could so well describe expatriate Westerners as this restlessness, readiness for displacement, this hunger for forward movement ("progress") represented in the drive to follow the Nile to its source. Predictable, common sparks of Western motives impel its representatives into contact with other societies: acquisitiveness if not greed, a "doing" as opposed to a "being" ideal, a belief in a historical line of progress, and the spiritual and personal restlessness that drive and are driven by the other qualities. After all, whites engage with Africans primarily because the centrifugal forces of their culture send them off to buy, exploit, study, "improve," "aid," and "develop." Thus in a broad sense the dedicated Drs. Danet (*The Lion of Africa*) and Murray (*A Good Man in Africa*) spring from the same cultural matrix that produced white slave-traders—individuals who believed that they could succeed in unfamiliar territory, individuals without enough mooring in their homelands to stay put and attend to their own, indigenous affairs. And the development worker or applied anthropologist is in some fundamental ways akin to the white diamond prospector in Africa: all believe in "scientific" exploration, followed by action, ending in "results."

What are we to make of the remarkable Schweitzer legend in light of these analyses? Surely the good doctor transcended equivocal motives in his work as a medical messiah—Westerners know his biography as a world-class theologian, a brilliant musician, finally educated in medicine through the patronage of J. S. Bach. A thoughtful English-language rendering of his work in French West Africa (*Schweitzer*, 1990) shines the camera on him and other Europeans but turns the lens towards Africans just enough to reveal contrasting realities. Not all locals celebrated his presence; for example, he threatened the role of traditional healers, medicine men, and railed against certain "premodern" beliefs as "superstition." Precisely because Schweitzer's commitment and accomplishments were extraordinary, his story serves as an unusually sharp illustration of the conundrums inherent when representatives of one culture exhibit "generosity" for another. His saint-like status in the West itself, after all, is framed by a certain ethnocentrism, in that the Nobel Peace Prize, the concept of (religious or medical) missionaries, and Western humanism and scientific logic are all products of non–African cultures. Yet by all accounts his (medical) work became a positive legend in Africa as well, even if the belief system that accompanied it has made inroads much more slowly.

Notwithstanding a common conditioning, the white stars of the most rewarding films provide an interesting study not only in similarity but contrasts as well. Yet they stand out in starker relief against an African background than set against each other. The opening scene of *A Good Man in Africa* or the marketplace scene from *Gorillas in the Mist* serves as a reminder that on African streets, even more than on the Big Screen, Westerners stick out like some manner of white sore thumb. There is more working than appearance, there is the question of place, and purpose. From the fumbling Leafy and the firmly rooted Dr. Murray in *A Good Man in Africa* to the elephant doctor Maria Di Conti in *The Ivory Hunters* to the iron-willed Dian Fossey in *Gorillas in the Mist*, Western expatriates always seem slightly out of place even when they intend to contribute generously of skills and self to local life. If the whites enjoy privileged lives high above indigenous standards while benefiting economically from local resources, they appear suspiciously close to being colonialists; if they have significantly "gone native," they risk seeming like lost or guilty souls—or even patronizing; intercultural imitation is not always considered the sincerest form of flattery. If, like Dian Fossey, they exhibit an iron determination to "save" African resources, they can be tagged as meddlesome, holier-than-thou, a category even less flattering in some eyes than that of the purely economic colonist.

Within the problem of finding a dignified role and a comfortable sense of place in an "alien" society, striking differences nonetheless emerge among the central white characters. Jimmy Dolan (*The Air Up There*), an optimistic, short-term business expatriate, is limited by the Western assumption that his offer will have global appeal, will carry the same meaning everywhere. In *A Good Man in Africa*, Leafy is the permanent outsider incarnate—the nineteenth century Englishman dressing for dinner in the jungle. He considers service in Africa a dim assignment, a detour on a career path which should, by all rights, take him to realms where custom, language, climate, politics and health care are all more familiar and "civilized," that is, closer to being English. Dr. Murray scolds him expressly for failing to engage the local culture. "Take a look around you, Leafy. Ask a few questions. Find out about the place you're living in." Murray seems well suited to his physician's role and expatriate life—though some locals consider him one more interfering European, and they undoubtedly celebrate his intention to retire not in Africa but Portugal. "Trader" in *Lion of Africa* has woven himself into the economy of his locality, but remains culturally and morally something of an enigma—for someone who married an African woman, and still commands the respect of her brother, he demonstrates surprisingly little interest in the land or the people. He rejects a paying offer to drive medication to dying Africans, pleading that he is really not in the mood. By film's end his heart is touched again—this time by an attractive American white woman—though it is not clear if his callousness has permanently softened. Denys in *Out of Africa* also demonstrates laissez-faire toward the suffering of Africans, although with a sense of a higher philosophy: it seems that Denys respects Africa as the primordial continent of Nature, thus best left to its natural devices and evolution. Set beside such "respect" for a continent as is, the physicians appear absolutely meddlesome, though the question of which group exhibits greater "respect" for their people might best be posed to desperately ill Africans.

Of course, not all white Africans are rank "outsiders." To pick the striking example, though Afrikaner culture springs from a European heritage, it has evolved from more than 200 years of experience on African soil. Strict patterns of racial segregation, however, appear to leave the dominant culture with much the same attitude as new arrivals—they consider their practices innately superior to the ways of black Africans without knowing what those ways are, for most don't know and don't care to learn much about indigenous cultures. They belong to, in fact dominate the region politically, economically, and culturally but within an apartheid so rigid that the only real exchange between peoples is economic, and of course unequal.

In *A Far Off Place* and *The Power of One* we see a different kind of native-born white African with a feel for indigenous culture and thus with bicultural moorings. The young Nonnie Parker in *A Far Off Place* has grown up both literally and figuratively on the edge of the Kalahari, and P.K in *The Power of One* is also explicitly a bicultural product, with his memory that "Mother taught us about England, Nanny taught us about Africa." Both young whites are secure in their sense of self and African citizenship, and for both it seems that their cultural roots are comfortably intertwined with little internal conflict or confusion. ("Bi-acculturation" from birth appears to be much less problematic than in later years, perhaps because cultural perception and "feel," like language, are most comfortably and accurately learned early in life.) P.K. was born, he informs us, "with the songs of Zulu rainmakers in my ears." These white characters suggest the best of both cultures, literally the best of both worlds. Nevertheless, they inhabit spheres of privilege and opportunity that set them apart; they enjoy the luxury to consider themselves bicultural with the security of being ultimately white, and their characters may hold limited meaning when set within the huge problems, the nagging contradictions, of a enormous continent.[5]

Whether brutal oppressors (*Cry, Freedom*), arrogant colonialists (*Chocolat, Coup de Torchon*), patronizing but harmless carpetbaggers (*Out of Africa*), cynical expatriates (*Lion of Africa*), hapless expatriates (*Good Man in Africa, The Gods Must Be Crazy*), well-intentioned visitors (*The Air Up There*), morally tormented souls (*Cry, the Beloved Country*), or white heroes of indigenous causes (*Cry, Freedom; The Power of One*), the centrality of whites in film portrayals of a non-white continent serves to remind us of the insidious nature of ethnocentricity. From the rigid presence of Afrikaners to white diplomats, from attractive female teachers to quietly effective physicians, a majority of camera time focused on a small white minority revisits the question of what constitutes a sympathetic character—for Western audiences—and what should constitute a truly central one. When blacks stand at the center of an American-made African film, it is symptomatic that American film stars such as Danny Glover (*Boptha!*), Whoopi Goldberg (*Sarafina!*), and James Earl Jones (*Ivory Hunters*) are used to bring a familiar presence to the screen.

If Westerners in Africa have a delicate road to finding a graceful self at the intersection of cultures, for Africans themselves the challenges are significant. When Africans as portrayed in these films come under Western influence, there is always the question of how the new and old imperatives will mix. Henry Piggot in *The Lion of Africa* uses his Cambridge education only to reign cynically over fellow Africans. When Saleh from *The Air Up There* is "borrowed" to St. Joseph's University—to be returned four years later "with a first-class education"—we assume a positive Western-African mix in the making, given his gentle and dignified presence; yet "living in two cultures" is rarely simple. Exposure to a new culture does not merely foment new beliefs and behaviors but results in concomitant losses as well. In other words, as a person is becoming more culturally "Western," for example, he or she is simultaneously becoming less African or Chinese or Caribbean.[6] In these films, the African characters with "Western" skills vary widely from the deeply dignified, cosmopolitan

Inspector Nkuru and Jomo of *Ivory Hunters* to the portly Western-style hustler of *The Air Up There*. Few characters in real life may be as fully poised and socially secure as inspector Nkuru, as nakedly corrupt as Henry Piggot, or as torn in loyalties as the elephant-protector-turned-poacher's-informant Kenneth in *Ivory Hunters*, but the fact remains that to live between cultures is often to live in a tug-of-war between contrasting identities. For some Africans the new and old continuum may mean little more than a sense of personal "sophistication," as with Leafy's lover who rejects Voodoo. "No, I modern girl!" For others it may represent a substantial tension between competing values (*The Air Up There*). What Western audiences may all too readily remember are the snapshots of North American or European life encountered on a distant continent—talk about the National Basketball Association, Stilton cheese, or fax machines. Filmmakers often cannot resist the surprise value of such entertaining moments. Too easily missed is the fact that such Western snapshots are set in distinctly African frames, that basketball, for example, has its culturally African context, style of play, and local meanings that are ultimately much more interesting than any novelty of hearing Michael Jordan's name on the lips of Winabi tribesmen. Only a satellite dish is needed to receive raw images of Western life, but the folkways developed over thousands of years are needed to digest and interpret them. The worldwide fame of North American icons emerges as one of the most noted phenomena of the modern "global" culture, but as a stand-alone fact it proves one of the least useful.[7]

In the North American and European industrial world, it is politely assumed that social relations are completely post–colonial, that vigorous decades of civil rights debate and legislation, of education and of institutional change have rendered ethnic relations equal and ended exploitation. That proposition is of course at the very least debatable. What is in some ways subtler yet almost indisputable is that Western industrial society has bred an ideal of "modernity" throughout the formerly colonial world and continues to export it in myriad ways: not only "health care," "education," and "development," but everything from modern transport to nation-state systems to environmental problems and overpopulation are concomitant with this modernity. In this sense, the intra–African wars, even genocides, waves of refugees, and devastating famines are complexly but undoubtedly linked to the societal redefinitions, ecological shifts such as sub–Saharan desertification, and other byproducts of a complex modernity. Traditional Africa, for better or worse, can no more ignore modernity than can a fish ignore water.

While only some of the films considered here address the colonial legacy directly, all the Africa-West films cope with the advent of modernity. Grace Danet attempts to supply tribal medical care at the interstice of old and new societies in *The Lion of Africa*; we may ask whether the Kandinko have a cholera epidemic for indigenous or imported reasons, we note that the "modern" state medical bureaucracy cannot deliver emergency supplies on an emergency timetable, that the local powers are more interested in pandering for foreign aid than helping, that the local diamond trade commands much more attention from whites and blacks than does medicine and human development. Beyond the fact that this is an Africa in transition, however, it is sometimes difficult to weigh effects of modernity—what is clear is that Africans are impacted increasingly by a world with telephones, antibiotics, feasibility studies, and golf. The shape of modernity may change according to the main event. In the films that hinge upon the poaching economy, modernity is primarily seen as a foreign thirst for illicit products with the accompanying political and moral implications. What is clear is that modernity in some form has come to roost on the Oldest Continent, that modernity is a largely Western invention, that the West is viewed as inextricably linked with its fruits, and calamities.[8]

If one of the central habits of the mind is its tendency to organize "reality" within the context of a constructed framework, then Africans and Westerners have every reason to see the world differently. Heirs of the world's most traditional cultures and heirs of the most modern, non-traditional cultures have every reason to perceive two different worlds while looking at the same horizon. It would doubtless be instructive to ask both culturally African and culturally Western audiences about the interaction in the films discussed here—to ask who is having to bend further to accommodate the other group, and who does a better job of living at the intersection of cultures, of blending both sets of expectations in their daily behavior? Audiences of Westerners will likely stand on the same assumption as many of their films: that as members of "advanced," savvy societies, they understand not only their world but also grasp the workings of the pre-modern, "less advanced" mind of natives. They will see Westerners as adapting well when the situation, or their personal temperaments, allow it. Culturally African audiences, on the other hand, understandably offer a strikingly different judgment of the same interactions. To begin with, the less powerful partner in any exchange has greater motivation to scrutinize the more powerful, and Africans equally have reason to claim, in the words of Ten Bears in *Dances with Wolves*, "I have studied you more than you know." Africans as well may perceive their cultural representatives as much more adaptable and flexible, by reason of necessity but also by reason of an understanding of the human condition "grounded" in their heritage, mythology, the traditional wisdom of Africa. Although no ultimate right or wrong answer can be offered—such is the nature of "cultural perception" that any validity stops at the bounds of the framework—the interplay of characters provides challenge for further exploration.

The careful reader, studying the quotations at the start of the chapter, may have concluded that an error was made, that the quotes from *Gorillas in the Mist* and from *Out of Africa* must have been reversed. But such are the twists of the human story in Africa that the quotes are accurate, and illuminating. The sharp-edged story of Dian Fossey is graced by the eloquent words of a Western woman, her confidante, very much in love with and at home in Africa. The personalized reminiscences of Karen Blixen-Finecke in *Out of Africa* are leavened by philosophical conflict over ownership of the soul of the Oldest Continent. Once more, there are surprises in the heart of Africa.

Filmography

Film (aka), year, country (language), director, producer/distributor, minutes

An African Dream, 1990, S. Africa, John Smallcombe, Hemdale, 94
The Air Up There, 1993, USA, Paul Michael Glaser, Buena Vista Pictures, 107
The Battle of Algiers, 1966, Algeria (fr./arab.), Gillo Pontecorvo, Rizzali, 120
Black and White in Color, 1976, Ivory Coast (fr.), Jean-Jacques Arnaud, Allied Artists, 90
Bopha!, 1993, USA, Morgan Freeman, Taubman Entertainment, 120
Chocolat, 1988, France (fr.), Claire Denis, Cerita Films, 105
Coming to America, 1988, USA, John Landis, Paramount Pictures, 116
Coup de Torchon, 1981, France (fr.), Bertrand Tavernier, Quartet Films, 128
Cry, The Beloved Country, 1995, S. Africa/USA, Darrell Roodt, Miramax, 106
Cry Freedom, 1987, UK, Richard Attenborough, Universal Pictures, 157
Dilemma: A World of Strangers, 1962, S. Africa, Henning Carlson, Connoisseur Video, 89
A Dry White Season, 1989, USA, Euzhan Palcy, MGM, 97
A Far Off Place, 1993, USA, Mikael Salomon, Walt Disney, 100
The Gods Must Be Crazy, 1980, S. Africa, Jamie Uys, 20th Century–Fox, 109
The Gods Must Be Crazy, II, 1989, S. Africa, Jamie Uys, Columbia, 98
A Good Man in Africa, 1994, UK, Bruce Beresford, Gramercy Pictures, 94
Gorillas in the Mist, 1988, USA, Michael Apted, Peters Company, 129
I Dreamed of Africa, 2000, USA, Hugh Hudson, Columbia, 114
Ivory Hunters, 1990, TV, USA, Joseph Sargent, Turner Pictures, 100
The Kitchen Toto, 1987, UK, Harry Hook, Film Four International, 96
The Lion of Africa, 1986, TV, USA, Kevin Connor, HBO, 110
Master Harold and the Boys, 1985, TV, USA, M. Lindsay-Hogg, Lorimar, 90
Mister Johnson, 1990, USA, Bruce Beresford, Avenue Pictures, 97
Mountains of the Moon, 1989, USA, Bob Rafelson, Carolco Pictures, 136

Options, 1988, USA, Camilo Vila, Vestron Pictures, 105
Out of Africa, 1985, USA, Sydney Pollack, Universal Pictures, 150
Overseas, 1990, France (fr.), Brigitte Rouan, Paradise Productions, 94
Place of Weeping, 1987, S. Africa, Darrell Roodt, New World, 88
The Power of One, 1992, USA, John G. Avildsen, Warner Brothers, 127
Sarafina!, 1992, S. Africa, Darrell Roodt, Hollywood Pictures, 117
Schweitzer, 1990, USA, Gray Hofmeyr, Live Home Video, 91
Shaka Zulu, 1987, USA, William C. Faure, Prism Entertainment, 300
White Mischief, 1987, UK, Michael Radford, Columbia Pictures, 107
A World Apart, 1988, UK, Chris Menges, Atlantic Entertainment, 112

Chapter Five

AROUND THE WORLD IN FILM: A PANOPLY OF INTERCULTURAL DISTINCTIONS

"They have this huge heart, and this huge ignorance."
The Russia House

"I was not aware of the depth of passion seething in the Arab bosom."
A Dangerous Man

"I admire your persistence. It's so American."
French Kiss

Each body of films discussed in this book forms, in the end, a whole entity, a montage of stories, images, and beliefs. Even the contrasts and contradictions are part of the unity, the serialized epic which is the story of that cultural meeting, as told in film. And from each epic, from the composite of perspectives on a civilization or a meeting of civilizations, flows a central meaning, a tapestry onto which new colors may be added, but in which a basic design remains.

This chapter discusses some of the shorter stories told in film, not major epics. Some of the groupings of film, such as Japan and the West or The Native and The New Americans films, present the varied and sufficient material to represent the cultural junctures involved in some depth. Other categories, two of which are examined in this chapter, are but the shadow of what they might be, but important nonetheless. Still other categories, such as Old World/New World film, though composing subtle, sometimes vague categories, may still offer rich examples on different perspectives

132

meeting across the Big Screen. Thus, we take a whirlwind tour around the world of intercultural film.

Peeping Through Holes in an Iron Curtain: The "Communist and Free Worlds" in Film

The groups of Western film focused on specific areas reveal the Western perception (or at least the filmmaker's assumptions regarding popular conception) of the target culture. Eastern Bloc and Middle East meets the West films may be the extreme cases, at times not achieving an even minimal human range for the complexity of situation and personality. The uni-dimensional portrayals are consistent with popular Western notions of these target cultures, notions often susceptible to the flattest of stereotypes.

The "Iron Curtain" films, as they may be called, speak loudly of the power of ideology and political trappings to masquerade as culture, or at least as national character, and to routinely eclipse the other facets of a people and their lives. Watching several decades of films from the West on the meeting of the peoples of the "Iron Curtain" and the "free world" suggests that there never existed Eastern Bloc scientists, or doctors, or educators, or writers, bus drivers, or janitors—only professional communists. The national character of the Eastern Bloc countries, like the personalities of people within them, is reduced to a stilted polemic rooted in Lenin or Trotsky.

In this context, searching for meaningful definition and illuminating dialogue seems much like panning for gold—although brilliant speckles appear, they are rare and extracted with much effort. Overall, though, the fields where the Western and Eastern Blocs meet in film can be mined for worthwhile substance. Silences and absences can speak volumes: what isn't addressed on screen constitutes significant grist for study. For those willing to look between and beyond the scenes and the lines, Western-Eastern Bloc film can reveal both national and individual character, especially if we look in both directions.

Spies, Trenchcoats, and High Stakes

The Spy Who Came In from the Cold (1965), adapted from John Le Carré's fiction, anticipates an entire Cold War genre in which politics largely becomes personality, and one personality beams freedom, while the other scowls neo–Stalinism. In several ways this film illustrates the dichotomy especially well. Although the action pivots around Berlin the viewer comes away with a sense of having gone nose-to-nose with Moscow, and although Western operatives are cast as dark, murky, even nefarious, the Eastern agents emerge as doubly so. The central Western character is drawn as complex, emotionally conflicted, even brooding, and troubled by heavy drinking, but the audience is more likely to remember an interesting English agent in battle with dark forces than to register his rather "Russian" personality. Subtleties and contradictions are crushed by the polarized forces of West and East, swallowed by the vortex of spies.

Although espionage and intrigue dominate the Cold War genre, some East-West films, remarkably, nonetheless manage to humanize major characters. Also based on Le Carré's work, *The Russia House* (1991) runs on familiar energy—concentric circles of mystery and surprise as the superpowers duel over possession of critical Cold War information—yet at its core a sensitive, intelligent, engaging woman lends a dignified personality to Russia. Never mind that Katya, the "Russian" woman, is the U.S. American actress Michelle Pfeiffer; she does "look" the part, does "seem" reasonably Russian in behavior and soul. If a gifted actress can convey emotion and personality outside of her own experience, why not those from different cultural traditions, one might ask? Obviously Pfeiffer could as easily as not *be* Russian had she grown up with the Cyrillic alphabet and Russian parents. A charitable interpretation of American actors feigning Russian identities might even point to the commonality of the human vessel into which different identities are poured through socialization, might emphasize our "oneness" above and beyond culture's heavy imprint. Yet behind such an acceptance continue troubling questions. Can the body language, tone, and mood of events as experienced by Moscovites be completely captured by actors from different societies? And on principles of "truth-in-ethnicity," is the casting of a Hollywood star defensible when numerous Russian-born actresses are available?

Gorky Park (1983) likewise places a U.S. actor, William Hurt, in the role of Comrade Renko, searching for conscience and self-definition as a homicide detective within the Soviet system. Russian institutions, as icy as the Russian winter, serve as the corrupt permafrost upon which the grim drama (three exceptionally brutal murders) plays out. The screenwriters set the tone with official dialogue which may seem laughable, as when Renko assures a superior: "With the world's finest militia and the enthusiastic support of the peaceful Soviet peoples, I am confident we will apprehend the criminal elements involved, Comrad General." However wooden, such speech may be reasonably realistic for the time and place; moreover viewer-critics should consider how the official myths of *their* culture must sound in the ears of another. Overall, even a Red-blooded Russian shows not only intelligence but dignity, as Renko insists on honesty and excellence—not necessarily portrayed as integral parts of the Soviet system—in his investigation, which begins to implicate a U.S. American businessman. In stiff, spare dialogue, Renko teases issues of communicating across a cultural distance while subtly baiting a suspect. "You [Americans] are so different. Forgive me for staring.... You must have noticed many differences between a man like yourself, Mr. Osborne, and a man like me." Osborne in turn offers an enticement, a choice sable hat, which the officer declines judiciously, even enigmatically, while invoking the Russian capacity for patience, for waiting for desired ends. American impatience and matter-of-factness drive Osborne's response: "Do you want the hat or not?" Although police-versus-criminal drama rarely portrays average, everyday life, *Gorky Park* represents a significant turnabout in portrayals of U.S.-set-against-Soviet character. For once, the central American figure exhibits bald cynicism and corruption while the central Russian displays "American" virtues and competence. When Renko declines an attractive opportunity to defect to the West the depth of Russian roots, and soul, is at least suggested.

Doomsday and Doomsday Lite

In 1968 a temporary break in the ice of Cold War film appeared with *The Russians Are Coming! The Russians Are Coming!*, testing Mark Twain's assertion that "against the assault of laughter, nothing can stand": naked satire burned holes in the frosty assumptions of East-West relations. While Russians are drawn as sympathetic, down-to-earth individuals, the American fear of communism—or at least of individual communists—is caricatured as hopelessly overheated if not intrinsically foolish. ("There's a shore party of nine men off a Russian submarine, stranded." "Oh, my God, it's all over, it's finished.... We haven't got a chance, not a chance. Oh, my God, how could such a terrible thing happen?") By extension the Cold War itself begins to appear as a giant miscommunication, a misunderstanding. "In Union of Soviet, when I am only young boy, many are saying Americans are bad people," confides Russian seaman Alexei Kolchin to all–American girl Alison Palmer. "They will attack (us). All mistrust Americans. But I think that I do not mistrust Americans ... I wish not to hate anybody!" "Of course," agrees Alison, "it doesn't make sense to hate people. It's such a waste of time." Yet a second set of messages reinforces the notion of the West as clearly *the* desirable culture. Russians come ashore only because the commander's curiosity to take an upclose look at American soil runs his submarine aground, and a young Alexei, smitten with Alison and presumably the whole idea of "freedom," seems instantly at home in the U.S. At film's end an armed mini-showdown reminds everyone of the serious stakes behind the satire, but for many viewers Russians would never seem quite so uni-dimensional again. Almost twenty years later *Russkies* (1987) echoed the lighter side of Russians clandestinely among us, and while comedies often shred serious characterizations in pursuit of humorous moments, they often as well poke holes in worn, unhealthy stereotypes. The deliberately farcical *Spies Like Us* (1985) does little to present authentic personalities on either side of the divide, but from its daffy action emerges an unmistakable conclusion: those who run the opposing systems may be nefarious, but at the grass-roots, human level both U.S. Americans and Russians are down-to-earth, even fun and probably even lovable.

Based on a popular novel, *The Hunt for Red October* (1990) adds complexity to the central Russian character, around the edges of one more doomsday, especially chilling Cold War plot. The "Red October" is a nuclear sub, undetectable by conventional means, representing the potential and indeed the intention for nuclear first strikes by the USSR. The Russian captain, portrayed by Scottish actor Sean Connery, takes the sub to sea with the clear purpose of defecting, running both a Soviet and American gauntlet. The classically Cold War tenor—no one's motives are totally trusted by anyone else—is softened by Captain Ramius's love of poetry, by his sentimentality, intellect, and integrity. Russian officers intending to defect are further humanized by the innocence of their idealized love of the West. "...I will live in Montana," glows a senior officer. "I will have a pickup truck, or possibly even a recreational vehicle, and drive from state to state. Do they let you do that?" "Oh, yes." "No papers?" "No papers." Yet the very fact that "free world" worship is so centrally posed raises its own, troubling question. Can the import of a film ultimately be other than patronizing when the most sensitive, intelligent Russians defect? From the complexity of the military and political plot also emerges another consistency which flatters U.S. Americans: a superior cunning predictably leads the West to win. What in some ways thaws the portrayals of key Russians eventually sends the same stock, culturally divisive messages.

Humanity with Difficulty

Six years earlier *Moscow on the Hudson* (1984) had given genuine heart, depth, and humor to a Russian character, Vladimir Ivanoff—as played by

U.S. American Robin Williams. Although semi-comedic in intent, often lighthearted, the film actually presents a concise challenge of analysis equal to the finest of intercultural stories: so rich are so many scenes in cultural depiction, often ambivalent or multi-layered, that no summary can do it full justice. Many of the facets of the quintessential "Russian soul," as interpreted by Western theorists, find expression in Ivanoff's pensive, moody, warmly emotional manner in both his old life and new U.S. American one.[1] In *Moscow on the Hudson* the protagonist also defects, a fact which skews any possibility that his culture (or at least his nation as presented) will be judged without prejudice, or as equally worthy as the culture that receives the defector. From early scenes in Moscow, Russian life is cast as drab, oppressive, and the Russians in charge as virtually Orwellian—suspicion and repression are a way of life. In addition everyday existence, down to the bare necessities, has turned into a test of endurance, in which standing patiently in line for hours, under falling snow, is rewarded with quality toilet paper. From such seemingly sterile soil flower a poetic soul, Vladimir, who plays saxophone in a circus orchestra, and his best friend Anatoly, the circus clown.

At one level viewers may relax and enjoy straightforward vignettes of cultures in contrast. The grim Soviet Union spawns dual images of the West, one the institutionalized portrayal of insidious decadence, while in the opposite direction run the unofficial fantasies (often equally unrealistic) of the comfortable, unfettered Western life that make defecting a constant temptation. An audience mostly aware only of Russian scientific achievement catches the unmistakable message of sensitive emotional and artistic currents within the culture, currents that run beneath an institutional drabness which no Russian can love. "My soul is standing in line at the food store," rejoins Ivanoff when Anatoly chides him about a flagging spirit. In contrast, when the circus travels to New York, its members encounter a society almost literally bursting its capitalist britches, wide-open to everything: immigrants from all corners of the globe (including an immigration lawyer who is himself a Cuban refugee); private and public morality and "entertainment" of all genres; capitalism and materialism running loose, disorganized yet fruitful. Most of all, social and political "freedom." "This is New York City," rules the police officer called to Bloomingdale's to referee Ivanoff's defection. "The man can do whatever he wants." What much of the world seems to want is to migrate to the West, especially North America, as a rainbow of new Americans arcs across the screen in a spectrum of hues and personalities. The imports serve as a chorus for the immigrant experience. From an Indian physician to an Italian cosmetics salesgirl to a Jamaican government clerk, motley characters paint

New York as open, honest, and alive—everything that monotonal and monocultural Moscow supposedly is not. Though some may complain of a sugary Statue of Liberty film, *Moscow on the Hudson* effectively touches every issue in the immigrant's handbook, from the "bittersweet" duality of intoxicating freedom dampened by homesickness to the tribulations of making a living in the Land of Plenty.[2] The screenplay's writers, after interviewing numerous immigrants, put such ethnographic research to good purpose: in dialogue and detail they achieve an uncanny authenticity of tone except when their comedic reach is strained.[3]

For all the pure intercultural interest on the very surface of events, a host of more perplexing questions lies just below. Will Ivanoff's affection for this "strange and wonderful" country sustain him through years of estrangement from family, friends, the familiar? For that matter, what drives the human animal away from the familiar to experience the largely unknown? Discontent is not a sufficient condition for a successful defection. As alienated Anatoly cannot take the giant step, while seemingly resigned Vladimir suddenly is lit with defection fever, we may wonder what corner of the much-discussed "Russian soul" seeks "freedom," who may later crave companionship over vodka, whether poetic Russian voices will be stifled by an ambiance that eclipses other cultures and languages, pushing all expression toward English. We may muse that the United States is still fueled by the spirit of those willing to "get on the boat," willing to leave centuries of established predictabilities and comforts behind. From such ungrounded yearnings U.S. culture has created a menu of virtues. But *Moscow on the Hudson* may ask if the rush to U.S. shores results largely from ephemeral imbalances between nations in opulence and opportunity, for most world cultures have had, at various times, immigrants flow in and emigrants flow out. Likewise, the official Russian portrait of Western decadence may be all too casually dismissed as comically false propaganda. Yet as the Russian troupe, just off the plane, gawk at the lascivious billboard hawking Calvin Klein underwear—meant to be emblematic of American culture—the question of whether the seductive is also the "superior" fairly emerges. "Freedom," "opportunity," "happiness," and "progress," like all social artifacts, are culturally defined, and *Moscow on the Hudson* offers myriad points of reference from which to survey for their location.

The following year *White Nights* (1985) attempted to counterpose East and West across politics, dance, and personality, with ragged results, but Mikhail Baryshnikov, essentially playing himself as ballet legend Nikolai Rodchenko, adds authentic punch to the effect. The essential theme—a superstar of the arts sold on straightforward Western liberty—makes its impact in the form of a powerful anti–Soviet statement, one unlikely to engender respect for the timeless values of Russian culture. "Sunday supplement" critics, sometimes distracted by the superficialities of a film from the deeper values at play, nevertheless homed in on the clear intercultural import of this storyline. The Los Angeles *Times* tagged the "cold, claustrophobic" film as doing "wrong to two cultures," noting the stock, unidimensional nature of the Soviets and protesting the instinct to "reduce whole nations and cultures to this sort of shorthand."[4] For another reviewer the film succumbed to predictable "clichés," even "xenophobia," attempting "to denigrate a society and culture which it sees as inferior and impoverished,"[5] and even a relatively benign review by the New York *Post* reacted to the dark portrayal of Russian life, "where even the privileged are prisoners and only the sentences differ."[6] Another critic touched directly upon the most troubling twist of all, the implication, born of the Baryshnikov character's rebellion, that deeply Russian art must be smuggled abroad to survive, the "idea that a Russian can be truly Russian only in America."[7] It can be countered that for once, in *White Nights*, we also see a defector in the other direction, the disaffected tap dancer played by U.S. tap star Gregory Hines. He asserts in fact that U.S. American culture also imprisons and breaks individual spirits. Nonetheless the orgy of re-defections at film's end leaves no doubt as to whose culture is more desirable and just.

While centerstage is dominated by starkly judgmental messages the more revealing, often humanizing ones blink like beacons in the wings. When an aging "babushka" watches the final escape in silence, just short of winking her approval, the vignette represents not only a kindly spirit but a species of Russian heroism, for the old woman could have made her life much easier by alerting the authorities. Such a seemingly small act looms large on the screen because the parameters for the exercise of free will are clearly limited, in contrast with Western faith that free will conquers all. For example, when Nikolai Rodchenko's manager plans to go public about his detainment in Russia and "focus world opinion" she reveals very "American" reference points, especially the belief that open speech forces a solution to problems.

The questions suggested by the film, more than the film itself, shed insight on cultures in contrast. We first encounter Raymond Greenwood, the Vietnam War-era defector, entertaining Siberians with a burlesque—*Porgy and Bess* offered as if it depicted the contemporary United States. If Russians will heartily consume caricatures of the West, why should Western film-viewers think that they are not equally spoon-fed much that is spurious, albeit in entertaining form? In the broadest, metaphorical sense could *White Nights* suggest that the U.S. is "tap"—carefree, easily irreverent, multicultural and racial in origins and style—while Soviet culture is

A black U.S. American, shown here with his Russian wife, are drawn into the saga of a captured Russian defector who wishes to regain freedom in the West, in a cauldron of crossed perceptions in *White Nights* (1985).

ballet—constrained, of necessity quite disciplined, but ultimately an advanced, beautiful expression of human possibilities? But even such wider search for meaning echoes the fundamental cleavage, the postwar assumption that the two cultures are fundamentally opposed. The crudest films, such as *Rocky IV* (1985), pit American resolve against a diabolical Russian will to dominate as the boxers smash at each other's faces—representing the opposing system. *Streets of Gold* (1986) also stages the East-West battle in the ring, with Russian and U.S. American fighters slugging it out in Olympic competition; but, within the confines of a predictable plot, discerning viewers can see flickers of the sensitive "Russian soul," can ponder interesting contrasts in the nature of Eastern and Western character.

Popular film stereotypes of national character tend to endure. While they may occasionally break apart in richly serious screenplays on the one hand or irreverent comedy on the other, they are generally more vulnerable to minor changes in shape, or to gradual corrosion, than to complete destruction. In 1991 East-West film based on hackneyed plot-lines and characters kept coming, as not only *The Russia House* but *Back in the USSR* and *Company Business* were released. "I've been here two weeks, on a tour, with a group. I've seen it all, the monuments, the Kremlin, the Bolshoi ... but ... I wanted to see some real life, you know, the real Russia," explains the youthful Archer from Chicago in *Back in the USSR*. This could have made a promising beginning to meeting another culture. Instead he blunders into a tired plot of intrigue—in this case stolen art instead of stolen secrets of State—but the panorama of Moscow, and Moscovites, captures moments of redeeming interest. Young Lena may illustrate a complex contemporary Russia—as a prostitute, yet her own woman, also an aspiring clothes designer, and a temperamental entrepreneur all in the same, convincing package. An aging, confused, decorated soldier cared for by family echoes genuine experience, as do revealing myths about the U.S. ("Chicago? Al Capone, no?"), as does the behavior of several young Russians, yet overall the film seems frozen in the last days of the Cold War. The screenwriters would have done better to let the story reflect a thawing "glasnost" in plot and character, a liberating "perestroika" that finally goes beneath outworn images. Even less worthwhile, *Company Business* turns on the repatriation of an Eastern Bloc spy by a semi-retired, cynical CIA operative. At least a genuine Russian in actor Mikhail Baryshnikov gave some sense of a native-born personality interacting with an unusual, unflattering American one.

A Captive in the Land (1990) finally attempts to give cooperative interaction to a U.S. American and an injured Russian, stranded near the North Pole after a plane crash, struggling for sheer survival while hoping for rescue. Although the limited plot—very little happens while the two hole up in a wrecked fuselage trying to stay warm—provides quite limited interest, the script avoids hackneyed East-West dueling by giving the two a common fate. Predictably, the Russian speaks fluent English for the constant stream of dialogue. Perhaps significantly, the American, Royce, believes rescue is imminent, while Averyanov's thinking is not imbued with such optimism. Rather, his dignified, philosophical resignation to the fates stands in contrast to the American character. If a crippled Russian citing poetry achieves an authentic ring, so does Royce's refusal to abandon him as they make their escape. But when Royce ultimately tows Averyanov scores of miles on a sled, making an almost impossible passage, the question of whether the Russian would have done the same arises. Are we witness to only another twist on the message of U.S. American superiority, this time a starkly one-on-one moral contest won by the West?

Intercourse between cultures tends to follow the shape of the situation that creates it. International tension and war create their inevitable dynamics, of course, but even deliberately planned interaction will hold the

form of its design. "This is Anglo-Soviet cultural exchange" Nicki counsels Katya in *The Russia House*, "we smile and we exchange culture." The
cocktail reception scenes in *Moscow on the Hudson* certainly evidence a sincere interest between the peoples, but worthwhile meanings only spark
across odd, oblique points, humor and irony aside. ("Veronica Cohen, I
teach Marxism at Columbia University." "Vladimir Ivanoff, I am musician
with circus ... You don't look like a Marxist." "I'm not, I'm a humanist. What
does a Marxist look like?" "Usually has beard and mustache." "The women,
too?" "In Russia, especially women.") Communication, even when not over
the barrel of a Cold War weapon, may prove all too superficial, and characterizations overtly patronizing. "They just want to be like us," proclaims
British publisher "Barley" Scott Blair in *The Russia House*. This judgment
comes from a man who rates, no less, as one of least ethnocentric characters in any East-West film. Yet what are we to make of Westerners, like
Barley, who "love the place. It draws me ... Such a shambles ... Poor bug-
gers." His tone may bear a certain kindness, but not the beginnings of healthy
interchange and understanding. Not only can cheap psycho-social analysis
find labels for patronizing whole cultures — savior complexes and the like —
but such a dynamic tends to efface the important and delightful differences
in perspective between cultures that prove illuminating, as well as leaven-
ing, to the storytelling arts. The serio-comic BBC production *Letter to
Brezhnev* (1985) scores points as intercultural film largely because the plain,
prosaic meeting of Russians and English occurs on an even field, and no
one has cause to patronize anyone else. The story line follows the mundane —
two Soviet sailors, allowed a night of leave in Liverpool, meet a pair of
lonely, working-class women with whom they share casual romance and
conversation about their respective lives. "Well what about all the food
shortages?" queries Elaine after Peter has poetically praised his native land.
"There are no food shortages," he responds. "We read about it all the time
in the papers...." "We read the same about you." Such casual dialogue constructs more than the sum of its parts. It serves as a solid demonstration
that the face-to-face meeting of cultures often erases vague, fallacious images
of societies seen only at a distance, replacing them with sentiment in-the-
flesh, however eccentric or misrepresentative. If Elaine falls wistfully in love
after only one night with charming, expressive Peter, becoming intent
against all advice on joining him in Russia, we may wonder if her idealized
love represents any greater illusion than the flat, negative images of his
country generally held by the English. From the surprising reply to her letter to Brezhnev, inviting her to Russia on a free Aeroflot ticket, to the cold
portrait drawn for her by English officials, the issues of separating reality
from illusion and citizen from propaganda are subtly invoked; perhaps all

Russian Peter and British Elaine kiss through a fence that symbolizes the real distance between their lives, in *Letter to Brezhnev* **(1985).**

diplomacy should occur at the citizen level, one-on-one. As Elaine boards a flight for Moscow at film's end, the viewer may already imagine a cockney girl abroad; the situation begs for a sequel, a glimpse of crossing cultures in the other direction.

Films have too often depicted Russians as little more than hard drinking, frustrated Westerners, not as a unique blend of traditions and cultures, mixing influences from Europe, the Orient, and the Islamic world, formed through centuries of equally unique history. Russia meets the West film could, and hopefully will in the future, mine rich and suggestive differences for meaningful characters and stories. For example, the Russian character and the demands of daily life lend intense importance to interpersonal connections—Russians are known to develop friendships in the deepest, multifaceted sense of the term.[8] Expectations of friendship deeper and different than those encountered in Western, especially U.S. American culture, could drive sophisticated dramatic interest, and the famed Russian penchant for soulful, honest, passionate exchange over food and drink could enliven it. Comedic as well as serious plots wrap nicely around white lies, misunderstandings, and nuanced conversation, all predictably present when real-life Russians and Westerners meet. It is easy to imagine the storyline of *Gung Ho*, which featured Japanese management attempting to rule over unruly American workers, transposed onto a Russian and Western setting, the meeting of established Western capitalism with post–Soviet capitalism in its infancy. There are as well a host of real-life challenges to Westerners living or visiting in Russia, just as to Russians in the West, which lend themselves to the Big Screen in ways both illustrative and entertaining. From standing in lines to eating and drinking habits, from punctuality to the daily routines of city life, the everyday existence of ordinary people remains largely underportrayed.

Shifting Sands and Arabian Nights: The Great Gulf Between the West and the Land of Mohammed

The archetypal Middle East meets the West film could fittingly be represented by *Midnight Express* (1978). Set in Istanbul, it follows young Billy Hayes who, arrested for smuggling drugs, suffers years of misery, of "barbaric" experiences in prison before escape. In the broadest sense, for viewers, the court and prison scenes represent a system, that of an entire people and culture. Emblematic also is the reaction of Billy's father when he comes to Istanbul for the trial: once Turkish food makes him ill, he quickly decides not to take "any more chances. I'm going to eat at the

Hilton every night with steak and french fries and lots of catsup." Turkey is dicey, different, clearly non–Western without the saving grace of Far Eastern élan. In the end the impression left for Westerners is that Turks are at least slightly unsavory, unpleasant, unforgiving, and above all mysterious, their personalities as murky and ill-defined as their vaguely dark skin tones are to many a Western eye.

Anticipating the genre, *The Man Who Knew Too Much* (1956) spun a foolish tale of intrigue set in French Morocco, in which the depth of Western insight is mostly limited to remarking upon the similarity of the Middle East to the desert country of North America. City and interior scenes attempted an "Arabian" mood but achieved only weak, inauthentic ambiance, and everyone, everywhere in the film speaks English. Classic U. S. cultural icon James Stewart carries the baggage of supposedly archetypal "all–American" values straight into Morocco; if we believe the film they work as effectively there as on home soil. Shades of *Black Rain*, in which American police outshine Japanese police in Tokyo, the Stewart character beats Moroccan authorities at their own game. While the culture, the distinct nature of the Middle East is not exactly ignored, it is presented, understood, even validated only through a Western-centric lens.

If only rarely are a people portrayed in their full depth of character by the film products from other cultures, the granting of sovereign dignity to the Middle East has been especially alien to Western film. Even the magisterial *Lawrence of Arabia* (1962) cannot avoid patronizing Arabs, perhaps because the real-life story involved Arab puppets and Western strings, perhaps because film usually reflects not only deliberate social-artistic thinking by its makers but a range of unconscious biases as well. Granted, the apparently remarkable T.E. Lawrence stands against Western imperialism, or at least for Arab solidarity. Yet the film displays him leading Arabs across their own deserts, commanding enormous loyalties. When an Englishman is shown, in effect, to be a better Arab than the Arabs what message is finally conveyed? Ultimately steely and stoic, Lawrence is truly, effectively "English" even in the alien environment of the Nefud Desert. Middle Eastern tradition is once again presented through very "English" eyes, though at least some measure of supposedly authentic character, or at least dignity, is afforded to several major characters.

Lawrence of Arabia and the recent sequel *A Dangerous Man* (1990) give less focus to Middle Easterner than to the phenomenon of the extreme expatriate as object of fascination, some admiration, and much suspicion. Lawrence (as a serious Arabist who spoke the language and studied and region and its history intensely) was recognized by his countrymen as essentially, ultimately, no longer one of them. After leaking confidential information in *A Dangerous Man* about postwar diplomacy with the Arab world he was excoriated by a British official as having "turned on your country and your race.... You have betrayed your religion for heathen aliens." Beyond the blatantly racist words revealing the location of dominant biases, the fact that someone from the English world now had more empathy for the Arab was essentially unfathomable to English sensibilities. In spite of the rich character development it gives Prince Feisal, the film, much like ethnocentric English leadership of the era, essentially ignores Arabs as central players, even in their own lives and destinies.

There has been relatively little to fill in the void of the Middle East on the Western filmmaking map. *The Wind and the Lion* (1975) fictionalizes fascinating events in turn-of-the-century Morocco, as the expansionist U.S. of Teddy Roosevelt clashed with the ethnic pride of North Africans. "The (American Character) is a little blind and reckless at times," concedes TR, "but courageous beyond all doubt." His observations laced through the film sharply illuminate turn-of-the-century American character, especially his as emblematic of a nation's, yet North African character remains underdeveloped. Choosing a Scot, Sean Connery, to play the charismatic Raisuli represents ethnocentric blindness, even ethnic insult (though perhaps a sound box office decision). Other U.S. American characters, played by American stars, strut front and center while indigenous Moroccan culture remains lightly entertaining and quaintly exotic on the periphery. Sensitive moments do allow not only the perceptive observations of Roosevelt but corresponding clarity for Raisuli as well. "But between us there is a difference," he writes the President in delivering the theme. "I ... like the Lion ... must remain in my place ... while you ... like the wind ... will never know yours." While such eloquent moments reflect on real differences, overall the critical sense of the real is missing. Raisuli's English proves too good, his thinking and manner too Western, the entire film cast as Western fantasy upon Morocco, not the complex, intriguing Moroccan society itself.

The West meeting the Middle East takes strides in realism, or turns nastier still depending on point of view, in *Not Without My Daughter* (1990), set first in the U.S. and then Iran in the '80s, after the Islamic Revolution. The setting had enormous potential in the meeting of quite distinct cultures over life's real issues: family, marriage, in-laws, religion, education, jobs, money, prejudice, and frustration. But as Iranian-born, Western-trained physician Sayyed Mahmoody takes his American wife Betty and child back for a short summer visit to Teheran but soon announces that they will be staying, a claustrophobia descends that turns portrayals of Iranian characters devilish and chokes off the free expression of the few

Actors Candice Bergen and Sean Connery may cut handsome figures on the screen but at the expense of the realistic. Connery was not a credible choice to play the Moroccan tribal leader Raisuli in turn-of-the-century North Africa, in *The Wind and the Lion* (1975).

visible Westerners. While Betty's options are truly limited under Iranian (Islamic) law, the filmmakers' options remained open—they actively chose to so ominously veil Iranian culture, much as the culture veils women, that no connection to or sympathy for "Persian" tradition is likely to result for Western viewers. Though aware that "it's a different culture," Betty concedes that "I guess I just don't understand it," a comment presented as almost charitable given the circumstances. She studies Islam (through classes in English) after resigning herself to life in Iran, but no bud of those studies blossoms on screen. This contrasts significantly with films (e.g., *Amistad* [1997]) in which Judeo-Christian writings stir the thinking and spirit of new immigrants to the West, even those held against their will, as is Betty in Iran.

The stark portrayals do, if little else, underscore the point of vast, almost insuperable differences between current Western and Iranian civilizations—the viewer cannot but feel transported to a truly different, albeit alien realm. In odd moments, the opportunity to reflect critically on those differences emerges, for example when the music signaling the Islamic call to morning prayer awakens the couple during their earliest days in the

When Betty visits her in-laws in post-revolution Iran, she finds herself surrounded by a world beyond her comprehension in myriad senses, in *Not Without My Daughter* (1990).

country. When Betty comments disparagingly, her husband rejoins that "all religious beliefs seem primitive when they're not your own," the most perceptive line in the film. In fleeting scenes Dr. Mahmoody finds meaning in his work with Teheran's masses, suggesting a world unknown to Western viewers, but the film takes us no deeper. Iran is given just enough of a face to sour any Western sympathies, and Betty escapes toward the West with young Mahtob. The U.S. flag wafting over the American embassy in Ankara towers with the majesty of a religious icon, and may even suggest that secular freedom and Western social mores are, in fact, the religion of the United States.

Time rapidly heals scars, but not vast chasms between cultural blocs, at least as seen in *Hideous Kinky* (1998) and *Three Kings* (1999): even in contemporary, turn of the century film North Africa and the Middle East remain exotic, spooky, almost incomprehensible locations from another planet. Half-hearted attempts to develop sympathetic non–Western character do arise, but drown in a larger, dismal pool of confusion. One of the largest real cultural gaps, between individualistic Western culture and the Islamic world, in one sense stands justly represented in popular film.

"Lost Cousins": The Old World and the New

Ingmar Bergman's *The Emigrants* (1971) and *The New Land* (1972) gave compelling portrayals of the immigrant experience—often born of desperate circumstances in the Old Country—generally unromantic, predictably plagued by a gamut of economic and cultural frustrations. But the struggle often returned dividends, and semi-assimilated subgroups were born. Those European emigrant subcultures began changing almost instantly upon arrival in the New World: a new physical environment, economic system, and paths of social and geographical mobility assured rapid evolution. Americans of English descent were soon as distinct from the British as were French and Germans, as indeed Mexicans and Brazilians became different people from the Spanish and Portuguese. Though New World citizens of European descent may have quite properly perceived themselves as a new, evolving culture, European moorings remained strong. From the point of view of vastly different cultural traditions—Islamic, Japanese, and Chinese, for example—the "white men" from the New World differed from those from the Old in only minor details. A contemporary look at economics, education, and mores on both sides of the Atlantic reveals not only a strong political and economic alliance but *relatively* shallow differences in world view. Samuel Huntington's taxonomy of cultural blocs quite sensibly groups Europe and North America together as "Western culture," contrasted with Latin American, Shinto (Japanese), Confucian, Russian Orthodox, Islamic, Hindu, and African cultures.[10]

Though the differences between the Old World and New often fail to achieve the dramatic, sharply-toned contrasts that animate film, a number of screenplays representing those cultures in contact merit analysis. Only a representative handful are discussed here. In much cross–Atlantic film the mix of characters is incidental to a plot-line with its weight directed elsewhere, and in North American film European characters are often added, like spice, purely for flavor. Typical is *My Best Friend's Wedding* (1997), a comedy in which a male friend of the protagonist is strategically gay but gratuitously English. In *Notting Hill* (1999), spun around the charm of the same U.S. starlet, a British-American romance faces every imaginable challenge, except differences in cultural thinking which, to believe the film, are non-existent. Significantly *Titanic* (1997), Hollywood's most lucrative product of all time, enjoys the perfect raw material to display contrasting cultural perspectives (persons from numerous countries sailing from the Old World to the New together, sharing the confined space of the vessel) yet such differences, like the ship itself, are swallowed by tragedy in an unforgiving ocean. In other films, however, the subtle differences provide the grist for serious storytelling. *The Remains of the Day* (1993), driven by a very "English" story but exploring inter–European and cross–Atlantic issues as well, affords only a minor role to an "American," yet his speech to a room full of European leaders stands as a beacon in focusing attention on differences between Old and New World political thinking.

Other worthwhile films mix multiple levels of cultural encounter, as in *The Foreign Student* (1994), which places a sensitive French male in the Southern U.S., interacting not only with white culture but with the black subculture as well, in fact through forbidden romance with a charming, literate black woman (who's working earnestly at French through a correspondence course). Though the film suffered somewhat unkind reviews for tone-deaf, superficial treatment of a rich cinematic potential, it did merit the concession from at least one critic that Philippe "captured perfectly the culture shock experienced by a young man upon his arrival in a small college community" in Virginia.[11] He comes from Paris, after all, not hesitant to encounter anyone and "look them in the eye"—even black women in the Southern U.S., unlike white boys from the same racially and sexually charged, uncomfortably mixed society. Philippe's background does in fact serve to remind that the sociology of urban versus rural, and economic and social class, are all too easily missed while obvious differences in accent or ethnic identity are highly visible upon the screen. Many viewers (and some critics) will treat the raw, primitive *Straw Dogs* (1971) as the meeting of U.S. American and Cornish cultures. More meaningfully, however, the shallow, violent story pitted a professional mathematician against rural, uneducated, sporadically employed males (jealous of the professor's attractive, local wife) in a social and psycho-sexual dynamic that owes very little to differences in national culture.

More often, cross–Atlantic film story lines are packaged as comedic or serio-comic. The best of the genre, *Local Hero* (1983) involves the representative of a U.S.-based oil company, sent to a quiet, coastal village in Scotland to acquire land for a refinery. "Mac" McIntyre's stay abroad proves long enough to exercise all the potential stages of expatriation: at first holding a "strictly business" demeanor, Mac experiences a gradual seduction by friendly, eccentric people, by a relaxed pace of life, by centuries-old traditions and charm. All these qualities must be wanting in his home business culture of oil and money—his company chief is so neurotically curved in personality as to hire therapists whose job is to verbally demean him! Even the CEO, however, succumbs to the Old World graces on a visit to the striking village setting. Personalities from the differing cultures never clash openly; instead the differing orientations to—and the pace of—life influence the sojourners gradually, for the most part realistically. Does the film simply give an old fashioned city-country tale a Scottish accent for novelty, or are the essential differences really those of national and regional culture? Insisting on no conclusions, *Local Hero* takes urban viewers up close to feel the texture of life far removed from their everyday realities. When McIntyre returns to his upscale lifestyle in Houston and looks out his high-rise window at busy, neon landscapes, no dialogue is needed to capture his doubts: has he really returned home? The pull away from the once irresistible, fast-paced city life increasingly emerges in film representations from various, mostly Western, cultures (especially those with economic security, or alienation, as central characteristics), and film is well suited to convey the landscapes and human textures of country life. It's hard to keep them in Páreé, it seems, after they've smelled the alfalfa down on the farm.

Skyline (1984) and *Barcelona* (1994) bring Spaniards and North Americans into contemporary contact, each adjusting to the other's cultural environment. The little-known, underrated *Skyline*, set in New York City, offers a study of the loneliness of even the sophisticated immigrant. Gustavo, a professional photographer, hopes to prosper artistically in The City, but finds himself struggling to speak not only English but also the cultural language around him. Art, in one sense universal, creates its own subculture and subcultural language everywhere, superimposed upon the overall, ambient style.

Young executives from a Houston-based oil company suddenly stand transported in time and culture when they arrive at a slow-paced Scottish village to
negotiate a large land lease, in *Local Hero* (1983).

Yet Gustavo finds himself unable to grasp the language of his artistic profession in New York with sufficient subtlety to facilitate his entry. Generally worn from "culture fatigue," he resorts to such clichés as self-pity and
commiseration with other émigrés. Telling moments of interaction and
adjustment as well as nicely paced humor ring true, and give the film rewarding reach in depicting the upscale immigrant experience.

    Barcelona goes across the Atlantic the other way, as a young U.S. expa-
triate businessman and his naval officer cousin come to know one of Spain's
premier cities "in the last decade of the Cold War." The portrait of contemporary Barcelona is decidedly shallow: we see scarcely a sign of children, families, the elderly, religion, education, or the arts (all central to the
traditional culture) amid the montage of nightclubs, music, sex, and
superficial political debate. Yet the very lightheartedness permits relaxed
reflection on differences in the thinking of, at least, the young adults from
both countries. One less than analytical young woman, who learned her
English in Rhode Island, derides "all of those loud, fat, badly dressed people watching their eighty channels and visiting shopping malls" and continues, barely pausing for breath, "the plastic, throw-everything-away

Director Whit Stillman teases remarkable intercultural interest from the stream of dialogue among young U.S. Americans and young Spaniards in *Barcelona* (1994).

society with its notorious violence and racism, and finally, the total lack of culture." None of this is intended to be taken personally, however, as Americans are accepted on individual merit. U.S. interventionism in world affairs may be resented, the USO and the U.S. military uniform as symbols even draw direct assault from radicals, but individual Americans do fine, socially, in Spain. Characters from both sides of the Atlantic seem to transcend bumper sticker dialogue to achieve genuine rapport, for at film's end not less than three intercultural romances promise to prove enduring.

Big Night (1996) features recent Italian immigrants as restaurant owners in 1950s New Jersey, attempting to adjust not so much to American ways of business as to the local consumer mentality. "Old world idealism clashes with American pop culture," boasts the film's own promotional campaign. In fact, the chef as Old World food artist is loath to make allowances for less than sophisticated diners, but this merely symbolizes a larger truth. The difference in tone between Italian character, newly off the boat, and American character is consistent, if woven of fine and subtle thread. Behind the bumps of words and actions between Italians and those of their new environment lie quiet differences of spirit. Minor comedic slips lace dialogue and action consistently, serving to keep the package light while deeper issues play out.

While *Big Night* offers a tragically comic, somewhat delicate meal, *French Kiss* (1995)and *Green Card* (1990) serve up the fast food of American comedy, designed for easy labeling, facile ingestion, and pure entertainment. But while the canned, Hollywood products invoke the disappointingly predictable—the "French" lead in *French Kiss* is U.S. American star Kevin Klein—their counterposing of North American and French characters lacks neither interest nor merit. Behind Hollywood's slapstick and gags, viewers may contemplate the love-hate affairs between American and French personalities. True, *French Kiss* exploits stereotypes, such as French condescension (which drips from even the most polite words of a concierge at an upscale hotel), or foolish "American persistence" in the face of bald facts. In some measure, however, our self-consciously analytical society has given stereotypes a bad name: many stereotypes carry a degree of enduring truth, have indeed won their status as stereotypes by conforming to "reality" as popularly, consistently experienced. Luc does embody the interesting mix of Cartesian logic, roguish, sensual sophistication, and understated emotional attachment to roots and tradition that makes him quite believably "French," while Kate from Canada, originally from the U.S., embodies different strengths of character. Tagged by Luc as repressed, virtually Puritan, and mindlessly emotional, her dogged belief in positive outcomes may help shape her character predictably, but she does resemble the quintessential American.[12] *Green Card* cuts the national stereotypes from similar molds—Georges the composer is sensual while Bronte is stunted in her emotional growth beneath a North American veneer of openness—but with one welcome difference: Gerard Depardieu is so truly French that he cannot, convincingly, act the part of any other national identity.

Zorba the Greek (1964) is sometimes tagged by those who study the crossing of cultures as a "must see" film, a modern classic that sets a culture of propriety and restraint in stark relief against a culture of joy and vibrant tradition. The artfully drawn and superbly acted central characters may indeed invoke the shape that occurs when the branches of age-old cultures grow from the tree in different directions. What's more, the film's secondary players, noted in the credits as "the people of the Island of Crete," give a wholly fresh, authentic feel to the Greek setting, remarkable for Anglo film of the era. Yet however representative of their respective societies Zorba and Basil proved, the more subtle, useful message of the film may have been the surprising twists of putting dreams into action across large cultural spans—the adventures of Basil in Crete recreates many a real world experience in establishing a business across cultures. He finds, as have many before and after him, that a newly encountered culture (and for that matter each individual within it) tugs at emotions in unexpected ways, and invariably presents challenges that could not have been anticipated. The real import of *Zorba the Greek* is less an archetypal episode of "British character" interacting with Greek, but more the inevitable force and mystery of the expatriate experience, however difficult the phenomenon may be to classify convincingly.

Around the World in Film

The challenge of classifying film is especially relevant to this chapter. Film, with its infinite textures of character, dialogue, action, sight, sound, and final emotional impact may be the medium least expected to fall into neat categories. Yet the temptation to create intellectual compartments to house not only ideas but phenomena and experience is strong. This book needed logical rubrics for the discussion of hundreds of intercultural films and geographical chapters were chosen. Yet across those categories cut issues of expatriation and immigration, war versus peacetime stories, colonial and neo-colonial legacies, aristocratic versus common people, power differences and power distance, "white" and "people of color," international business and development themes, women as a culture apart within cultures, comedy versus drama, and so on ad infinitum.

How should *Zorba the Greek* be classified, in either general or cultural studies of film genres? Two-and-a half hours long, a sometimes drab black-and-white offering in a decade dominated by technicolor, the slow-moving film almost suggests that hues of color are provided only by a determined look at the human soul. In addition to the facets already discussed, *Zorba the Greek* offers hints of postwar and post-colonial dynamics, a glimpse at inter-Greek issues of class, the meeting of "educated" and "traditional" mind-sets, and a stark if brief portrayal of sexual politics across cultural confines—in the form of a feminist tragedy, a decent woman trapped by the biases of traditional mores. With these and other cross-currents running at various depths, it is fair to ask if the focus on Greek versus English culture distracts from more penetrating issues.

Many other films are at least as hard to categorize cleanly: does *Bread and Chocolate* (1973) reflect more on Italian-Swiss differences or the paradox of multicultural Switzerland? Is *Journey of Hope* (1990) about difficult life in Turkey, the highly different life in industrialized Europe, the contrast between the two, or the universal tribulations of the indigent immigrant? Should the modern classic *Babette's Feast* (1987) be primarily considered a unique meditation on the universal power of the human spirit to thaw icy social circumstances, or more prosaically the chronicle of a French female in conservative Danish territory? Is *The Remains of the Day* a pensive "Upstairs, Downstairs"-type examination of stratified English society on the brink of World War II, or more broadly a study of English, German, American, and French mentalities interacting? Should we compare it to other Merchant-Ivory productions with multicultural themes, note the international cast, or meditate upon such a seemingly "English" story orig-inating from the pen of Kazuo Ishiguro?[13] These films may all be placed under the broad rubric of "InterEuropean Film," for example, but the fact remains that the wrinkles of cultural identity in these films can prove almost endless.

Even when these films are classified by basic cultural geography, vari-ation may become more visible than theme. Given the hundreds of national cultures, each of which have multi-level involvement with each other beyond embassies or consulates, the geographical categories of intercultural film prove almost limitless. Of the nearly two hundred countries accepted as sovereign by the United Nations, each, in theory, could produce films featuring their countrymen in interaction with all of the others. The per-mutations would be such that almost 40,000 intercultural films could be produced without once repeating the combination of national cultures, to say nothing of the possible permutations of films featuring the interplay of several cultures at once.

In practice, however, representing cultures in film is an extremely lop-sided affair from several points of view. To begin with, relatively few parts of the world host the filmmaking infrastructure and investor capital to pro-duce feature-length films which are both credible and competitive.[14] The lack of global markets for many parochial products further frustrates the industry in many areas. If a filmmaking industry grew in "exotic" Tibet, perhaps a Western market would welcome at least a handful of its prod-ucts, but less so for films from Iceland, Hungary, or Afghanistan. Those areas that fall between the cracks of clearly recognizable "major" world cul-tural blocks may suffer in filmmaking identity and marketability—as pop-ularly conceived, Iceland is neither Europe nor America, Hungary neither Europe nor Russia, and Afghanistan neither Asia nor the Middle East. Even the production of film, to say nothing of distribution, artistic and political intent, and artistic and political reception, is thus driven at least partly by recognizable cultural geography. The former Soviet Union repub-lic of Kazakhstan, now a resource-rich, independent nation with roughly the territory of India, is not likely soon to have clear international identity nor world markets for its film products.

Overwhelmingly, the major films from North America and Europe dominate the global market, even if India and Japan produce more films each year, primarily monocultural films for internal consumption.[15] The cultural visibility and image of the major characters and setting are critical to the product's international appeal. Not only would a film featuring Bolivians on vacation in French Guiana tend towards minor appeal outside those two countries, it might even be outpaced at the box office within those countries by North American or European fare, other factors being equal. Of course, "other factors" seldom are, from technical and artistic quality to the image of the host culture in international entertainment. U.S. American, Hollywood-quality film is unlikely to be merely "equivalent" when the cachet of American entertainment, reach of the English language with American usage, and recognizability of U.S. film stars are considered.

In turn, the widely distributed film products enjoy a life of their own in defining popular culture. Ironically, many Mexicans may receive their mass media impressions of Colombia or Brazil from imported action-adventure products filmed in English, rather than more directly from Colombian or Brazilian imports or from their internal filmmaking industry (in spite of Mexico's second-tier status of producing nearly one hundred films a year). Caribbean natives can learn much about United States, Canadian, and European citizens of African heritage from film but scarcely find themselves represented on the Big Screen; when Caribbeans are the focus they will often view themselves in U.S. American (*Clara's Heart*, 1988; *Cool Runnings*, 1993) or European (*No Fear, No Die*, 1992; *Cafe au Lait*, 1993) film, not homegrown products. At times, "minor" countries or cultures will emerge on the world film scene through sheer merit: the Czechoslovakian *Kolya* (1996), as the superbly touching yet subtle and original treatment of a Russian child "adopted" by a Czech intellectual, enjoyed a positive worldwide reception, and many films from unexpected corners have surfaced through such channels as international film festivals. Nonetheless, sheer output and recognition remain the province of major cultural blocks. All "major" world cultures enjoy at least some film output, and the variations on the themes, including intercultural ones, are almost endless. For example, *Window to Paris* (1995) features the delightful romp of Russians through Paris, trampling French folkways and customs as they go, while *Close to Eden* (1992) meditates masterfully on a Russian working in Mongolia as two Asian cultural traditions intersect. Every major culture exhibits its own identity not only in the films it produces for domestic, popular consumption, but also in the films that interact with other cultural traditions. U.S., Canadian, English, and French films all produce engaging stories that invoke their colonial past or international present, as well as films set at the crux of their current multicultural dilemmas. Such films mirror the status of the societies themselves as among the most affected by immigration, and most open to internal multicultural debate, and most involved in international business, "development," and consequent placement of expatriates. Reflected on the Big Screen as well is a measure of apparent collective guilt in these societies about their colonial and neo-colonial legacies. Surely they have a disproportionately huge share of worldwide film distribution largely because of Anglo-Franco economic and political hegemony; additionally the films may travel well because of an openness to the issues of crossing cultures.

If modernity develops, as Huntington and others project, along the axes of eight major and a host of minor cultural systems, will popular film as well develop an increasingly varied set of faces? It would be enlightening to see feature films produced by Middle Easterners, for example, that turn the tables on the woefully inadequate portrayals coming from the West. A post-perestroika Russian industry already shows signs of re-creating what Russians look like, for the world as well as the internal market. And if "minor" cultural traditions continue to re-emerge from under the shadow of "major" ones, the unqualified success of films like *Kolya* will become more rule than exception. That could only be considered a positive development. A single set of cultural lenses never was adequate to capture the diversity of peoples.

Filmography

Film (aka), year, country (language), director, producer/distributor, minutes

Iron Curtain & the West

Back in the USSR, 1991, USA, Deran Sarafian, 20th Century–Fox, 87
A Captive in the Land, 1990, Soviet Union/USA, John Berry, Gloria Pictures, 96
Company Business, 1991, USA, Nicholas Meyer, MGM, 99
East-West, 1999, Russia/France (fr., rus.), Régis Wargnier, Sony Pictures, 120
Gorky Park, 1983, USA, Michael Apted, Orion Pictures, 130
The Hunt for Red October, 1990, USA, John McTiernan, Paramount Pictures, 134
Letter to Brezhnev, 1985, UK, Chris Bernard, Palace Pictures, 94
Moscow on the Hudson, 1984, USA, Paul Mazursky, Columbia, 115
Ninotchka, 1939, USA, Ernst Lubitsch, MGM, 110

Reds, 1981, USA, Warren Beatty, Paramount Pictures, 194
Rocky IV, 1985, USA, Sylvester Stallone, United Artists, 91
The Russia House, 1991, USA, Fred Schepisi, MGM, 122
The Russians Are Coming!, 1968, USA, Norman Jewison, MGM, 120
Russkies, 1987, USA, Rick Rosenthal, Lorimar, 100
Spies Like Us, 1985, USA, John Landis, Warner Brothers, 102
The Spy Who Came In from the Cold, 1965, USA, Martin Ritt, Paramount, 110
Streets of Gold, 1986, USA, Joe Roth, Vestron Video, 95
White Nights, 1985, USA, Taylor Hackford, Columbia, 136

The Middle East/The West

Bagdad, 1949, USA, Charles Lamont, Universal Pictures, 82
A Dangerous Man, 1990, TV, UK, Christopher Menaul, Anchor Bay, 104
Every Time We Say Goodbye, 1986, USA, Moshe Mizrahi, TriStar, 95
Hideous Kinky, 1998, UK/France, Gillies MacKinnon, BBC, 97
Ishtar, 1987, USA, Elaine May, Columbia, 107
Istanbul, 1989, Sweden/Turkey, Mats Arehn, Magnum Entertainment, 84
Lawrence of Arabia, 1962, UK, David Lean, Columbia, 187
The Man Who Knew Too Much, 1956, USA, Alfred Hitchcock, Paramount, 120
Midnight Express, 1978, UK, Alan Parker, Columbia, 120
Not Without My Daughter, 1990, USA, Brian Gilbert, Pathe Entertainment, 115
On Wings of Eagles, 1986, TV, USA, Andrew V. MacLaglen, Taft Entertainment, 221
Three Kings, 1999, USA, David O. Russell, Warner Bros., 116
The Wind and the Lion, 1975, USA, John Milius, MGM, 119

New World/Old World & US/Canadian

Alice in the Cities, 1974, Germany (gr.), Wim Wenders, Pacific Arts Video, 110
America, America, 1963, USA, Elia Kazan, Warner Bros., 177
Barcelona, 1994, USA, Whit Stillman, Fine Line Features, 101
Before Sunrise, 1995, USA/Austria, Richard Linklater, Warner Bros., 101
Big Night, 1996, USA, Campbell Scott, Samuel Goldwyn Co., 107
Bye Bye Blues, 1989, Canada, Anne Wheeler, True Blue Films, 110
Canadian Bacon, 1995, USA, Michael Moore, Gramercy Pictures, 91
The Emigrants, 1971, Sweden (swds.), Jan Troell, Warner Bros., 151
Far and Away, 1992, USA, Ron Howard, Universal Pictures, 140
The Foreign Student, 1994, France/USA, Eva Sereny, Cathago Films, 93
French Kiss, 1995, USA, Lawrence Kasdan, 20th Century–Fox, 111
The Good Mother, 1988, USA, Leonard Nimoy, Touchstone Pictures, 106
Green Card, 1990, USA/France, Peter Weir, Touchstone Pictures, 103
Local Hero, 1983, UK, Bill Forsyth, Goldcrest Films, 106
My American Cousin, 1985, Canada, Sandy Wilson, O'Kanagan MPC, 90
My Best Friend's Wedding, 1997, USA, P. J. Hogan, Sony Pictures, 105
The New Land, 1972, Sweden (swds.), Jan Troell, Svensk Film, 157
Notting Hill, 1999, USA/UK, Roger Mitchell, Universal Pictures, 125
Oxford Blues, 1984, USA, Robert Boris, MGM, 98

Ready to Wear, 1994, USA, Robert Altman, Miramax, 132
Shadowlands, 1993, UK, Richard Attenborough, Savoy Pictures, 130
Skyline, 1984, Spain/USA (sp.), Fernando Colomo, Pacific Arts, 84
Straw Dogs, 1971, UK, Sam Peckinpah, ABC Pictures, 118
Titanic, 1997, USA, James Cameron, 20th Century–Fox, 195

Down Under

The Chant of Jimmy Blacksmith, 1978, Australia, Fred Schepisi, Filmhouse, 124
The Coca-Cola Kid, 1985, Australia, Dusan Makavejev, Cinecom Itnl., 94
The Fringe Dwellers, 1986, Australia, Bruce Beresford, Ozfilm, 98
The Last Wave, 1977, Australia, Peter Weir, Ayer Productions Ltd., 103
Once Were Warriors, 1994, New Zealand, Lee Tamahori, Avalon Studios, 99
Walkabout, 1971, Australia, Nicolas Roeg, 20th Century–Fox, 95
We of the Never Never, 1982, Australia, Igor Auzins, FCWA, 136

InterAsian

Ah Ying (Banbianren), 1983, Hong Kong (cant.) Allen Fong, Feng Huang MPC,
110
Close to Eden, 1992, Russian (sub.), Nikita Mikhalkov, Miramax, 109
Dersu Uzala, 1975, Russia (rus.), Akira Kurasawa, New World Film, 140
The Flor Contemplacion Story, 1995, Philippines, Joel Lamangan, Viva Films,
120
The Go Masters, 1982, China/Japan, Ji-Shun Duah, Bejing Film Studio, 123

InterEuropean

Babette's Feast, 1987, Denmark (dns., fr.), Gabriel Axel, Orion Classics, 102
Bread and Chocolate, 1973, Italy (itln.), Franco Brusati, World Northal, 100
Foreigners, 1972, Sweden (swds.), Johan Bergenstrahle, Swedish Film Inst., 113
Grand Illusion, 1937, France (fr.), Jean Renoir, Home Vision, 120
In the Name of the Father, 1993, Ireland, Jim Sheridan, Universal Pictures, 133
Journey of Hope, 1990, Turkey/Germany (gr., trk.), Xavier Koller, Miramax, 109
Kolya, 1996, Czechoslovakia (czech.), Jan Sverak, Miramax Films, 105
The Remains of the Day, 1993, UK, James Ivory, Columbia Tri-Star, 138
Schindler's List, 1993, USA, Steven Spielberg, Universal Pictures, 200
The Swissmakers, 1978, Switzerland, Rolf Lyssy, T & G, 104
Window to Paris, 1993, Russia (rus.), Yuri Mamin, Sony Picture Classics, 87

Intermediterranean & Mediterranean/European

Fear Eats the Soul, 1974, Germany (gr.), Werner Fassbinder, Tango Film, 93
Mediterraneo, 1991, Italy (itln.), Gabriele Salvatores, Miramax, 96
Pascali's Island, 1988, UK, James Dearden, Avenue Pictures, 106
Wedding in Galilee, 1987, Israel (arab.), Michel Khleifi, Kino Video, 113
Zorba the Greek, 1964, Greece, Michael Cacoyannis, 20th Century–Fox, 142

Anglo/Caribbean & European/Caribbean

Burn!, 1969, Italy/France, Gillo Pontecorvo, United Artists, 112
Café au Lait, 1993, France (fr.), Mathieu Kassovitz, MKL Distribution, 94
Clara's Heart, 1988, USA, Robert Mulligan, Warner Bros., 108
Cool Runnings, 1993, USA, Jon Turteltaub, Walt Disney Pictures, 95
How Stella Got Her Groove Back, 1998, USA, K. R. Sullivan, 20th Century–Fox, 124
No Fear, No Die, 1992, France (fr.), Claire Denis, First Run Features, 93
Sugar Cane Alley, 1984, France (fr.), Euzhan Palcy, ORCA Productions, 103
Wide Sargasso Sea, 1993, Australian, John Duigan, New-Line Cinema, 98

Tourism Lite

Around the World in Eighty Days, 1956, USA, Michael Anderson, Warner Bros., 175
Death on the Nile, 1978, USA, John Guillermin, EMI Films, 140
If It's Tuesday, This Must Be Belgium, 1969, USA, Mel Stuart, United Artists, 99
The Last Fling, 1987, TV, USA, Corey Allen, Academy Entertainment, 95
National Lampoon's European Vacation, 1985, USA, Any Heckerling, Warner Bros., 95

Chapter Six

"FROM A DIFFERENT SPIRIT": THE NATIVE AND THE NEW AMERICANS

"There was a time when the New World didn't exist. The Sun set in the West, on an ocean where no man had dared to venture, and beyond that, Infinity."
1492: Conquest of Paradise

"You are the first white man I have ever seen. I have thought about you more than you know.
Dances with Wolves

"Do you know how hungry people are out there for your world, the authentic voice from the wilderness?"
Grey Owl

"As landlord of this continent, we're gonna collect the rent."
Lakota Woman

"He wouldn't lower himself to speak English—would you, Stab— but watch out, because he understands it perfectly well."
Legends of the Fall

The meeting of Native Americans and Americans of European descent is the story of the transition, on a colossal scale, in an entire hemisphere of the earth over the last five hundred years. It is a story of such staggering proportions, both past and present, along moral, social, economic, and political axes that our capacities to fully appreciate, even face the story must at some level fall short.

By definition, it is a story seen in dramatically different terms by the Native and the New Americans. For the entire hemisphere itself to have been named after a European, long before significant numbers of Europeans had relocated to it, speaks volumes about whose language the story would be told in. The standard history texts referred to what year various nooks and crannies of the new hemisphere "were discovered" for the European world, or often, simply when they were "discovered," as if no other world, meaningful or otherwise, existed.

Against this "trail of tears," this backdrop of pathos, tragedy, tension, and even contemporary struggle, the making of film and the analysis of films that feature Native Americans raise questions of no small delicacy. Issues of authenticity, voice, point of view, and dignity in these portrayals are hotly debated. Thus, the analysis of these films is fraught with peril for the unwary. Yet such analysis represents an opportunity to look at one of the most remarkable sets of episodes of intercultural contact in world history, and represents also a unique opportunity to cut to the core of what film can and cannot do in illuminating the contact between cultures. Admittedly a somewhat daunting prospect, a detailed look at the meeting of the Native and the New Americans, as expressed in film, is a challenge that must be met head-on.

The ethnic backgrounds, the social and economic systems, the collective experiences and worldviews of the two peoples were so utterly different that any voice used to tell of the meeting would inevitably come from only one side of the cultural divide. The meaning of land and ownership and livelihood, the spiritual life, the senses of self and meaning of self-expression, all were significantly different and sometimes diametrically opposed. The voices would have been sharply distinct even had the cultures managed to live side by side, harmoniously; the state of war, or acts of genocide that characterized the collision of the peoples has further assured different universes of perception. Of course, they have not been universes of equal weight, visibility, or influence in Western learning or social and political thinking. To the victors has always gone a wide array of spoils including intellectual and philosophical privilege—they have written not only the "factual" history texts but the popular philosophies and manuals of etiquette as well. Many of the modern films, and my analytical viewpoint here, attempt to compensate for historical imbalances, although, of course, not all Indians were imbued with noble qualities nor did all whites behave badly. Rather, the sharply differing perspectives led to broadly differing goals, and to the inevitably painful clash that largely ended Native ways of life.

The repertoire of Native meets New American film finally, and essentially, highlights the meetings between technology and change-oriented cultures and essentially static, pre-technological ones. Collisions of Western civilization with "advanced" cultures, such as the Chinese and Japanese, assumed quite different outcomes perhaps because those other cultures were national and literate, even technological, capable of imperialism within their own domains. While strained, communication was at least possible along the axis of similar economic goals, and somewhat parallel systems of political and social organization. As New Americans met Natives, however, communication was complicated not only by mutually alien values but also alien ideas about the goals of society. If what made "white men" go into social motion were goals such as "land ownership," "profit," "expansion," and "progress," in most Native cultures such concepts were foreign, as demonstrated in films from *The Mission* to *Geronimo* to *Thunderheart*.

The Native American Canadian-born actress Tantoo Cardinal, who has appeared in numerous popular films depicting the American Indian, has commented on the differences in background and perception that set the backdrop for the meeting of cultures. "Our concept of life, of the earth being a living ... a living thing ... that natural forces, winds, everything, is a part of life, was an alien concept to the people who came here," she stressed. She has nicely summarized the essence of the meeting of worlds: so different were the "cosmic views," the essential conceptions of the forces that drive life on the planet, that all of the communications and negotiations closer to the surface suffered from the chasm of non-understanding at the deeper levels. Truly and finally, these cultural traditions met each other "from a different spirit." That chasm, the different spirit of the cultures, dominated five hundred years of contact across an entire hemisphere of the earth.

The films portraying the Native and the New Americans are subject to every stripe of criticism: verisimilitude is often egregiously lacking in characters and in geographical settings; Indians are played by white men speaking English. Points of view, of sound, of meaning bear the bias of white-culture consciousness in even the "sensitive" films, which indeed are the product of white minds, money, technology, and way of life. There is some measure of compelling truth to each facet of these assaults on films that portray Native Americans, and it might be reasonable to conclude that immeasurable harm to the cause of understanding has been wrought by all such films, that having no portrayals would have been far better than highly skewed ones. Nevertheless, any level of familiarity, albeit misguided, with the culturally different may be more socially useful (giving one culture some awareness of and some empathy for representatives of another) than total lack of exposure. For better or worse, the media images abound and do shape popular perception. Relatively few U.S. Americans, for example, have visited contemporary Indian reservations or had direct exposure to large numbers of expressly Native Americans, while virtually all have seen more than a few films depicting "Indians" in either historical or contemporary settings.

The reigning assumption is that Western mainstream film has depicted "Indians" through the most heavy-handed and unflattering of stereotypes, as persons virtually with no intra-group culture but that of naked savagery, until American film began with *Little Big Man* (1970) a process that continued admirably through *Dances with Wolves* (1990) and beyond. A more thorough appraisal of the record reveals a somewhat more complex history. Granted, there has been no more stock a set of clichés in American film than war-whooping, Old American West horse-culture Indians, brandishing bow and arrow, preying on the wagon train, the fort, or the homesteading family on the prairie. Such films often offered neither realism nor dignity for the Indian, nor enlightenment concerning their societies. Yet even in early film, Indians sometimes offered other dimensions. Consider the so trite as to become "camp" *Lone Ranger* films, with the "faithful Indian companion, Tonto." Although the sidekick and subordinate of a white hero, this Indian and others like him in similar films did have dignity: their loyalty, honesty, and courage were beyond question as they successfully fought "evil," usually embodied by white criminals and other n'eer-do-wells. Nevertheless the early period of Native-and-New American filmmaking did evolve into a more perceptive phase that began in the 1970s.[1] It has produced a remarkable lineup of films to consider, in many ways an embarrassment of riches.

Virtually all analyses of The Native and the New Americans are vulnerable to charges of carelessness with distinctions and even fact: that in North America alone some five hundred fully distinct peoples, spread across a vast continent and living in dramatically different climates and circumstances, with differing economies and customs, usually speaking mutually unintelligible languages, in many instances at war with neighboring Native peoples, should so often be lumped as simply "Native Americans" or "Indians," should so often be assumed to be virtually the same people, constitutes an insult to them as well as to common intelligence. And to dump all pale-skinned arrivals into the catch-all category of "whites," when they came from more than a score of cultural locations, and from significantly different social roots and economic circumstances may similarly commit bald oversimplification. Indeed, much of the diversity of the North American continent since Columbus has been shrunk down to stereotype by myths purveyed through various media, whether deliberate or casually ignorant. To once again explore the story of the meeting of the Native and New Americans provides an opportunity to revisit those groupings that popular lore has too often failed to nuance for difference and complexity.

In films where Native American meets European Americans, however, and perhaps in reality, the similarities of Native peoples far outweigh
the differences, and "our concept of life" as described with simple eloquence
by Tantoo Cardinal seems to refer not narrowly to her Cree tribal roots
but to "Native peoples" in a broader, more inclusive sense. The filmmakers and scriptwriters have done either a poor job of distinguishing between
Native peoples or an admirable job of recognizing the vital core of similarities which transcended their differences. The truth probably lies somewhere in between, as older films often differentiated but crudely, casting
Native tribes as "good" (e.g., Sioux) or "bad" (e.g., Pawnee) Indians, and
as newer films have moved steadily toward some measure of anthropological realism. The filmmakers have likewise portrayed a largely consistent
character in the immigrants with whom the Indians interacted. Whatever
the ignorance of largely white filmmakers concerning Native cultures, they
presumably are more familiar with their own variegated European roots,
yet in Native meets New American film the whites also are not sharply
differentiated by ethnic grouping. The relative consistency of the driving
motivations of European cultures—economic expansion, missionary zeal,
cultural self-aggrandizement—meant that the shape and character of European interactions with Natives would be substantially similar, at least in
popular film.[2]

First Meetings and Colonial Times

Western film has portrayed the meeting of the cultures across all of
the major epochs of a half-millennium, from the landing of the first white
explorers. Two contemporary releases that portray the "discovery" of the
"New World" fall short of laudable cinematic art, yet suggestively illustrate the meeting of cultures. In *Christopher Columbus: The Discovery* (1992)
an expert who speaks "all the languages of the known world" accompanies
the expedition to the New World. In a scene which could serve as metaphor
for many such encounters, he attempts to talk with the natives but can make
absolutely no sense of their vocalizations. "These people don't speak a
language," he pronounces. The natives stand outside of all previous European experience, their vocalizations must be less than linguistic, and by
extension they must be less than human. Only as spoils and as circus-like
exhibits are natives worth kidnapping back to the Old World. In a scene
at once acutely touching and symbolic a Native jumps ship when well out
into the Atlantic and starts methodically swimming back in the direction
of home, a Native thrust into a world of size and scale he has no basis for

comprehending. Or perhaps a Native who rejects white men and their ships in favor of a sea he knows, a Native who would rather drown than surrender freedom.

In *1492: Conquest of Paradise* (1992), starring Gerard Depardieu, another take on the same historic years rises as Hollywood spectacle. Although a disappointing film—perhaps little enlightenment can be expected from a director who casts a Frenchman attempting to speak English as an Italian leading Spanish explorers—the story line and script provide redeeming moments for the analyst. "I think we have returned to Eden," reports Columbus's journal. "Surely this is how the world once was in the beginning of time ... I believe no man will ever see this land again as we do for the first time."—accurately prophesying the transformation thus set in motion of a continent and its peoples, but echoing the theme of the "noble savage" as the inheritor of primal beauty and virtue. With some subtlety the film shows the first meetings and awkward attempts at exchange between extremely different peoples; the script allows a local chief to reply to Columbus's promises to bring God and medicine to his people by asserting that they already have God, and already have medicine as well. The inevitable crumbling of goodwill begins with small frictions—essentially intercultural misunderstandings—which soon escalate into enmity and finally war. Eventually, when Columbus's Native interpreter flees, without goodbyes, into the jungle, Columbus belatedly yells, "Utapan, talk to me!" "You never learned to speak my language," is the reply at once cryptic and profound. In contrast, *Cabeza de Vaca* (1991) affords the insight of a Spanish-language depiction of early 16th century exploration of the new continent—highly appropriate in that English was little spoken in the New World until the 17th—and brings an air of realism, bordering on nihilism, to the colonial experience. Opposite the "Eden" discovered by Columbus the scent of danger, even death—intercultural mismatch grown lethal—hovers in every encounter. If Spain of the Inquisition offered only an unforgiving God, what kind of gods, if any, ruled the New World?

Set in the Colonial period in what is now the United States, *Squanto, A Warrior's Tale* (1994) also offers a negative, though much more conventional portrait, as it addresses early colonial history from the perspective of the Natives. Although a "feel-good" adventure in classic commercial style—Squanto's pure, Native heart brings "peace" for a time—the film does serve to depict the consciousness of another age. Whatever Indians were or were not, in the Western conception of the era they were certainly not human. "There's a divine order to life," proclaims the arch-evil Sir George, lecturing the kidnapped Native. "First there's God, followed by the Angels, then the King, then the rest of us according to our position in the world. Your position, Indian, is lower than the animals." While it's tempting to discount such youth-oriented, Walt Disney productions as too specious for serious consideration, they at least humanize the Indian, as Squanto's marriage, family and tribal life, and love of nature and of peace are all brightly lit upon the screen. But the primal elements of Native American Myth are too facilely presented, from Native American loyalty and courage to a spirituality so pure that it touches an order of monks who offer protection.

The meeting of colonists and Indians surely was never so simple. Rather it perhaps was as starkly brutal and unfair as suggested by the outcomes. The basic heartstrings of Right and Wrong are tugged by such imagery. Another example: *Tecumseh* (1995) with its wooden and clichéd portrayals is hardly sophisticated cinema but depicts the frustrations of the Shawnee Indians convincingly, as their society begins crumbling several years before the American revolution. From kisses of young Indian lovers and touching wedding ceremonies (mimetically dubious but resonant with the average movie viewer!) to the Native version of soccer to grieving over death or separation, Indians are made almost "white" in speech and emotions. The result: a failure to present the Shawnee realistically, or a positive, sympathetic portrayal of a misunderstood people, depending upon point of view.

Other films take fewer pains to imbue Indians with qualities sympathetic to the white culture but offer a more politically, historically accurate feel to early meetings of the peoples. *The Last of the Mohicans* (1992, loosely based on the literary classic, and *The Broken Chain* (1993) tell familiar stories of the colonial period in the Northeast of the continent. French pitted against English imperialists for control of the region with Indian peoples as pawns provide the authentic historical backdrop. The character Nathaniel Poe (Bumppo) himself provides a study in the meeting of cultures, for he lost his white parents while a young child, was adopted by a Mohican father, but learned the English language and customs at a colonial school. His bi-cultural wisdom and tolerance are sometimes limited however, as when he first matches perspectives with the daughter of the British Colonel Munro. "My father ... Chingachgook ... he warned me about people like you.... He said, "Do not try to understand them ... Yes, and not try to make them understand you. That is because they are a breed apart and make no sense."" A frontier as well as Hollywood love chemistry between the two soon transmutes the epic tale into romance shared by a rough hewn semi–Native and a young woman of European refinement who experiences the frontier as "more deeply stirring" than she could have imagined. At story's end a solitary old Mohican remains, symbol of the dying purity of a continent of Natives, but a new saga has only begun—the accommodation of European and American exigencies and traditions. The challenges to Nathaniel Poe and Cora Munro are significant. One wonders how they will carve out a life, rear children, approach education, what their lives together will be like in five years, or in ten.

Set in South American jungles in modern times, *The Emerald Forest* (1985) dramatizes the first contact of an aboriginal society with what they term "The Termite People," rapaciously gnawing through their homelands. The film depicts both "good" and "bad" representatives of whites of European descent and of Natives as well—"The Fierce Ones," for example, are a violent, threatening tribe as predatory as any "primitive" people ever brought to the screen. Collectively the whites present an entirely new world of values and practice; while some whites sympathize with aboriginal peoples, collectively the whites represent not only a material threat to traditional cultures but a world apart, a people as if from another planet. The human story turns on the kidnapping of a white boy, Tommy Markham, by a relatively peaceful tribe called "The Invisible People," and on his coming of age in the jungle culture (and later rediscovery of his dominant culture roots). His swift, complete reacculturation to Native life may support the argument that nurture rather than nature essentially shapes all humans; his refusal to return to a more "advanced" culture testifies to both the power of socialization and the seductiveness of warm, close-knit, traditional societies. Allegedly based on "real events" the film only at times achieves a convincing sense of the possible. Nevertheless it elicits many aspects of the contrasting cultures, such as the wholly different artifacts and customs of pre-technological life set against modernity, and most notably the Native emotional and spiritual life set against a system of rationality. From the other side Bill Markham, Tommy's father, is thrust into an extraordinary experience through re-meeting his son by chance, and his response to the challenge provides one of the most provocative dimensions of the film.

In the low-budget and unpretentious *Amazon* (1990) a white-collar European encounters the jungles of Brazil through improbable circumstances, trading a comfortable life for day-to-day struggle against the elements, both natural and cultural. The theme of a primal and stable way-of-life-invaded sounds again, in realistic tones, less rhapsodically than in *The Emerald Forest*. Indigenous or semi-indigenous life around the edges of Brazilian poverty is by no means idealized as Edenic, but the question again is joined: what does "modern" civilization offer, with certainty, to indigenous peoples, besides the certain doom of their time-tested ways of life?

Finally, the Canadian-made *A Map of the Human Heart* (1993) explores the life of Avik, an "Eskimo" from the far north, and his multi-faceted, lifelong involvement with whites. Although flawed in construction the film serves well for exploring crises of traditional cultures "discovered" by "civilization" and the agonies of individuals as they choose between divergent worlds.[3]

Missionary Zeal

In *The Mission* (1986), Portuguese determination to exploit the South American natives directly as chattel parallels their view of the natives as a species apart. A telling scene features a debate, before a visiting dignitary, on subjugation of the Natives, as enlightened clerics oppose exploitive ranchers. A delicate operatic performance by a Native youth opens the scene, with the dignitary exclaiming, "How can you tell me that child is an animal?" "A parrot can be taught to sing, your eminence." "Ah, yes, but how does one teach it to sing as melodiously as this?" "Your eminence, this is a child of the jungle, an animal with a human voice. If it were human an animal would cringe at its vices. These creatures are lethal and lecherous. They will have to be subdued by the sword and brought to profitable labor by the whip."

In *Black Robe* (1991), 17th century French missionary zeal characterizes the penetration by white Jesuits into the Canadian forest of the Algonquin, Huron, and Iroquois, with the goal of converting them "because they are uncivilized. Just as the English or Germans were before we took our faith to them." There is at least a willingness by the missionary to put the Indian on equal terms with the European heathen, and a willingness as well to reach out with earnest effort. As young Father Laforgue's odyssey with Native guides is being considered, a seasoned French Canadian warns that "He must paddle with them twelve hours a day or they will not respect him. He must smile and not show anger. He must carry a pack animal's load on his back, as they do." Another replies that Laforgue is well prepared and well suited, "dedicated and devout," and well studied in the Algonquin and Huron languages. His vigorous study and the use of authentic, subtitled Indian tongues in the film contrasts refreshingly with the underemphasis on language in most films where culture meets culture, but also serve to illustrate that the linguistic tools, by themselves, do not assure productive communication. There must be a deeper basis for the meeting of minds, a compatibility of worldviews as well. The missionaries are driven to share their own "more advanced" spiritual as well as material

Attempts to impress other peoples with technology are as old as intercultural contact itself; here missionary Father Laforgue show Natives the "magic" of writing, in *Black Robe* (1991).

life—even in 1630s Quebec the temptation to dazzle with technology is already alive, as the young priest proudly shows that paper and the printed word can transmit thoughts as if by magic.

Perhaps no other film so incisively depicts missionary contact with Native cultures, and the potential for crossed meanings in spite of "good intentions" as *Black Robe*. An Indian shaman personifies the spiritual traditions in conflict, and articulates the judgment that the white priests are "devils," one of the countless instances of polarized perceptions. At least a young white French Canadian who has accompanied the mission party becomes steadily more attuned to Native viewpoints and even praises Algonquin civilization: "They are true Christians. They live for each other. They forgive things we would never forgive." Confronting the statement that the Natives have no concept of the afterlife with an account of their highly developed beliefs in a hereafter, he asks "Is theirs harder to believe in than our paradise where we all sit on clouds and look at God?" Natives are not romanticized, however; predatory tribes war viciously on the more peaceful, and Indian belief systems contain dark and nihilistic as well as optimistic aspects. Overall, missionary efforts had at best marginal success, perhaps, because they were only offering what Native cultures already had—strong spiritual and metaphysical systems of belief. The missionaries were well schooled, but not in the anthropology of religion, in the knowledge that spiritual systems must mesh with and adapt to the encompassing social system.

At Play in the Fields of the Lord (1991), the epic of contemporary missionaries at work with the pre-modern Natives deep in the Brazilian jungle, mixes evangelical religion, Western urges for quick profits, a tribe with virtually no knowledge of the outside world, and the torn soul of an American with Native heritage in a cauldron of crossed values. Like *Black Robe*, the film amounts to an insightful meditation on differing belief systems, on the large gap that must be crossed to communicate between them, and the sacrifices incurred in the process. The portrayal of missionaries is far from flattering—at best they are self-righteous interlopers and at worst whining egoists virtually out of touch with reality—while Natives are depicted as lacking guile or fault as surely as they lack sophistication. Though the plot centers on a man reared by modernity, he has gone Native and personifies the clash of cultures, as he struggles with the demons of life in the modern world. Disease, one often forgotten accompaniment of the first meeting of peoples, claims victims on both sides but threatens the very survival of the Natives. While the tone is often dark and depressing, the film elicits questions that lead to meaningful analysis.

Similar challenges to the Western conception of the psyche occur in *The Mosquito Coast* (1986), in which brilliant, eccentric inventor Allie Fox takes his American family deep into the bush of "Mosquitia," to design a rational community with all the know-how of a latter-day Thomas Edison. The film fits only ironically into the category of the missionary films—Fox detests the missionary persona, considering himself a messiah for a more rational, non-hypocritical order. While the film turns on the odd and obsessed personality of its white protagonist, it provides grist for analysis, as the Harvard-educated Anglo-Saxon expects not only his family but also members of vastly different South American cultures to share his disdain for modernity's excesses and his passion for ecologically sound solutions. Scenes of Fox lecturing (dirt poor) Natives on the evils of an affluent, capitalist economy achieve wry comedic effect, as does a scene in which he coaches his Native hirelings to confront him if he fails to work hard enough —"You just come up to me and say, 'Mister, you gotta do a whole lot better than that.'" Although offbeat in approach and offering no ultimate answers, *Mosquito Coast* at least elicits questions central to understanding among cultures.

Also set in the threatened Amazonian jungles, the charming *Medicine Man* (1992) features a different kind of missionary, the medical/scientific. Dr. Robert Campbell, doing bio-medical research in the bush, has largely "gone native"—in many ways he respects Natives more than his own civilization, which he regards as superficial, hypocritical, and destructive. Natives enjoy the white guests, observing their foibles and romances and sharing judgments and customs in both directions. In Campbell's clash with the local medicine man the differing philosophies are nonetheless outlined: Western science as a dominant rationale, virtually a religion in itself, set against traditional healing with its own metaphysical system and the resources of a "pharmacological superstore," the flora and fauna of the jungle. Indeed traditional wisdom is anchored by bio-diversity, a diversity fast disappearing before the bulldozers of the "more advanced" culture. Campbell never patronizes Natives, although he's shamefully arrogant with Dr. Rae Crane, his female research assistant, displaying a male chauvinism in place of ethnocentrism, and demonstrating again that sensitivity to one set of different perspectives does not guarantee sensitivity to all.

The Frontier

Warriors outfitted with war paint and bow and arrow, cowboy characters stiff as boards mixed with "Indians" flat as paper, such is the pattern, not without reason, underlying much film criticism of the Native American-flavored frontier genre. The stock characters from central casting, the endless war whoops and scalpings, all invite jaded and negative responses. Yet popular film, with substantial budgets and talent devoted to pleasing low common denominators, has always formed a complex melding of the predictable, the nakedly profitable, and unexpected moments of artistic brilliance, if not truth and light. Depending on point of view, *I Will Fight No More Forever* (1975), recounting Chief Joseph's principled, heroic stand late in the nineteenth century against the U.S. Army to defend his people's way of life, achieves either an advanced version of a primitive or a primitive version of a modern film of soldiers and Native Americans. While the Nez Percé speak English, and are given syrupy lines of dialogue at that, they emerge as infinitely more admirable than the most rapacious of the whites. The clash on the Big Screen goes far deeper than military issues, is moral and spiritual, even if the sympathetic star is the pompous General Howard, who in the end enforces a genocidal policy after making turgid speeches about conscience. Nevertheless, in spite of the almost painfully stock portrayals the script is at least mildly elucidating, affording the Nez Percé a "human" form as well as genuine courage and dignity.

Though some consider the watershed point in American Indian portrayals to be *Broken Arrow* in 1950,[4] the first genuinely meaningful splash in a dull pond of filmmaking may have been made by *Little Big Man* in 1970, with its central character socialized in both cultures, its multifaceted and humorous look at two peoples, its recasting of Custer's last stand. Poorly textured by contemporary cinematic standards, careless with realistic detail by any standards, the film nonetheless represented a leap in the portrayals of Native and New Americans together. Going beyond the old Western, the story evolves from shifting and relative perspectives, inviting the audience to poke its head out of its ethnocentric shell to view afresh the meetings of these peoples. Tongue in cheek while also serious throughout, this playful epic wraps a hundred lighthearted ironies around its portraits without romanticizing characters from either side of the divide.

In contrast to the straightforward Cheyenne manner, much of the white world is confused or repressed at best, grossly dishonest at worst. "The one that ruined you was that Indian," says a grifter to young Jack Crabb, alias Little Big Man, disappointed to see him clinging to scruples. "He gave you a vision of moral order in the universe, and there isn't any." And while loosely constructed comedy-drama does not always elicit contemplative thought, here the vignettes tease virtually every stereotype of Indian interactions with whites. In one typically illustrative parody, Jack's sister Caroline braces for certain rape when their wagon train is attacked, only to have the Indians ignore her completely. Indians, labeled by whites of the era as treacherous, or ruthless, fight with far more principle, essentially as a matter of honor. The reputedly ultra-warlike Pawnee are recruited by whites to help war on the relatively peaceful Cheyenne, at a time when the white world feels free to describe all Natives with ringing damnation. "The Indians know nothing of God and moral right," thunders a white minister, "they eat human flesh, fornicate, adulterize, misogynize, and commune constantly with minions of the Devil."

Far from accepting whites as superior, Natives feel a patronizing pity for the emptiness of their society, and even for the physical appearance of whites and their former slaves. "The black white men ... mostly they are strange creatures, not as ugly as the white, true, but they are just as crazy." Overall, white culture is depicted as complex in the pejorative sense, wrapped in an official religious code so tight that hypocrisy squirts out at every seam, a people distinctly lopsided and unhappy. While the sympathetic Cheyenne come across as genuinely in touch with supernatural powers, even here idealized notions are playfully punctured, as when Chief

Old Lodge Skins, who ceremonially lies down intending to die and pass to the spirit world, only to be drenched in rain, concedes offhandedly, "Sometimes the magic works, sometimes it doesn't." Some of the cultural contradictions, or at least surprises to those unschooled in Native American anthropology are evoked—there truly were "contraries" who rode horses backward and codes of tolerance for gays within the warrior societies. Overall, *Little Big Man* took the first important steps to transcend the flat simplicity of the earliest Native and New American films and their painfully stereotypical characters.

Another part of the same turn in Native American subject films, *A Man Called Horse* (1970), based on Dorothy M. Johnson's fiction, has also deservedly become a modern classic. With its (inferior) sequels *Return of a Man Called Horse* (1976) and *Triumphs of a Man Called Horse* (1982) it offers depth and some sense of refreshing authenticity—at least Indians speak Indian languages and not English on screen. Sir John Morgan has traveled halfway around the world to "shoot a different kind of bird" than he hunted in his English leisure, when capture by Sioux warriors abruptly curtails his gentlemanly adventures. Consistent with the expectations of the dominant cultures in myriad settings the Sioux expect their captive to conform and show no interest in his culture or language. His re-acculturation frames the major issues that emerge when cultures meet—the tendency for bias against the other bordering on or even exceeding cruelty, the inevitable challenge to understand foreign language and comportment. Happily a half–Indian informant, also a captive of the tribe, serves as cultural informant—"I've a lot to learn, Betisse, and you are going to teach me." Although his study of his captors displays an Englishman's cool purposefulness, since his ultimate goal is to understand the Indians well enough to escape, the inevitable effects of immersion do indelibly change Sir John. *A Man Called Horse* is laudable for its extensive use of Sioux dialogue, unsubtitled, for its arresting portrayals of rituals such as the Sun Vow Initiation, yet a sobering caveat remains. A film set almost entirely in a Sioux camp offers an arrogant, aristocratic European male as the sole fully developed and sympathetic character, presenting the truth through his eyes. In the end he proves a "better Sioux" than the Sioux, excelling them in their own skills, teaching Western military strategy at a crucial moment, winning the heart of a desirable Sioux woman. *A Man Called Horse* lacks humility, if only less than consciously; at least in the later *Dances with Wolves*, also approached through the eyes of a sympathetic white here in contact with the horse-culture Sioux, the white protagonist falls far short of omniscience, and the Natives display numerous cultural patterns worthy not only of respect but also emulation.

Jeremiah Johnson (1972), the contemplative rendering of a lone mountain trapper, portrays the interchange of Native Americans and settlers uneasily sharing the further reaches of the Rocky Mountains. In such sparsely populated areas there would seem to be relatively little grist for conflict and much reason for cooperation between all humans; nevertheless the differing traditions co-exist as uneasily as do differing Native tribes themselves, and indirectly even modern Western society intrudes. Another mountain man, Del Gue, is asked what he intends to do with the scalps on his saddle—"Sell 'em to the English ... London is wallpapered with Indian scalps." The film features a host of informants ready to judge indigenous peoples, yet none conscious of trespassing on their lands. The narrative turns on Johnson's decision to help desperate settlers, "Christian women and children," traveling West through mountain passes sacred to the Crow. "This is Big Medicine," warns Johnson. "They guard this place with Spirits." "You don't believe that," scoffs a preacher from the low country. "It doesn't matter, they do." "You've been up here too long Johnson, believing in this," rejoins the Reverend in classic intercultural ignorance. Cooperating against his better judgment Johnson pays a bitter price. Overall, *Jeremiah Johnson* is distinguished by its measured, meditative pace and balanced characterizations, by the quiet chemistry that develops when Johnson acquires and begins to appreciate a Flathead bride. Understanding between Johnson and his wife, and between whites and Indians in general, grows realistically through gestures and other non-verbal expression long before linguistic communication can develop.

As wide open as was the American frontier, peaceful coexistence was less common than friction between the Native and New Americans, especially as expressed in popular film. Also sensitively framing body language and subtle behaviors, the notable *Cheyenne Warrior* (1994) elicits the tensions that are palpable when even the smallest gesture might be misinterpreted. Many honest attempts at exchange distinguish this film as seriously evoking the differing viewpoints characteristic of each society. It displays the range of personalities on both the "white" and "Indian" sides, including a kindly settler, widower of a Cheyenne woman, trusted by the Natives for his candor and integrity. A young white woman and a Native thrown together by circumstance develop deep "feelings" for one another; they test the possibilities of enduring romance, though in the end Rebecca Carver does not wish to live like a Cheyenne while Soars Like a Hawk "will not live like a white man." If pioneers were often loners, bred for individualism, Natives were tribal; "my people must come first in my life," declares Hawk. Still the bond between Rebecca and Hawk is not lightly cast aside.

Romance, in fact, is the hook for much of the Native/New American interaction. On the wide-open frontier, tolerance of other peoples was often hard to find, but so were romantic partners for lonely souls. Several films (e.g., *The Last of the Mohicans*) show white women deeply "stirred" by some primal quality in Indian males. *Stolen Women, Captured Hearts* (made for TV in 1997) even asks the viewer to believe that an Anglo woman kidnapped by Indians in the racist, Indian hunting 1880s quickly changes acculturation, or more nearly finds her Indian love interest deeply engaging in ways that her devoted frontier husband could never hope to match. Interestingly and perhaps surprisingly, however, the majority of mixed relationships flow the other way—involve white males responding to some form of indigenous beauty—and in *Broken Arrow, Black Robe, Jeremiah Johnson, A Man Called Horse, Little Big Man,* and numerous other films we meet men from the white culture who learn to love Indian women. Possible interpretations run a wide gamut, from the history and sociology that made such mating inevitable to a subconscious yearning for a Mother Earth—the notion that white men experience both the purity and allure of "noble savages" as embodied in indigenous women. Far from patronizing their Indian loves the white men exhibit a respect at times bordering on worship, in an era when women of all races were taken anything but seriously. The implication may be that such worship, as well as myriad circumstances, at times drew the interest of Indian women away from their own natural matches; the phenomenon as expressed in myth and erected in film suggests a special commerce across the bounds of culture, of which heterosexual romance may be only the vessel.

Consider the Pocahontas myth in its numerous incarnations, the most recent a delightful, animated "family" film. *Pocahontas* (1995) displays a panorama of natural beauty (not just hers) and the smooth, comfortable linkage of Natives to the wisdom of the natural world. However narrow and prejudiced society may prove on both the Native American and colonial side, somewhere underneath a pan-humanness yearns for expression. Indian-white mistrust is such that an arc can most believably spark across the space of heterosexual attraction, and so a romance that is larger than personal energizes the meeting of warring worlds. Yet the story's ending is grounded in the stark social facts of the era, for with their worlds still, literally, oceans apart, Pocahontas and John Smith must face the inevitability of their separation, albeit with horizons widened forever. (The irony: for once film, in all its fancy, was more "realistic" than the historical record, for the actual Pocahontas did marry another officer, John Rolfe, and return with him to England where she died, no doubt, of exposure to Old World germs and weather. Popular film, always with the last word, has produced a Disney sequel in which the New World Princess encounters the English on their territory.)

Whatever the recipe of reasons, the cross-chemistry remains lively in films that represent numerous times and places. In the oddly heartwarming *Where the Rivers Flow North* (1993) Tantoo Cardinal, as the co-protagonist of a white husband driven from his land by "development" in late 1920s Vermont, emerges as both foil and worthy partner in a struggle to hang on to dignity and tradition in the face of "progress." Noel Lord and his Indian wife Bangor engage in the constant teasing and sparring of caring partners with differing mind-sets; she achieves a very Native mixture of common sense, folk wisdom, and "superstition." The power that romance exerts across cultures is always arresting, and many films suggest that differences in background and mindset can be spanned by partners motivated by the fruits of the relationship.

The fact that the Native was gradually enveloped by modernity, and that as the "frontier" eroded so did the traditional options of Indians, emerges as the dominant theme in numerous films. In *Geronimo: An American Legend* (1993), starring Native American actor Wes Studi, the Chiricahua Apaches, having run out of frontier, have retreated into the deserts and hills of the Southwestern U.S. and Mexico while continuing raids on the settlements. A perceptive U.S. Army Lieutenant, Charles Gatewood, plays cultural informant to a younger trooper. After describing the reasons for the quiet, reserved behaviors of the Apaches, he explains why some are at war with others: "There are lots of different Apache tribes that don't much like each other. Most of all Apache go where the best fight is. It's a morality once you understand it." The surrender of Geronimo and the attempt to turn semi-nomadic warriors into desert farmers mark the end of one epoch in the West, the beginning of another dominated by technology, bureaucracy, and a set of values anathema to most Natives. In fact, an alternative take in *Geronimo* (1993) presents the legendary figure in old age as virtually a cigar store Indian, perhaps the bleakest outcome of all, as the meaningful fiber of an autonomous people was reduced to trinkets by invading, restless Americans preoccupied by conquest and "progress." Films of the Indians' last stand on a fading frontier keep coming, as inexorable as was the New Americans' march across the continent. *Crazy Horse* (1996) recounts one more appealing tale of Indians against strong odds; Native cultures may die out, but the Indian Tale will apparently live forever in Hollywood as Western, saga of courage and masculinity, and morality play.

Fading traditions and lost dignity for the Indian also frame *Tell Them Willie Boy Is Here* (1969), which follows the manhunt for an Indian who killed the father of his girlfriend in self-defense (and loosely recounts actual events from 1909).[5] In many ways standard Western fare complete with posse, tracking, and ambushes, the film meditates nonetheless upon a disappearing authentic ambiance for the Indian as white America devoured the Old West. One veteran Indian fighter, on his last campaign to track Willie Boy, laments the passing of the old times—there will soon be no more Indian wars, no one to hunt down and kill. "Your daddy was lucky," he tells Sheriff Cooper, "he died while it was still good to live."[6] A female expert on Indian matters spices the mix, as she fights a rearguard action for needed services and for understanding of the Indian subculture. Although she is Dr. Liz Arnold, Superintendent of the Marango Indian Reservation, the white male society around her grants her deference but not serious respect. "You're just gonna hang around here mothering these Indians until you're sick and tired of it, then you go off somewhere, I don't know, Europe, East, some damn place looking for somebody else to save." The larger society of the time sees the Indian "problem" only in the most superficial terms, shaped by newspapers full of shallow truths if not lies about Indian encounters while agog concerning the Western tour of President Taft. In the end the rough-hewn sheriff shows a grudging respect not for Indian culture exactly but for sheer courage and purity as represented in Willie Boy, especially in contrast to the softness and shallowness of the cityfolk who experience Indians simply as myths and mementos. When told that people will want to see some tangible scrap from the manhunt, Cooper delivers a scornful reply, "Tell 'em we're all out of souvenirs."

The frontier of permafrost and the Northern Lights is represented in *Shadow of the Wolf* (1986) set in Canada's Great Bay territory in 1935, as the Inuit were finally forced to recognize the inevitability of the invasive culture, which had been making inroads on their traditional life for decades. Resistance toward the whites and their material world is central, with the young Agaguk exemplifying bone-deep suspicion and resentment toward the encroaching system. A surface co-existence between Inuit and whites masks mutual distaste in settings such as the trading post, and other settings elicit still less understanding and trust. Questioning by police, for example, reveals the same evasions and games with words that less powerful groups use in numerous cultures—questions from whites are answered with questions, with plays on words, but never with candor, never motivated by trust. The suspicious disappearance of one white policeman triggers the descent of a group of agents. Knowing that the Inuit have become utterly dependent on modern paraphernalia they threaten to take away all rifles and other modern tools until the guilty confess.

Also set in the far north country just before the turn of the century, the youth-oriented film *Warrior Spirit* (1994) shows Wabi and his white-culture friend come of age on the frontier. The early boarding school scenes are chock with confrontation, as when Wabi counters the Christian story of the creation by sharing in class the teachings of his people. "Do you actually believe that rubbish?" sneers the teacher. "Do you believe yours?" he shoots back. Numerous such encounters make the film worthy of attention.

Contemporary Portrayals on the Reservation: A World Apart

As the American wilderness disappeared, many of those Native Americans not exterminated in the process were relocated onto reservations, in theory territories that were to be almost as self-governed as sovereign nations, where Indian culture could be lived in freedom and dignity. In practice these reservations, chosen not by Natives but by the dominant nation and surrounded by its environmental and social practices, were often difficult places for Indians to lead lives consistent with their cultural moorings.

Those films set in and around reservations starkly portray the worlds apart enveloped by the very different forces of modern North America; for outsiders, experiencing life inside becomes a journey into an unexpected, unpredictable environment. Even the nakedly dark, violent *Shadowhunter* (1992) set in Navaho country powerfully elicits a sense of indigenous forces at play as an Anglo detective, John Cain, hunts for a renegade Navaho killer. In the excellent, even captivating *Thunderheart* (1992) FBI agents enter the Sioux lands of South Dakota to investigate a reservation murder. Wound around the spine of the police action, however, is the engaging portrayal of agent Ray Levoi whose Native American father abused alcohol and died when his son was seven years old, and the young agent's spiritual journey to his nearly forgotten, repressed roots. Core fibers of Sioux wisdom are nicely woven into the narrative, as when two elders of the tribe meet Ray and instinctively have faith in him, in his roots, being, and spirit. The granddaughter of one elder had clashed sharply with Ray when he criticized tribal existence, arrogantly asserting that "this is the twentieth century." "I've seen your world," she snarled. But in a later scene she softened to say "my grandmother says you come from very brave people." Grandmother, in effect, had seen through the modern veneer to the core, the soul, of the man. Also central to *Thunderheart* is internecine struggle among factions of the Sioux, as "pure," honest traditionalists confront a faction that wants a modern economy and in fact enjoys cozy financial dealings with corrupt whites. Ultimately the struggle resurrects the "good Indian-bad Indian" dichotomy long prevalent in American storytelling.

FBI agent Ray Levoi, a Sioux by birth and on assignment to investigate murders on a Sioux Reservation in South Dakota, renews his feelings for his roots partly through a regard for the tribal elders, such as Grandpa Sam Reaches, in *Thunderheart* (1992).

Although a murder mystery also anchors the plot of *The Dark Wind* (1993), set on Hopi and Navaho lands in the southwestern United States, refreshingly the only police presence (except for a thoroughly corrupt FBI agent) is Native. Navaho policeman Jim Chee solves the crime and exposes the drug trafficking behind it through an interesting blend of "modern" deductive reasoning, knowledge of tribal culture, and intuition.

The old frontier battles between soldiers and Indians are figuratively and literally reenacted in *War Party* (1989), set in a small Montana town and nearby reservation. The town's white mayor with some Indian support hits upon a scheme to attract more tourists—a one-hundredth-anniversary reenactment of an Indian-versus-Cavalry shootout, with locals hired as actors for the day. "Nobody's out to open old wounds or rewrite history," he explains at a town meeting. "All we want to do is put on a good show, help all of our people." After one young white racist in Union uniform sneaks live bullets into his revolver, however, and uses the playacted battle to settle a real grudge with a local Indian, nothing less than a racial war along the range ensues, raking old wounds dangerously open and prompting a television reporter to ponder how a "local incident like this could have unearthed all the racial prejudice that's obviously been buried here for decades." Sonny, one of the Indian boys involved in violent revenge, concludes that this is the "Same old shit. Nothing's changed in a hundred years." He had been critical of his Indian father as a sellout to whites, the same father who now laments that "All my life I've tried to understand the white man ... never learning a goddamned thing." In one of the many ironic twists and turns, the renegade Indian boys, during their last standoff, ask for the counsel of their old, home-town medicine man whom they had always considered, until then, a drunken embarrassment.

"It's simple and easy. You don't dig in our graveyards. We won't dig in yours," angry Indians warn archeologists in *Lakota Woman* (1995), one of numerous scenes of crossed perceptions, values, and expectations striking sparks like swords in battle. The film recreates the standoff at Wounded Knee in 1973 between the government-backed repressive tribal regime and the radical American Indian Movement, revisiting the territory of *Thunderheart* with a blunt, striking political candor and much accurate historical detail. It permits no gray areas, as running abuse of Indians and shortsighted officials form central motifs, and fiery young Mary Crow Dog encapsulates the conflict when arrested and threatened. "The joke is, you have no clue who we are." The girlhood reminiscences of Mary, before her political coming of age at Wounded Knee, in fact reflect a ubiquitous white culture as ignorant as it is dominant and arrogant. When, at a parochial school, a priest stumbles upon a note about himself which asserts, "Father Hochbauer knows nothing about Indians and should only teach white people," his response is swift and punitive. Sadly, relations between the cultures show an absence of a sincere interest in the other's thinking, of mutual respect, of genuine exchange on any level.

In some ways the most realistically packaged, and subtlest, of the modern films set on the reservation is *PowWow Highway* (1989), offering a glimpse into Cheyenne life within and outside its boundaries. In an opening scene Buddy Red Bow, at a tribal council, opposes a developer armed with charts, graphs, and a smooth manner. "...I've read every damn contract since the Ft. Laramie treaty of 1868, and it's always the same deal, ain't it, you get what you want, and we get the shaft.... This ain't the American Dream we're living here, this is the Third World." Most of the conflict between basic values is cast more indirectly, however, as when a televised commercial features a local car salesman's patronizing pitch, "This old cowboy's on the Warpath with Heap Big Savings." Philbert Bono, driving across country with Red Bow in his sacred "pony," vaguely in quest of his Native powers, affably mixes sincerity and blissful ignorance. Cheerfully,

In a tale of reservation live at once serious and painfully humorous, Philbert Bono leaves an offering of great personal significance, a Hershey bar, at a site sacred to many Indians, in *Pow Wow Highway* **(1989).**

he tells another Cheyenne that an episode of *Bonanza* left him inspired by an Indian prophet, though the role was played by "a white guy." "Bonanza? That's not where you learn about the Prophet!" Consistently, events return Bono and Red Bow to present realities, as when they shop for radio equipment and encounter insensitivity, even racism. "You don't understand. No gettum' special deal on this one, chief."

The poverty and blight of reservation life for most Indians appear closely related to the indifference, sometimes disdain, of surrounding whites, and to the complex identity issues among the Natives themselves. Few speak more than token words of Cheyenne, it seems, or use traditional trappings apart from ceremonial events. "I hate these goddamned things," complains Red Bow of a "Pow Wow" with traditional dress and music. "Look at these people ... they think a few lousy beads and some feathers was a culture or something." Moments later, however, he joins in the rhythmic dancing, personifying perhaps contemporary Indians caught between extremely divergent worlds, often feeling somewhat out of place in both. In a parallel scene a radical-movement Indian is moving his family away from violent Pine Ridge and into a condominium in suburban Denver, but it is left unclear if he can find a sense of home in one place any more than the other.

Contemporary Portrayals Conflict in Values: A Failure of the Melting Pot

Arguably no film has more compellingly portrayed contemporary Western society as distinctly in discord with the traditional world as *Koyaanisqatsi* (1983), yet remarkably, during the entire eighty-seven minutes not a word is spoken, except for the mantra of the title itself as a background score. The film consists entirely of images, from high-rise buildings razed by explosives, to the striking web of city traffic, to the lost, alienated faces on the street in the urban jungle. *Koyaanisqatsi* can reasonably rank as a "must see" for all serious students of the relations between the Native and New Americans, ironically so for a film without direct reference to the traditional cultures except for "Koyaanisqatsi," which apparently means "Life out of Balance." Viewer sensitivity, insight, and imagination must do the rest, must extrapolate broader meaning from ordinary images presented in extraordinary fashion. So engaging are the images that most viewers will infer some powerful message, whether fully that intended in the mystic Native American sense or not.

The Native and the New Americans saga perennially returns to the matter of divergent cosmic views, and all the films with contemporary settings focus on mismatches of fundamental belief and purpose, in one form or another. In such films as *The Burning Season* (1994), *Clearcut* (1992), and *Journey to Spirit Island* (1988) at issue is the voracious consumption of resources squarely in conflict with traditional peoples' needs and values. "Based on the true story" of Chico Mendes, *The Burning Season* pits aggressive "developers" of the rain forest against its long-time residents; the attitude of the developers recalls the Portuguese of *The Mission* who choose the whip as the appropriate driving force of "civilization." Mendes's steadfast navigation by moral principles starkly contrasts, throughout, with the opportunism of what might be called a "Development Culture." *Clearcut* raises other moral issues, most saliently the justice of fighting violence against nature with violence against the violators. Graham Greene stars as the almost chillingly alienated Native who, exasperated with the environmentalists' failure to stop predatory logging in western Ontario, administers personal justice when he kidnaps the head of the logging company. In one sense Native American spiritualism rises as especially poignant in this film—a deep reverence for the land and its natural fruits has been systematically abused for too long, and the frustrated resistance escalates into retribution. Other analyses, however, might speculate that a more general alienation and anger brewing in some Natives has simply manifested itself in violence against convenient targets. *Billy Jack* (1971) and a pair of sequels had years earlier burned the fuel of countercultural anger at The Establishment to achieve cult success, invoking every stereotype of North American subcultures while simultaneously hoping to smash them. Combining karate, prejudiced ranchers, mistreated teens, drug-use debates, wildlife concerns, issues of pacifism, and the ultimate would-be-pacifist-angry-Indian-warrior in Billy Jack himself, the film in many ways served as specious countercultural potpourri. Nonetheless it sounded many fundamental tones of frustration that youth, and Natives, were feeling.

Coming of age in a white world as an Indian, finding a Right Path along a trail of moral and practical uncertainty, remaining true to the spirit that has guided ancestors—such are the issues of the "family" movie *Journey to Spirit Island* and its youthful, as well as adult, protagonists. Developers wish to break ground on an island sacred for the Nahkut, but it is protected under law because eagles are nesting there. The resulting drama, although Disney-like in its predictable adventures, nicely and at times delicately gives outline to the spiritual, moral, and worldly shape of the meeting between opposed traditions.

Sioux City (1994) strikes to the heart of the dilemma of roots versus modernity, for Dr. Jesse Rainfeather Goldman is "Indian" by birth and appearance only, adopted as a young child by white, upper-middle class Americans. As the young physician takes vacation time to search for his mother back on the Lakota Sioux reservation, memories of his origins are quickened for the first time. He discovers she has died days before under suspicious circumstances, and while this mystery drives the intrigue of the film his quest becomes a search for a larger truth. As he seeks to know his mother's fate, the circumstances of his adoption haunt him—why was he tossed away to the white world, albeit to caring, wealthy parents? "Don't judge her," enjoins Jolene, a young Sioux woman who soon becomes his love interest. "You have no idea what it's like to be an Indian woman then or now, and you never will." In fact, the entire Native experience is distant from his own in an upscale, Jewish subculture. Should a scientist respond to mysticism, a doctor to traditional healing, a professional from Los Angeles to the bucolic life of the reservation? Like Ray Levoi in *Thunderheart*, he initially perceives the Lakota as backward, stuck in the previous century, and his adopted spiritual community serves as his frame of reference. "Yes, the Jews live among the dominant culture. They do so throughout the world. But they have never lost their sense of identity," he says in touting Jewish adaptation and "success." Yet something in his Nature wars with Nurture, as he circles, moth to flame, powerful memories and urges. He submits to the emotional support and even mysticism of his Native community, yet in the end returns to California, even with the ravishing Jolene asking him to stay, the tug of both roots and romance. A more realistic ending than the modern life abandoned and the impulsive move "home," so common to this genre of story? Or a fatuous best-of-both-worlds, candy-coated ending as Jesse renders medical services to Native Americans back in Los Angeles, and even fields a promising visit from his love? She hopes to coax him into returning, he wishes her to stay, and so the pull of the different worlds is felt while the question of identity is cast once more. The mystery of his mother's death was solved but another remains: who, really, is Jesse Rainfeather Goldman?

Medicine River (1993), *Smoke Signals* (1998), and *Naturally Native* (1998) rise to stand alone as quality, authentic-flavored renderings of contemporary life among Native Americans with all its dignity, pathos, foibles, and humor. These films, featuring modern Native Americans as protagonists and whites as only shadow players, have turned the tables on decades during which whites were central and Indians all too often mere window dressing. So Native American-based are these films that they might scarcely convey the meeting of cultures at all, except for the palpable tension within the communities themselves, grounded in traditional ways but surrounded by a powerful, seductive society. Young Indians leave to live in the "white world," and their elders wonder if they will ever see them again. In *Medicine River*, the essential dilemma of new generations in traditional communities everywhere—to stay with their roots or engage with a larger world—is enacted by a world-class photo journalist as he returns home, after twenty years absence, upon the death of his mother. Complete with neckties, he arrives seeming out of step, consulting his wristwatch for punctuality, now uncomfortable with the Native pace of life. When told his brother will probably be back in town "soon" he inquires with Anglo impatience, "What is "soon," a couple of days, a week?" "Yeah." He has seen, literally, a larger world through the professional lenses of his work. "There's nothing for me here," Will proclaims at first, yet soon feels the subtle, then constant tug of informality, affection, and community. The two women in Will's life represent attraction in the opposite polarities; Ellen from Toronto, blond and polished, radiates the cosmopolitan, while his new relation with Louise speaks to earth-bound values, to an honest, relaxed sense of place. Ethnic, small town life stands brightly but honestly portrayed as economically depressed but rich in compensations, and the life of elders on the margins offers honesty and paradox as well—Martha Old Crow seeks a reclusive, highly traditional life in her stunning valley, but she sits outdoors in a padded recliner when not enjoying her modern housing.

Medicine River, Smoke Signals, and Naturally Native do for contemporary Native Americans what *Dances with Wolves* did for the nineteenth-century plains Indians—Native personalities and emotions emerge from the haze of previous filmmaking to stand with greater individuality and clarity. *Smoke Signals* and *Naturally Native* are among the most authentically "Native American" commercial films ever, largely produced, directed, and of course acted by Natives, and squarely face Native problems—such as the destructive power of alcohol—while giving sympathetic characters the dignity of their daily lives. Too many earlier films imitated the apartheid of real life: Natives only seen through police contact or during emergencies, around the edges of white characters and their stories, the two peoples estranged from the warmth at each other's kitchen table. Now the white audience enjoys a front row seat at an "Indian soap opera" which will surely afford Indians a humanity much less distant from white emotions and experience, and afford Natives a self-reflective look, lit brightly by effective drama.

Smoke Signals showcases the contemporary Native life of Coeur d'A-lene, Idaho, but flashbacks and stories from recent decades echo memories and collective experience. A baby, thrown from a window just before his parents perished in a burning house, was caught by Arnold Joseph, who had started the fire in drunken carelessness. But beyond such poignant facts, emotions are interwoven with tales, myth, and even magic, all of which inform daily life as the bedrock of a certain Native Truth.

The title of *Smoke Signals* holds at least a triple entendre: it may fairly refer not only to the stereotype of Indian communication, not only to the deadly fire that forged the lives in the film, but also to such a haze hanging over Indian identity that Natives themselves have been unsure of what image would shine through when the smoke had cleared. "Don't you even know how to be a real Indian?" Victor chides Thomas, but the sub-cultural search for the "real" is hindered by layers of bitterness, confusion, and self-doubt. Indians, painfully aware of their stereotypes, often behave both naturally and self-consciously at the same time. Victor, assuring his mother he will return from a pilgrimage to Phoenix where his dad has died, asks if she wants a signed promise. "No way. You know how Indians feel about signing papers," she responds, invoking collective Native experience on several levels. When Thomas and Victor need a ride from two young Indian women, one playfully asks what is offered in return, because "We're Indians, remember. We barter." Thomas offers a story, an outlandish tale that arouses disdain from Victor, but she cheerfully calls the narrative "a fine

Victor Joseph and Suzy Song share memories, pain, and hope, in a film renowned for its believable, sympathetic portrayal of contemporary Native life, *Smoke Signals* **(1998).**

example of the oral tradition," with apparent humor and sincerity wrapped in the same complex package. In the home of another Native in Arizona, Thomas glances toward a television screen flickering with Cowboys and Indians. "The only thing more pathetic than Indians on TV," he wryly comments, "is Indians watching Indians on TV." Thomas draws on the "oral tradition" consistently; as philosopher and raconteur, spokesman for relaxed lifestyles and forgiving attitudes, is he the prototype of a new and genuine prophet, or merely another lost Native looking for himself?

Naturally Native advertises its emergence as "the first mainstream feature film funded and produced entirely by Native Americans" (with funding from the Mashantucket Pequot Tribal Nation), and the life created onscreen mirrors that purebred status. As in *Medicine River* and *Smoke Signals*, the audience feels invited into Native homes and offered basic hospitality, but no phony politeness or dissimulation. Three adult sisters, taken from their tribe as children and raised by a foster family named Lewis, confront decisive moments in their identities. Even Indian males are bumped off center stage as these women's lives unfold, grappling with mundane realities, but again echoing the broadest questions of all. Are they their roots or their adoptive society? Can they find a way to live, in the social and economic ambiance wrapped around them by the "white" world, consistent with their sense of being Native?

Voices from the Earth

Most American filmgoers probably remember *Legends of the Fall* (1994) as the battle of a Montana ranching family against the elements, change, and each other; they will remember the seductive radiance of Julia Ormond as she wrenches the emotions of three brothers, the visceral appeal of Brad Pitt, and the tragic climax of bloodshed under the Big Sky. Some may remember the film in a different way, as rich in the perceptions of indigenous culture, as leavened by the spirit and presence of Native Americans.

Although decorated with white film stars, the legend is framed by the "Indian issues" that were part of the land and the times. Colonel Ludlow's military career had ended with an angry resignation over federal handling of the "Indian question"; among the ranch's staple figures are a wizened Indian, One Stab, as well as an Indian woman married to a white man, and their child. The charismatic protagonist Tristan, a white with rugged, frontier, "Indian qualities," projects a stoicism mixed with profound emotions. His very beginnings presaged that his life would be guided by Natural powers, for after his difficult birth the Colonel brought him to One Stab, who "wrapped him in a bearskin and held him all that night." Later, One Stab taught him the Hunt, the Natural World. "His place was with me," recalls the old Cree warrior. In turn the Colonel is almost a second father to the young girl, Isabel, born of the bicultural marriage, and insists that she needs "education." "What will she do with all this education?" asks her father. "She'll have a richer, fuller life, of course." "She's a halfbreed, Colonel." "Not in this house, she's not." Another bicultural marriage later joins Tristan and Isabel, yet in effect each represents both cultures, each integrates the knowledge and spirit of both the "white" and "Indian" worlds.

The richest indigenous flavor, though, comes through the narrative voice of One Stab in old age, telling the legend of the Ludlow ranch. This is a major turnabout of white movie-making tradition—instead of all other cultures being judged through white eyes, members of the dominant culture are defined by the indigenous. "I think it was the bear's voice he heard deep inside him, growling in low, dark, secret, places," recalls One Stab, remembering Tristan. "His grave is unmarked, but it does not matter. He had always lived in the borderland, anyway, somewhere between this world and the other."

The Last of His Tribe (1992), based on the true story of Ishi the sole surviving Yahi, also records the quiet tones of voices from the earth. In 1911 in Oraville, California an Indian was discovered who had survived the massacre of his tribe years ago. Now literally the last of his people, he could talk only with an anthropologist, Kroeber, who had studied his people and language. Poignant throughout, the action becomes a clinic in intercultural dialectic, from subtly or overtly patronizing behavior toward Ishi to delightfully crossed attitudes. As Ishi boards a train for San Francisco, a woman representing her social club gives him a sort of hospitality basket and adds the hope that he will not "find our civilization too disappointing." Though well intentioned, the woman neatly embodies a mix of patronizing and ignorant behaviors, seemingly unaware of the gulf between reality and her hopeful perceptions. The trained anthropologists and government "Indian experts" in contact with Ishi earn mixed reviews for insight. Shortly after Ishi's discovery the official from the Bureau of Indian Affairs attempts to remove him to Oklahoma "where he can be with his own kind," thus assuming that one "Indian" will happily take to other "Indians," and forgetting that a Native who grew up over a thousand miles from Oklahoma and speaks no other Indian language might have relatively little in common with his "own kind." Kroeber performs with significantly more sensitivity. While of course from a different world and not tuned to parallel emotions he intuits some margin of Ishi's mental system and some of his fundamental values. In fact, the name Ishi was given by default when Kroeber warned that it would be "the height of rudeness" to directly inquire as to his Native name, highlighting the importance of protocol in intercultural encounter. Kroeber "comprehends" Ishi well, falling short only in ultimately "understanding" him, that is in rising to the emotional, even metaphysical levels that are central to Ishi's experience.

In the end the power of *The Last of His Tribe* arises from Ishi's memory of his people, his sense of Nature, of a living and suffering Earth, of a traditional spiritual realm with which the dominant culture has manifestly lost touch—by definition it otherwise would not so violently have become the dominant culture. The film suggests that not only people but cultures themselves can die, that their spirit, not just their artifacts, can disappear into the soil of Mother Earth.

The most popular of recent films set at the meeting of white-Indian worlds has been *Dances with Wolves*; although of course a horse-culture, plains Indian, frontier tale, it deserves separate analysis because of its distinct impact and status as a modern classic. It may well prove the archetypal new Native American film, conferring a charm and dignity upon Native cultural values to the point of sounding a distinct reproach to previous Western attitudes.

The Sioux youth display the spirit of curiosity and mischief that elicits smiles in many cultures the world around, and Chief Ten Bears radiates graceful, aged wisdom, as when he entrusts exploring the white culture to a balanced team, a hotly fired brave and the deliberate medicine man. Perhaps putting a "likable, human" face on indigenous plains Indians like no other film, it shows both the promise and foibles of direct cross-cultural interactions, such as Dunbar's introduction of coffee to Indians and his use of charades to bridge the gap of language. Though the central characters are a white couple who find a home in Indian culture, that culture itself is in many ways the protag- onist, the worthy hero and star, though seemingly doomed to be driven back into the earth by socio-political change. Ultimately, *Dances with Wolves* evokes a sense of history, a past come alive to speak in the form of the diaries of John Dunbar. Although his diary might seem trivial, swallowed by prairie-wide vistas and epoch-making events, it stands quietly as a centerpiece. A diary lost and floating down the stream of time, then finally returned to Dunbar to speak again with the quiet voices of the earth.

Quintessentially, the Indian story, to the dominant culture, is one of mystery disappeared below the soil, of the imaginations of young boys

Although the real star of the film is a dignified village of Lakota Sioux, the white audience is brought into their lives through the bridge provided by Dances with Wolves (Kevin Costner) and Stands with a Fist (Mary McDonnell), both adopted by the tribe, in the film *Dances with Wolves* (1990).

stirred by finding arrowheads as they roam the fields or stalking game in "Indian" stealth with their slingshots, of boys and men yearning to rediscover primordial survival skills and their own primordial being. This is much of the pull, the apparently inexhaustible allure, of "Indian culture."

Toward Conclusions

As depicted in these films, contemporary exchange between the cultures is strained and insensitive where it most often occurs, primarily in the arenas of police contact and business relations. A refreshing exception is the very blond Rabbit in *PowWow Highway*, a childhood friend of the Indians, with whom they can talk candidly. Most whites, it seems, either consciously or inadvertently patronize Natives, just as John Cain initially fails to realize Ray Whitesinger's competence in *Shadowhunter*, as liberal lawyer Peter Maguire brings the well meaning but alien messages from a white legal world in *Clearcut*, as even Indian-by-birth Jesse Rainfeather coaches Indians on joining the modern world in *Sioux City*. In turn, many Natives are loath to endure what are perceived as the self-satisfied, even narcissistic personalities of whites. In real life and even in film, they usually suffer in polite silence, but not always. In an instantly classic scene from *Smoke Signals*, Victor blasted a chatty young white who lamented her lost opportunity to compete in the Olympics, making it clear he considered her all mouth and no substance. Far from idiosyncratic to the film, the scene echoed generations of Native distaste for the self-absorbed, highly individualistic tendencies of whites, especially set alongside the struggle of Natives for basic rights and survival.

The overwhelming majority of the Native and New American films, however, attempt to portray "traditional" Indians in "traditional" settings, with all the ritual, myth, and metaphysical trappings thereby implied. While it stands tempting to lament the speciousness of films that reduce "the essence of Native American culture to a patronizing melange of peace pipes, mysticism, and inscrutable tribal elders," Georgia Brown, reviewing for the *Village Voice* replies that, quite simply, "mysticism, pipes, and the wisdom of chiefs and elders really are essential components of Native American cultures."[7] She has driven to the heart of the matter. The very fact that the intelligentsia of the dominant culture often seem so uncomfortable with the fundamental myths, morality plays, and spiritual commerce of Native American stories may speak less to the realities of those cultures, past or present, than to the conflicted and complex souls now living complex white lives. And along two critical axes the traditional Native

American and white culture are almost completely opposed. The traditional "way of knowing" was strikingly different (in both method and outcomes) from the analytical, positivist modernity, and as well a set of white taboos concerning central human events, notably death itself, contrast with a Native openness. Thus, in *The Last of His Tribe*, Ishi, while appreciative of the anthropologist who speaks his language, feels a need to counsel Kroeber as someone too analytical and ill at ease with both life and death. Ishi senses that the anthropologist, who cannot grieve and fully face his wife's death, may be hiding from life through science. If Kroeber is "vitally interested" in encountering the last Yahi still alive in California, the interest does operate as largely scientific in the Western sense—noting, comparing, classifying, concluding. Kroeber's understudy, who first encountered the living specimen, exclaims that the very sound of the "cracked consonants" of his speech will arouse marvel. In contrast the Native "anthropologist," evaluating humans and their cultures, would follow highly qualitative and intuitive research strategies of not only listening and observing but of direct engagement with the peoples and texture of a culture as well.

Indeed, modern popular film almost unerringly portrays Native protagonists as "centered" on the vital issues of human existence, however temporarily befuddled by the details of a modernity that is not of their making. Thus Ishi seems to penetrate to the core of the matter when he observes that Kroeber "has put Ishi in there" (the anthropologist's notebook) and not "put Ishi in here" (the anthropologist's heart). In *Thunderheart* Ray Levoi's Sioux heritage wells up as he proclaims that the sacred South Dakota badlands, and by extension the souls of the Sioux people, simply "are not for sale." In *The Dark Wind* Jim Chee explains that to traditional Navaho, punishment for antisocial behavior is both unnecessary and irrational—a "dark wind" blows through the souls of those who behave badly, and like all other winds will blow its course. In *Dances with Wolves* Chief Ten Bears summarizes the impact of Europeans as uninvited guests in the New World: "They have all been the same. They take without asking." In one rendering of the Geronimo story, the aged chief tells Theodore Roosevelt that he had guided his Apache tribe, "and they trusted me. It was right that I should give them my strength and wisdom." Chief Joseph counsels his angry young warriors that "It is easy to raise the rifle, it is hard to put it down." In *Little Big Man*, Chief Old Lodge Skins observes that the white man does not "know where the center of the Earth is."

Such consistent reductions of life's core issues to eloquent simplicity, to graceful, even spiritual truths are a staple in these films created for the mass audiences of modernity. While they may or may not accurately reflect

Native wisdom, they clearly appeal broadly to the audience of the dominant society. Students of film as popular culture are squarely confronted with the most pivotal of questions: why are the evocations of fundamental "Native" perceptions received so empathetically by the mass audiences of the very culture that developed from almost diametrically opposed precepts, that clashed with almost all and even annihilated numerous Native cultures? By definition the perennial messages of Native and New American films must deeply resonate with the emotional chords of audiences. Though some observers wonder if an enormous collective guilt drives the contemporary resurrection of the Native American, that theory does not hold. The best films, such as *Dances with Wolves*, played to excellent box offices in Europe and other non–North American venues, and tourists from numerous industrialized countries have consistently displayed a fascination with the myths, the Cowboy and Indian landscapes, of the Old West. And a host of other potential sources of American guilt, from the historical abuse of immigrant groups to the razing of Dresden, Hiroshima, and Nagasaki are no more than occasionally evoked in North American film.

There appears to be some ingredient at once simpler, and more complex, at work in the Western psyche: the need for psychological antidotes to the particular stresses and twists of modernity. The spirit of the Native, at least as imagined or as portrayed in popular film, appears to be the very medicine the doctor ordered for psyches poked, pushed, and disoriented by what Freud called "civilization and its discontents." The desire to escape to a simpler time and way of life, anchored by honest, earth-bound values, appears deeply rooted. Such escapism is of course not confined to films with Native American themes—the entire narrative genre in which a complex modern life is gleefully abandoned to follow a rustic, Edenic life bears a first cousin relationship to the "feel" of Native American pastoralism. Such escapism must face challenging questions: what would in fact happen if an office worker told off his boss and built a cabin on a lake with his bare hands, or what would life truly feel like long-term, inside the Sioux camps of *Dances with Wolves*, for someone with modern acculturation? *The Mosquito Coast*, drawing its dramatic energy from the tension of plans gone awry and life turned chaotic, posed a stark counterpoint to the Polyanna outcomes of leading the "natural" life. Nevertheless it stands as an exception, and the "call of the wild," in all senses, is perennially seductive.

In film, the most attractive elements of traditional Native cultures and characters center on the qualities of trust and reliability, courage and "masculinity," and on what are portrayed as primal connections to both the physical and the emotional universes. A man of his word, the Algonquin in *Black Robe* explains a nearly suicidal trek through the wilderness to guide white men to a remote location, "I may be stupid, but I agreed to take them to the Huron mission." The Chiricahua Apache "doesn't give his word often, but when he does, he keeps it," asserts Lieutenant Gatewood in *Geronimo: An American Legend*. In *The Last of The Mohicans*, an unequivocal sense of honor guides the actions of Chingachook, his son, and Nathaniel Poe, as they attempt to keep the British from harm. The Lone Ranger, whose own principles were above reproach, was always accompanied by a "faithful" Tonto whose trustworthiness was absolutely unquestioned. In *I Will Fight No More Forever*, and in fact the majority of films set on the receding Indian horizons as "civilization" inexorably overruns them, the Native American handshake is worth its ethical weight in gold, a doleful contrast to the white man's flimsy commitments.

Equally basic to Indian character is physical courage, as most essentially tested in *A Man Called Horse* through the Sun Vow rituals. Whether the courage, literally under the gun, of a Billy Jack, who also faces the rattlesnake's fangs in ritual ceremony, or the fearlessness and endurance displayed in *Black Robe*'s far North setting, or the final lone battle of Willie Boy, the daring needed to take a dangerous stand in *Thunderheart*, or the youthful bravery displayed in *Journey to Spirit Island*, the fiber of courage is woven into the tapestry of most film portrayals of the Native American.

Related closely to courage is the spirit of defiance that infuses the story of *Billy Jack*, that fuels the standoff at Wounded Knee in *Lakota Woman*, that courses through the veins of the honest Indians in *Thunderheart*. Drawing a line in the sand, the defiant Indian will retreat only so far, evoking nearly universal emotions to which the captives of "modern civilization" can readily relate. Only one step beyond defiance is the open manifestation of a "warrior's spirit." In *Tell Them Willie Boy Is Here*, an Indian trapped by impossible circumstances decides to make a warrior's statement—even though he aims his bullets not to kill but merely slow down the posse, he makes headlines as a renegade, so that "at least they'll know I was here." In *Clearcut* the unstoppable rape of natural resources and the futility of Anglo legal remedies drives an Indian over the edge, as he aims retribution squarely at the white rapists of the forest, even ritualistically cutting away some of the corporate manager's skin, "debarking him" as his company does to trees. *War Party* with its playacted scenes turned painfully real may suggest that, as conflicting cultures meet, frictions are never more than a spark away from igniting into real violence: the contemporary murder—even a scalping—of Indians in *War Party* leads two youths to the ultimate act of warriors. One of the most metaphysical moments of *Geronimo* is also the most violent, as the legendary leader experiences visions "of his powers," his warrior powers. In *The Last of the Mohicans* "good" and "bad" Indians alike demonstrate the ability to fight valiantly for pride, honor, or retribution, often with less hypocrisy than the French and English. From the colonial frontier of the Mohicans to the southwestern terminus of the frontier in Geronino, and all the territorial fights in between, the Indian pushed to the limit displays his ultimate identity: a warrior without fear. "It is a good day to die, my son," declares Chief Old Lodge Skins with dignity and without pretense, in *Little Big Man*, displaying the ultimate courage, facing death with serenity.

The Native American additionally attracts Anglo audiences as a fellow being who has remained in touch with primal forces, especially those of the natural world. Even the contemporary *Naturally Native*, replete with the details and stresses of modern life, draws much of its resonance from these overarching qualities and myths: the Native enterprise of the same name derives its curative products from genuine, inherited traditions, but also banks on the popular (white and Indian culture) perception that the "Native" and the "natural" offer enduring value. The theme across films remains remarkably consistent. From language laced with the similes of life forms—"my heart soars like a Hawk to see you, my son," says Chief Old Lodge Skins—to quiet evocations of holistic relations to Nature, such as portrayals of the horse-and-buffalo plains Indians in which Native and other fauna and flora mesh completely, the Indian was and is the first and quintessential naturalist, perhaps ecologist. When other species were killed for food, at least the act itself bore the dignity of spiritual process, as when Mukoki in *Warrior Spirit* counsels his initiates that "Hunting is not a sport; it's a prayer." In *Legends of the Fall* One Stab taught young Tristan the "great joy of the kill, when the hunter cuts out its warm heart and holds it in his hands, setting its spirit free." In *The Emerald Forest* an aboriginal chief says simply of clearcutting that "They are taking the skin off the world. How will she breathe?" Even tribal decisions in times of crisis are informed by natural wisdom, as when the remnants of the Cheyenne were told by the Wolf, one hundred twenty-eight winters ago, to remain in the OxBow in *The Last of the Dogmen*, and even Ishi's lost people are remembered in terms of the Earth in *The Last of His Tribe*—"Do you feel Her breathing? Do you hear Her singing?" asks Ishi. Chief Old Lodge Skins in *Little Big Man* perhaps speaks for all Native peoples, at least in popular film, when he declares that the Cheyenne "believe everything is alive," in contrast to whites, who "believe everything is dead ... even their own people."

Concomitant with the Native's primal sense of the land are the survival skills needed to cope with the unforgiving elements. In *Shadowhunter* the ruggedly masculine John Cain is lost, helpless compared to his Indian guide, the daughter of a renowned Navaho tracker. The missionaries in

Black Robe and *The Mission* depend on the Natives for sheer survival, and the latter-day colonist in *The Mosquito Coast*, believing he can superimpose Western science on the jungle, discovers painfully that Native practices have their compelling reasons. And several films reflect the reality: European colonies in the New World only proved viable through the tutelage of natives in survival skills. Remarkable men such as *Jeremiah Johnson*—Robert Redford as "white Indian"—achieve no more than the Natives who handily survive the mountain wilderness. *Tell Them Willie Boy Is Here* shows both the resourcefulness of a savvy Indian on the run, but also the imitative skills of his white pursuer, once more Redford as Sheriff Cooper, who echoes the Indian with his taciturn ways, tracking instincts, rough-hewn principles, and ultimate reverence for courage.

Transcending particular qualities, the crowning dimension of Native character as conceived in Anglo films may subsume such traits as courage, trustworthiness, and natural ties with the land: a sort of primal wisdom, a philosophical and spiritual intimacy with almost self-evident truth. Only in an occasional film, such as in *PowWow Highway* where an elder snidely declines her role as a repository of wisdom, is there rejection of the belief, the expectation that Native culture knows a path to a vital core of understanding. *The Education of Little Tree* (1997) invokes his instruction in "The Way," interpreted by elders, as every significant event in life arises. In *Legends of the Fall* it is One Stab the elder who interprets the remarkable legend of the Ludlow family as if the Native can best feel human drama at its pulse. "It was then that Tristan came into the quiet heart of his life. The Bear inside him was sleeping. It is hard to tell of happiness. Time goes by, and we feel safe too soon." In *Little Big Man* the elders share wisdom as naturally as drawing breath, and in *Journey to Spirit Island* "Grandma" Jimmy Jim warns younger Indians that "cold ... will capture your souls, if you do not respect the sacred...." In numerous films the wisdom of elders is expressed in subtler fashion, as a sort of wordless intuition in *The Dark Wind* or *Jeremiah Johnson*. In *Thunderheart* a subtle but powerful theme underscores the wisdom of old Sam Reaches as well as Maggie's grandmother—they offer a quiet, resonant wisdom to younger Indians, even the most disillusioned of whom never patronize or fail to the respect the council of elders. *Cheyenne Warrior* gives to even the younger braves the dignity that comes from quiet knowledge and understanding. In *The Last of the Dogmen* Spotted Elk inherits not only a chief's blood but a chief's carefully sifted wisdom, and in *Dances with Wolves* Ten Bears archetypically yet believably, without pretense, sagely quides a tribe, as in the scene when he deftly elicits the troubled feelings of his medicine man about the coming of the whites. The Native may even know our soul better than we know ourselves. "I don't think I believe in visions," protests Jesse Rainfeather, adopted away from the Lakota Sioux at birth. "I think you do," his grandfather replies simply. The Indian way of knowing, reaching beyond surfaces, includes the metaphysical; in *Geronimo* an Apache medicine man foretells the time and manner in which the leader will appear, and the wisdom of the elders in *Thunderheart* includes more than may be known by the five senses. In *Little Big Man* a chief's wisdom extends to visions in dreams that, sooner or later, play out in reality. Ultimately and fundamentally, the Native is someone with a primal wisdom we covet and wish to share.

It matters little whether such remarkable, even metaphysical wisdom is "real" in the sense of that word to current Western culture. What matters fundamentally is that a faith in such wisdom forms a tangible, undeniable part of the belief system of the traditional cultures themselves and also a seductively attractive belief to general non–Native audiences. Those beliefs are elicited powerfully, creatively, in these films, in a way intended to drive the imagination of the popular viewer.

Many, even most, of the films discussed here are admittedly not tightly reasoned, and critics who delight in dissecting the internal logic of plot and action will find ample targets. Yet the most useful films are those widely seen and discussed, in short those that captivate audiences, and many of these will use the elements most likely to attract the jaded film-goer. Those experts who justifiably raise questions of historical accuracy must remember that a medium so powerful as film achieves lasting influence: its power to shape our perceptions and beliefs, to emerge as almost larger than History and Truth is resoundingly, essentially real. Films that so superficially portray a group as to grow obviously, painfully clinchéd may influence only children and the intellectually careless; films that more deservedly ring true as well as sympathetic, such as *Dances with Wolves*, may more deeply entrench themselves into the common, even the intellectual's psyche. Most U.S. American film-goers have seen *Dances with Wolves*, and most have exited the theater, whether consciously or not, with a visceral sense of the plains Indians and with some sense of cultural issues raised, with a reoriented sense of relation to traditional cultures, even a sense of having been in the skin of John Dunbar.

This penetrating reach of popular film is at once exciting and sobering—to revisit one core issue, how "authentic" and how mimetically "accurate" are the portrayals themselves? Though several reviewers researched the anthropology and history of the plains Indians enough to note a somewhat careless treatment of detail in *Dances with Wolves*, they generally gave it good marks for combining entertainment with integrity of message.[8] In the simplest of terms, is the essential meaning of the film likely to inform or misinform, to enlarge the insights of an audience? How important is it that Chief Ten Bears would never have had a Spanish morion in his tent, compared to his observation that whites had displayed the same avaricious character through the generations? How important is it, really, that the white man's bison-slaughter-for-sport may be several years premature, historically, when the scene, encapsulating beliefs and practices a universe apart, is absolutely striking and effective?

The value of *Dances with Wolves* and the other films lies in their potential to help humanize, not romanticize, lives culturally different from that of the audience, to offer alternative views of both history and contemporary reality, to challenge the ethnocentric views that all peoples naturally hold and may slide back into all too easily. The wife of a Sioux medicine man may or may not have subtly urged him toward matchmaking for a daughter, the wife of a chief may or may not have teased him publicly about an incident in his youth when he fled from bears. Such touches nevertheless give a much more "human" texture to individuals, as members of a community. In real life the Culturally Other is almost never "just like us" on the one hand (as Dunbar romantically describes the Lakota in his diary) nor a totally alien creature, as if from Neptune, on the other. For representatives of other cultures to figure effectively in film, or for that matter any of the story-telling arts, they must have a "human" face, meaning characteristics to which the audience may relate, while at the same time have their own identity, perceptions, and world view.

Native meeting New American film has been effective in resoundingly, if rather carelessly at times, rewriting the popular history of the settling of the continent. School children from the dominant culture have always learned to think in terms of an "expanding" civilization, rather than a receding one of Native peoples, and have vaguely assumed, when considering the matter at all, that Natives were naturally and inevitably swept aside by "progress." A more powerful antidote to such ethnocentric perspectives than any progressive print curriculum emerges in the vividness of the human stories in the best of these films. Even the least imaginative person will look at Colonial history anew in light of *The Last of the Mohicans* or *The Broken Chain,* in fact may view the "discovery" of the "New World" afresh after seeing *Christopher Columbus: The Discovery.* Classic stories of the Old West and The Frontier will never seem quite the same after such films as *Little Big Man, Dances with Wolves, Tell Them Willie Boy Is Here, Geronimo,* and *The Last of the Dogmen,* and the human side of Natives will be less distant after such films as *Cheyenne Warrior, Thunderheart, Medicine River, Smoke Signals,* or *Naturally Native.*

In her insightful *Primitive Passions* (1997), Marianna Torgovnick suggests that ultimately, in film portrayals and perhaps social reality, the ultimately successful Indians have really been whites.[9] That is, after the last Mohican, last Yahi, and countless other Indians have become as extinct as dinosaurs, "white Indians" like Nathaniel Poe, John Dunbar, Jeremiah Johnson, and Tristan Ludlow not only absorb "Indian values" but survive to carry them forward. While all around them individual Indians, and whole Native societies, may be dead (or dying) these whites nonetheless embody admirable "Native" qualities admired by the victorious culture. The futures of these particular whites who have "gone Indian" may be doubtful, but the deeper question does effect an eerie echo: why do whites so often emerge as the successful, "Indian" protagonists? Does the weight of white perception always gravitate to packaging all sympathetic characters in white persona, in ethnocentric if not racist representation? Interestingly Grey Owl, the most famous Canadian "Indian" of the 1930s, was really the Englishman Archie Belaney, Indian only by virtue of a boyhood "dream," a radical change to a Canadian wilderness lifestyle, and the nurturing of a legend. As the wilderness man wrote and spoke publicly under his adopted identity, was it he or his ingenuous audience who wished to live in a mixture of truth and fiction?[10]

Much as George Bernard Shaw mused that youth was too fine to waste on the young, are Indian qualities too coveted to waste on Indians? In the end the question leads squarely to another: how have the surviving Indians peoples fared as white culture finally, definitively overtook them?

In many ways the most illuminating of these films use contemporary settings for Natives after several generations of "assimilation"; several of the films discussed here depict an uneasily modern subculture, often fitfully searching for a centered sense of self. In the nineteenth century the wife of Chief Joseph of the Nez Percé had presaged a bleak future—the Natives in the white man's school, with clipped hair, in white man's clothes, were sadly "Not Indian anymore. Not white. Not anything." Although peoples with Indian identities have survived, even the Big Screen cannot romanticize the troubled subcultural picture. *Thunderheart* and *PowWow Highway* do not flinch from unpleasant realities, unabashedly showing the economic and social warts of reservation life. Of course, the "third world" life that Red Bow laments in *PowWow Highway* serves on many levels as an effect of the first world—Indians only live in "squalor" or "destitution" relative to the larger society and its constructed perceptions. Obviously Natives thrived in traditional ways for centuries without a sense of subsisting on the margins, there being no wholly different society to be on the margins of. Native culture cannot fairly be compared, dollar-to-dollar and nose-to-nose, with the greater society that surrounds it. *Thunderheart*, *Sioux City*, and most of the contemporary films thus create a space outside of the Western experience to stage the essential difference of peoples who truly are driven "by a different spirit." As created in these films the wealth of Indians, both individual and collective, lies not in the "trinkets" of the material West, but in land, tradition, ritual, courage, and the spiritual alchemy that turns earth and memories into gold.

Yet a sense of place, purpose, and fulfillment at times remains quite elusive. Philbert Bono from *PowWow Highway* engages in a quest, traveling in a decrepit jalopy as his "pony," more sure of who he is not—white— than who he is. In *Lakota Woman* Mary Crow Dog rejects a Catholic school as an alien place with alien people and messages, yet finds no replacement home until her anger and defiance find a purpose, for a time, at Wounded Knee. "I'm a modern Indian," asserts Russell White in *Sioux City*, but the question remains flatly open: what *is* a modern Indian, exactly? The young, almost middle-aged Lakota "floundered," he said, abused drugs, then came to a new inner peace through respect for "the old ways." *War Party*, like *Lakota Woman*, offers a plot wrapped around alienation and conflict, while identity issues remain central. Young Natives compare fractions of Native blood—"Hey, I'm three eighths"—apropos in the sense that their existence, around the social and economic margins of their Montana community, does not bear the full, undivided dignity of either white or traditional Native American identity.

In most of the contemporary films, whites have been reduced to bit players, instead of commanding the audience's sympathies like John Dunbar of *Dances with Wolves*. Especially in *The Dark Wind*, *PowWow Highway*, *Medicine River*, and *Smoke Signals*, whites all but disappear, magnifying Indians to the full size and power they always deserved. Yet the white world as an enveloping ambiance is not so easily dismissed, even if Arnold Joseph in *Smoke Signals* boasts of a spirited fantasy in which he simply goes "Poof!" and the whites are gone, "gone back to where they belong."

However much a modern Indian subculture may wish to banish its presence, the white world looms large just offstage. Every Indian knows that the larger society controls much of the land and resources so dear to Natives: the youths in *War Party* sit by a beautiful lake in Montana and dream of taking it back for their people, while in *Sioux City* land with beauty and significance is described as "not reservation land, anymore" due to "some sort of treaty way back when." In *Thunderheart* the whites, and co-opted Indians, threaten the remaining Sioux lands in their greed for uranium. Historically the white world is there, atrocities and all, never far from the consciousness of Indians, even the least schooled of whom know of Wounded Knee and the dismal nineteenth-century history of American Natives. Past events assure that present Indians are part historian; furthermore "storytelling" remains socially and emotionally important. In even the low-key *Medicine River*, seemingly far removed from the politics of Canada, an elder remembers the journey of old Coyote to Ottawa, where no lesser a dignitary than the Prime Minister greeted him warmly. "Boy, are we happy to see you!" exclaimed the Prime Minister. "Maybe you can help us with our Indian problem." "Sure," said Coyote, "what's the problem?" Such wry, understated dialogue does more than reveal ironic twists in Native stories and the events that spawned them, it suggests the ever contentious dialectic between quite distinct societies and spirits. Except in times of interracial crisis the white world can, and often does, ignore the very existence of Native peoples, but denial from the opposite side is more difficult. Most broadly of all, the white world exists as sets of expectations—to have "education," "careers," "property," and the like—expectations transmitted through myriad institutions as well as the surrounding media. Thomas and Victor pick at each other in *Smoke Signals* about not having "jobs" in the modern sense though they do have "jobs" in the more traditional: Victor lives with and cares for his mother, while Thomas does the same for his grandmother. Of course, Indians may prove just as goal-oriented as whites (*Billy Jack*, *The Dark Wind*, *Lakota Woman*, *Medicine River*), assuming the goals are consonant with culture and belief. Working too hard to meet the broader culture's ideals might prove unsatisfying in the end, anyway, because they are of, by and for the white world, not the Native.

The "successful" Natives shown in these contemporary films generally achieve a more traditional competence. The admirable Ray Whitesinger in *Shadowhunter* may be unlucky in love and uncomfortable in the non–Indian world, but she has legendary skill as a tracker. Jim Chee of *Dark Wind*, also a Navaho, works for the tribe as a rural police officer, a sort of tracker with a modern car and equipment. A number of characters seem satisfied with lives and jobs that serve Indian communities, from Trading Posts *(Sioux City)* to Community Centers (*Medicine River*). Those Natives that have entirely left, whether in childhood or as adults, may excel in the white world (*Sioux City*, *Thunderheart*, *Medicine River*), but the implication remains that they have strayed from their Right Place in the order of things. Other Natives live bonded to the Native center by their basic feelings, while also pushed out by modern centrifugal forces. Susy Song from *Smoke Signals* works in health administration, and due to competence and promotions now does "too much traveling." She represents as well a positive feminist sub-text, combining intelligence, honesty, and an attractive sense of self. Her relationship to Arnold Joseph, never fully explained, nevertheless afforded her full autonomy, an autonomy Arnold's wife had also achieved by declaring an end to living with his drinking. In *Naturally Native* three sisters command the screen as they negotiate Indian identities and specifically "Native" livelihoods within a white economy and society. From Jolene of *Sioux City* to Ray of *Shadowhunter* to Maggie in *Thunderheart* to Louise in *Medicine River*, a new generation of Indian women seek to combine a sense of roots with a grounded sense of self, feminism in a modern-traditionalist form.

In the primal tale of *The Last of the Dogmen* (1995) a white tracker and his companion, an expert in plains Indian history, follow a hunch to an unbelievable discovery: Cheyenne fleeing from army pursuit deep into the Montana mountains over a century ago, believed to have perished with the winter, have survived to maintain a nineteenth century tribal life in the most remote wilderness. Over the years, to protect the secret of their existence, the renegade band has killed the few white intruders who penetrated their remote Oxbow region, but Dr. Sloan speaks Cheyenne, and a relationship which crosses time is established.

If *Dances with Wolves* and *Smoke Signals* represent archetypes of new, and relatively realistic, Native American film, *The Last of the Dogmen* rises as a logical, ultimate extension of the myth of Indian culture as heritage lost. It powerfully captures the more ethereal side of what the Indian story means to our popular culture, evoking as it does a magical sense of what has escaped us, or what may be just beyond the next valley, re-creating the "different spirit" of Native culture as tenaciously enduring. Beyond that raw fanciful power, it offers a forum as wide as the Big Sky country itself to revisit central questions. Does Lillian Sloan truly respect these Cheyenne as equals and friends, or simply consider herself to have struck an anthropologist's mother lode? Does modernity have something to offer even these self-sufficient people, as symbolized in the healing penicillin brought from outside? Are these nineteenth-century Cheyenne in the OxBox now truly doomed, with waves of investigation as inexorable as the original march across the continent by whites? Is the inevitable fate of these Cheyenne the continuing fate of Native peoples everywhere, sooner or later to be hounded out of existence by a modernity which nonetheless consecrates the resources of universities to their study? Beyond the significance of such questions, the contrast of the modern white world with Natives frozen in time for a century brings into painfully sharp contrast the different peoples, from a "different spirit," awkwardly sharing the experience of meeting, and of attempted accommodation.

Filmography

Film (aka), year, country (language), director, producer/distributor, minutes

Aguirre: The Wrath of God, 1972, Germany (gr.), Werner Herzog, N. Yorker Films, 90
Amazon, 1990, Finland/USA, Mika Kaurismaki, GNS, 88
At Play in the Fields of the Lord, 1991, USA, Hector Babenco, Universal, 186
Billy Jack, 1971, USA, Tom Laughlin, Warner Brothers, 115
Black Robe, 1991, Canada, Bruce Beresford, Samuel Goldwyn, 101
The Brave, 1997, USA, Johnny Depp, Filmax International, 123
Broken Arrow, 1950, USA, Delmer Daves, 20th Century–Fox, 93
The Broken Chain, 1993, TV, USA, Lamont Johnson, Showtime, 76
The Burning Season, 1994, TV, USA, John Frankenheimer, HBO, 123
Cabeza de Vaca, 1991, Mexico (sp.), Nicolas Echevarria, New Horizons, 111
Cheyenne Autumn, 1964, USA, John Ford, Warner Brothers, 165
Cheyenne Warrior, 1994, TV, USA, Mark Griffiths, Libra Pictures, 90
Christopher Columbus: The Discovery, 1992, USA, John Glen, Warner Bros., 120
Clearcut, 1992, Canada, Ryszard Bugajski, Northern Lights, 102
Crazy Horse, 1996, TV, USA, John Irvin, Turner Pictures, 90
Dance Me Outside, 1994, Canada, Bruce McDonald, A-pix Entertainment, 84
Dances with Wolves, 1990, USA, Kevin Costner, Orion Pictures, 183
The Dark Wind, 1993, USA, Errol Morris, Seven Arts Production, 111
Dead Man, 1995, USA, Jim Jarmusch, Miramax, 134
Eagle's Wing, 1979, UK, Anthony Harvey, The International Picture Show Company, 104
The Education of Little Tree, 1997, Canada, Richard Friedenberg, Paramount, 112
The Emerald Forest, 1985, UK, John Boorman, Embassy Pictures, 110
Father Damien (Molokai), 1999, Belgium/Netherlands, Paul Cox, ERA Films, 109
Fitzcarraldo, 1982, Germany, Werner Herzog, New World Films, 158
Follow the River, 1995, TV, USA, Martin Davidson, Hallmark Home Entertainment, 99
1492: Conquest of Paradise, 1992, USA, Ridley Scott, Paramount Pictures, 149
Geronimo, 1993, TV, USA, Roger Young, Von Zernick-Sertner Films, 102
Geronimo: An American Legend, 1993, USA, Walter Hill, Columbia, 115
Grey Owl, 1999, Canada, Richard Attenborough, Renstar Distribution, 117
Hawken's Breed, 1987, USA, Charles B. Pierce, Vidmark Entertainment, 93
A House Made of Dawn, 1987, USA, Richardson Morse, Firebird Productions, 90
I Heard the Owl Call My Name, 1973, USA, Daryl Duke, Tomorrow Entertainment, 74
I Will Fight No More Forever, 1975, TV, USA, Richard T. Heffron, ABC, 110
The Indian in the Cupboard, 1995, USA, Frank Oz, Paramount, 96
Indio, 1989, Italy, Antonio Margheriti, R.P.A. International, 94
Jeremiah Johnson, 1972, USA, Sydney Pollack, Warner Brothers, 108
Jim Thorpe-All American, 1951, USA, Michael Curtiz, Warner Bros., 105
Journey to Spirit Island, 1988, USA, Laslo Pal, Academy Entertainment, 93
Killian's Chronicle (The Magic Stone), 1994, USA, Pamela Berger, Ed Cruea, 112
Koyaanisqatsi, 1983, USA, Godfrey Reggio, Island Alive, 88
Lakota Woman, 1995, TV, USA, Frank Pierson, Turner Pictures, 113
The Last of His Tribe, 1992, USA, Harry Hook, HBO, 90

Chapter Seven

"THE UNFINISHED SYMPHONY": MULTICULTURAL VOICES IN AMERICAN FILM

"You're so American. You're such an optimist."

Show of Force

"Maybe your son ripped you off. I've seen it a hundred times."
"In your world perhaps. Not in ours."

A Stranger Among Us

"You're an American citizen. You're not really an American."

Dragon: The Bruce Lee Story

"These are the eighties, man. It's the Cosby decade. America loves black people."

Soul Man

"Now, I'm sure they've got their own account of the Alamo on the other side, but we're not on the other side."

Lone Star

Introduction

Anyone attempting to discuss Multiculturalism in North America, as this chapter does in the context of popular film, must apologize in advance for the limitations of the effort. It is sure to leave many a subcultural stone unturned, and will surely not satisfy every perspective on the multicultural issues in play. Beyond the highly politicized, emotionally charged turns that many a debate on some form of Multiculturalism takes, many if not most

206

of the issues, and subcultures, resist clear definition. Such fluidity may echo North America's greatest strength and confusion: a multicultural democracy is eternally under construction not only in political shape, but in self-image as well. Honest questions, and seeming contradictions, can be posed wholesale: why would a market economy launched largely on the backs of slaves then showcase one of their descendants for the Olympics in Atlanta—an ill, aging black boxing champion who once openly defied the government of the United States but now holding the Olympic torch, as if he represented the core and pride of the country and its official culture? The title of Roof and Wiegman's book *Who Can Speak?* frames a critical question: who holds the torch of our national cultures, our subcultures, who may speak for them in this, a time of especial ethnic and multicultural ferment?[1]

"Only the dead know Brooklyn," insists the narrator in the story by Thomas Wolfe, and even they couldn't know it "t'rou and t'rou," so profound are the histories that run through it. No statement could better evoke the depth and complexity of the "soul" of major North American cities. As waves of immigration have washed over the cultural shores of the United States and of Canada for over two centuries, apparently fated to continue indefinitely into the twenty-first century, it is again clear that North America is a land of varied, tenacious subcultures within a larger, dominant culture, and it is also clear that awareness, analysis, and even specific celebration of our "multicultural" societies will remain an abiding part of our national dialectic. Not only are groups of recent immigrants that naturally represent distinct subcultures freshly resupplied, but long-term subcultures, most conspicuously Americans and Canadians of African heritage, Hispanics, and other "persons of color" experience at times a renascence of their consciousness of "otherness," and reassert their visibility.[2] The almost uncanny popularity of Alex Haley's *Roots* series in the 1970s amply testifies to the appeal of heritage and the resurgence of cultural identities, an appeal of such force that it should remain part of our cultural landscape for the foreseeable future.

In more than one ironic sense the realities of the multicultural genesis of U.S. American and Canadian societies have contributed to a trivialization of the constituent cultures themselves: so present is variety in facial shapes and skin tones that it is quite usual in many businesses and other public venues to encounter "ethnicity," quite visible yet presumably at the service of a bland general culture and devoid of values that contrast starkly with that general culture. Ethnicity can become literally and figuratively the "face" of an office or organization—perhaps through strategically chosen receptionists or advertising campaigns—while the corporate body itself reflects solely the dominant culture in values and goals. And beyond the use of ethnic veneer for public relations purposes, there are thorny, diverting questions of definition: both the concepts and the day-to-day realities of "culture" and "subculture" become slippery, elusive, hard to pin down, even self-contradictory. The hugely successful U.S. American black humorist Bill Cosby, for example, can narrate documentaries in which he decries the myth of the "melting pot" and observes that blacks "ain't melted in yet," while making comedy series for television in which black families of harried professional parents, indulged youngsters, and identity-seeking teenagers seem to function precisely like archetypical, middle-class "white" families.

It is often asserted that mass media, including film, represent if not a microcosm then a reflection of the larger society.[3] If so it is easy to spy the mirrored "face" of diversity there, just as in the "multicultural workplace," but harder to discern the realities that lie behind the images. Setting aside the films that specifically focus on ethnic groups in collision, an outside observer might conclude that the ethnicities mix like assorted chocolates in a box, offering different flavors but essentially equal value. Too easily missed is the gravity, the sheer pull, of a very visible, talented, media-competent central culture grown from Anglo-Saxon roots. Minority actors most often deliver lines in scripts produced by the dominant culture, much like dough placed in a mold. The psycho-social dilemma of countless minority artists is a complex topic of limited relevance here, but the litany of conflicted artists should remind us of an almost self-evident truth: the central culture predictably and consistently commands the cultural center. What is a black or Hispanic or Native American actor to do when offered work, but in roles that are at least subtly out of step with an ethnic sense of the "real"? What are talented minority playwrights to do when their purely candid efforts cannot achieve commercial success, but slight adulterations will produce scripts that at least reach audiences, while putting food on their table? For the purposes of the analysis here it serves to remember that the surge of minority visibility in film is relative and often adulterated by commercial processes, that most film scripts are touched and retouched by committee before being shot, that the industry of Fantasy and Illusion offers those commodities whole while offering "truth" in a much more refined, processed form.

At the broadest and most superficial levels, popular films with at least some multicultural decoration abound—the most ordinary of films may show faces of color or sounds and sights apparently designed to invite an illusion of the exotic. Many good films present stories of North America in which a subplot at least brushes upon the meeting of cultures, although the cinematic weight of the film is directed elsewhere. Even films which consciously and meaningfully portray some dimension of subcultural differences are far from rare, although setting, story, approach, and of course quality vary wildly.

North American films that touch upon multicultural themes, or present subcultural characters at least tangentially, are far too numerous to treat comprehensively—numbering in the thousands by the most inclusive counts, and at least in the several hundreds by more rigorous definitions. From the crazy-quilt of film depiction of "cultural diversity" within North America, this book focuses on a select number of representative and also unusually interesting, notable films, films that define the broader tendencies as well as provide a base for the analysis of similar films. This study of North American multiculturalism as expressed in modern American film seeks only to frame some of the clearest, most expressive voices, to give them contextuality, not to form final judgments on a fluid process. The multicultural cast speak for themselves—the voices, images, and stories are theirs. For all of the tendencies of a dominant society, multiplied in power by all the tools of the media age, to trivialize diversity and homogenize the cultural flavor of everything within its reach, there remain to be heard the clear chords of different cultural voices.

Classic Encounters of Black on White

The subcultural story of the one immigrant group that didn't choose the American Dream plays at once the simplest, starkest, and perhaps most complex instrument in the multicultural symphony. An instrument of impressive power and range, it has offered over one hundred fifty years of realism and fantasy in literature, and currently finds sophisticated expression in the novels of Toni Morrison and numerous other gifted voices. Modern popular film, from the late 80s and the 90s, has added powerful perspectives to the American family portrait in black and white. No longer is it necessary to flog the primordial racist symbolism of an old nag like *Birth of a Nation* (1915) or dissect the now quaint-seeming *Guess Who's Coming to Dinner* (1967), as important as these and other classic statements of the black-on-white experience may be. From film that recaptures black contributions to a white nation, such as in the Civil War setting of *Glory* (1989), to the near warfare of black against white suggested by *Malcolm X* (1992), American society's most conspicuous subculture has come onto the screen in a host of provocative settings.[4]

One of the classics, *Black Like Me* (1964) based on the book by John

Howard Griffin, bears in one sense a striking thematic resemblance to a more recent oering, *White Man's Burden* (1995): in both, inverted experiences and therefore perspectives afford dramatically different "realities." In *Black Like Me* a real-life "white man" John Howard Griffin did chemically darken his skin and turn himself into a "black man" and thus quite instantly and literally change social worlds, experiencing the other side of every black-white interchange he had ever known. Unlike Griffin's authentic chronicle, *White Man's Burden* is fanciful, essentially a form of "social-science fiction," as a dominant class of blacks rules a society filled with poor, striving, hapless underclass whites. The simple, straightforward inversion of social status has impact, with blacks as bosses and whites as laborers, blacks as police and whites as the common suspects, black as the color of dolls that white children covet. "There's something inherently wrong when a people historically and repeatedly burn down their community," says a black business mogul, speaking of riots by frustrated whites. "The bottom line is a very simple question, 'are these a people who are beyond being helped?'"

The expectations of the races also stand upon their head in the uncannily illustrative if heavy-handed *Trading Places* (1983) in which an elite white investor makes his brother a wager: if a black petty criminal switches roles, switches lives, with their company manager he will soon act and think like a privileged professional, and their manager will sink into the degradation of street life. Not only does *Trading Places* give the major characters, and therefore the viewer, a *Prince and the Pauper*-like sense of the view from a different perch, it as well exercises the classic debate of nature versus nurture. "Like racehorses," proclaims one investor, "it's in the blood." But the exponent of nurture, of the sociology of situation and life chances wins his bet, and through even a highly comedic vessel a message loudly asking for a reassessment of prejudice, and for level playing fields, is heard.

The equally farcical *Soul Man* (1986) is equally serious about exposing the superficiality of skin pigment: young Mark Watson is given a full scholarship to Harvard Law School on the strength of his grades ... and his phony black skin. As in *Black Like Me* he deliberately changes his race, but for different reasons and with different results, because he rides the wave of affirmative action—ethnicity turned into an advantage. He soon begins to receive more than merely an education in law—he has to act black, to *be* black. Race as a superficial fact translates into, if nothing else, assumptions and expectations—before even attending a class Mark receives an invitation to meet with the Black Law Students Association. In the gym, his prowess in basketball is simply assumed, and he's soon approached by women for his imagined prowess in bed, while on the unflattering side a white woman in an elevator nervously shifts herself and her pocketbook

Just like in "The Prince and the Pauper," Billy Ray Valentine is catapulted to life at the top, seen here introduced to upscale responsibilities by a pair of high-flying financial investors, in *Trading Places* (1983).

away from him, and later the local police follow his car for blocks. At a delightful dinner episode with the parents of a white girlfriend, cutaway scenes show the fantasies that each member of her family holds—in her father's he is abusive, in her mother's the ultimate "stud," in her younger brother's the ultimate rock musician. As Mark functions like a "black" law student his outlook steadily alters, old abstract issues of race become concrete. In one string of brief scenes woven throughout the film, student racists offer a steady diet of "black jokes," which seem less humorous to Mark each time. The use of blatantly racist humor provides a painfully realistic touch, because it stands as a ubiquitous, timeless dimension of human society whenever culture meets culture. Ordinarily, in spite of its clear "entertainment" value, racist humor is surprisingly absent from contemporary film, perhaps in an attempt to avoid offense. One argument holds that pulling explicitly racial humor out of the closet would represent an honest, healthy development, at one and the same time exposing the contours of racist thinking and allowing the targets of the humor a chance to respond, as Mark finally does in decided fashion.

With his masquerade discovered in the end, he appears before a disciplinary board and his advocate turns all the liberal arguments about race inside out to offer an ironic, spirited defense. "Can you blame him for the environment in which he was raised? For the warped values which he learned from earliest childhood? For the people with whom he was surrounded…? In short, can we blame him, ladies and gentlemen, for the color of his skin?" A clever argument, in the movies at least, that poor Mark is a victim of the "deteriorating moral fiber" of the community which socialized him, in this case, a wealthy and privileged yet self-centered and obtuse white community. And while clichéd views of cultural deprivation are turned on their head to ask pardon for someone raised within the moral sterility in the dominant culture, the stakes of a scholarship system based on ethnicity emerge in specific, human terms. Mark's co-student Sara Walker, black, a single mother and without means, would have been the bona fide recipient of the scholarship he fraudulently received. In the end Sara is reimbursed in cash, but she is rich throughout in intelligence, drive, and moral fiber, cast as a quiet and dignified statement incarnate for feminism and black pride.

If inherited ethnicity, accidents of birth, prejudice, and culturally molded expectations supply the philosophical fodder of *Trading Places* and *Soul Man*, they are still more explicit in *A Family Thing* (1996), as Earl Pilcher discovers that his real mother was a black who died in childbirth, that his half-brother Ray has known the secret, and has hated it, these long years. "Blood don't mean shit," says Ray. "I'm not your brother." Common bonds of blood may lead to contact and discovery, but it is the sociology of differing experience that invariably forges different lives. "You're right about that, I don't know what's it's like for you," concedes nearly ninety-year-old "Aunt T." with the folk wisdom of an aged black woman from the South. "Nobody ever knows what it's like for somebody else, that's always the problem." The dialogue of the races throughout is Faulkneresque—the present is haunted by the past, infused with it. Earl's "mother" shares the secret on her deathbed, apparently unable to carry such knowledge with her to the grave. Ray sees in Earl the memory of Earl's father toward whom he harbors undying resentment as his mother's white lover.

As Earl struggles in the small ways realistic to both daily life and the mental shock he has received, he experiences internal conflict and some enlightenment, but surely no pious transformation. And Ray's son, Virgil, astonished to meet a white "uncle" he never knew existed, experiences nothing more than the minor softening of his racial irritations, with no immediate dent in his view of the white world. Aunt T.'s calm, outspoken acceptance of family history exemplifies a theme below the surface of the film's events: while "polite" white society was often shocked by racial and sexual realism the same stories were accepted as everyday life in the black community.

Though film, as a means to deliver a message, rated as one of McLuhan's "cool media" it has the temperature, nonetheless, to get inside the skin and infuse the viewer with the emotions of others—no medium is so powerful for the direct injection of empathy, no experience as effective except John Howard Griffin's personal change of direct reality. *Nothing But a Man* (1964), *A Raisin in the Sun* (1989), and *The Long Walk Home* (1990) are among the best of the to-be-black-in-a-white-man's-world films, all offering variation on a constant theme: black subcultural life sculpted into numerous painful shapes by the rough, unfeeling dominance of the powerful white society. *The Long Walk Home* features Southern apartheid at the breaking point during the bus strike of 1955 in Montgomery, Alabama. It also captures the paradox of well-to-do white women, some of whom weakened the strike by chauffeuring their domestic employees themselves— reliable domestic help, it seems, was more important than standing against black political insurgence. *Nothing But a Man* and *A Raisin in the Sun*, based on Lorraine Hansberry's famous work, go inside the black subculture for a look at dignified life, under very difficult conditions. *A Raisin in the Sun* presents as well the emotional dynamics surrounding one of *the* critical issues in multicultural cities, that of breaking away from the ghetto to move into a dominant culture ("white") neighborhood.

In spite of all of film's power to broker empathy, especially for the sympathetic, downtrodden character, lively debate targets the political messages of interracial film. Are both blacks and whites portrayed accurately, commensurate with their real roles and actions, and does the camera patronize one group, or lionize another? Critics have protested, for instance, that blacks receive little visibility or credit for militancy in *Mississippi Burning* (1988). Nevertheless it brings a visceral understanding to the emotions in play in the race-torn Deep South (based on the real-life murders of James Chaney, Michael Schwerner, and Andrew Goodman in 1964), even if white heroics tend to obscure the reality that to be black and dignified in pre–Civil Rights Mississippi was in itself a courageous act, often a suicidal act. From beauty parlor to barber shop, the camera captures the deep divisions of a small, Southern town. "Simple fact is ... we got two cultures down here," proclaims the mayor, "the white culture and the colored culture. Now that's the way it always has been, that's the way it always will be." The film's scriptwriters prove admirably aware of subculture detail on numerous levels: not only is there a chasm to be crossed between white and black societies, but the invading federal agents import yet another mentality, as ignorant of local mores as if in a foreign country. White FBI Agent Anderson, himself a former sheriff from small-town Mississippi, stands stretched between his subtle knowledge of Southern culture and his federal bosses, who remain intent on using conventional methods in an alien setting. In one telling scene the lead agent, against Anderson's advice, chooses a public setting to question a black—who nearly loses his life in swift retribution. Anderson's intimate knowledge of Southern people and temperament contributes to the solution; it is he who teases out the location of the buried bodies of the slain civil rights workers.

Flashpoints in the battle for civil rights may drive much film of the genre, but stories painted on less dramatic backdrops carry rich portrayals as well. The touching *Places in the Heart* (1984) is powered by the most fundamental cinematic fuel of all—believable, compelling characters trudging through the genuine emotions of prosaic life—to chronicle the very American, Southern fight of a widow to keep family and farm together by bringing in a cotton crop. In this tissue of poignant ironies, the woman whose husband was accidentally shot by a drunken black places great trust in a black laboring drifter; a night raid by the Ku Klux Klan is foiled by a blind white man's ability to identify the hooded marauders by their voices; through the joint efforts of black and white a farm nearly given up as failed brings in the year's most profitable cotton crop. Respect and friendship between black and white develop across the gulf of their castes, although in the South of the Great Depression the apartheid context is so powerful that only small gestures across that gulf are possible. The philosophical messages sound with even greater clarity due to the recognizable, everyday hues and tones of life presented.

The clash of good and evil forces announced by *Birth of a Nation* has come full circle in *Malcolm X*: the black Islamic movement in the United States had branded the white race as devils, the root of evil and decadence, while celebrating black heritage as the cradle of civilization and holy human values. In a film primarily intercultural by virtue of the *reaction* of black separatists to white supremacy, white society plays a contextual role, having created the framework in which racial injustices and hatreds are seething. In a brief yet contextually huge moment a well-intentioned young white woman asks Malcolm what she and others can do to "help" the cause—"Nothing," she is flatly told. For some observers this represents a critical moment in American racial history, in which useful dialogue between the black and white cultures deteriorated, replaced by silence and suspicion; for others it may represent a naked truth, that American black subculture is both literally and figuratively on its own.

In some ways *Malcolm X* is the magnum opus of Spike Lee, the black director who may have contributed more fresh and original subcultural drama at the popular level than anyone before him, one of the truly original figures in U.S. American film. Some of his earlier films, however, pack an even greater punch for the study of black on white, culture on culture. While portraying the social and sexual chemistry of the races bluntly yet thoughtfully, *Jungle Fever* (1991) features a gifted black architect searching for fairness and dignity in the maw of a white-owned firm. He comes to work each day from Harlem, in contrast to his colleagues, and as opening scenes of New York City maps and street signs suggest, ethnic geography determines everything in The City. At times perceptions and attitudes seem as predictable, as easily charted, as the clearly-bounded neighborhoods from which the characters come, and real knowledge of the other's neighborhood is often nonexistent. "You've never been to Harlem?" Flipper asks Italian secretary Angela Tucci. "I've never met anybody from Harlem," she honestly admits, although she proves at least an exception, open to the experience of knowing blacks.

If numerous white characters are depicted as narrow-minded bigots, Lee never flinches from honest portrayal of either the hypocrisy or depravity in the heart of the black ghetto, as in the pathetic Gator, drug addict brother to the successful Flipper, a shameless leech upon his own family, even conscious of his degraded moral state. "I really hate having to resort to knocking elderly people in the head for their money, but I'll do it ... You know I'll do it," threatens Gator to extort fifty dollars for crack. The unabashed depiction of certain black ghetto characters grows all the starker because of Lee's clear drive toward societal and historical meaning—Flipper's father, "Papa Reverend," is a walking text of the social psychology of the races, a scholar of the hypocrisy of whites. Nonetheless the actors and their actions achieve the effect of being nakedly, convincingly real, with no apologies given, none expected. Flipper's white lover is ethnic-neighborhood Italian, from an overtly racist family, but black racism makes ugly appearances as well, as when Flipper and Angie simply attempt to dine in a Harlem restaurant.

Race, in fact, is the fuel that lights both sexual tension and strong social irritation throughout. Flipper's wife Drew flies into a rage upon discovering his affair with Angie, a fury that is clearly several decibels more powerful because the "other woman" is white. Drew, herself the child of a racially mixed marriage, concedes later in a calmer but still impassioned moment that color is an extremely charged issue for her. "This color thing has got you all messed up," Flipper says. "And that is why it hurts so very much," concludes Drew. Race often defies logic, as when Angie argues that race is relative, pointing out that Flipper's own wife had one white parent, but Flipper simply asserts that his wife and child "look black, they act black, so they *are* black." Flipper rejects the prospect of children with his white lover, observing that "a lot of times the mixed kids they come out all mixed up, a bunch of mixed nuts."

The attraction, laced with danger, between the sexes of the different races is ever present—the moth and flame. Sheer fantasy and exploration drive many of the liaisons, doomed to at best a rocky road. "The truth," Flipper informs Angie after their love affair has run its tortuous course, "[is that] you were curious about black ... and I was curious about white."

Not only the volatility of black on white but the mix of, as well, Korean and Puerto Rican communities charges the chemistry of Lee's *Do The Right Thing* (1989), already deservedly a modern classic.[5] Few fictional portrayals, in any medium, so compellingly depict pockets of ethnic groups living together, in daily contact, yet so utterly apart. "This is *my* pizzeria," bellows "Sal" in his business that serves an all-black clientele. "[Pictures of] Italian Americans on the wall only." In a beautifully directed sequence white cops drive slowly by and stare with distaste at unemployed ghetto blacks, who stare back with the same regard. Inside the closed car a cop comments to his partner "What a waste!" while moments later one of the men on the street offers the same observation, in the same words, in regard to the police. And in one of the more telling yet wordless scenes of modern film, a black faces off with a Puerto Rican in a battle of the boom boxes, each gradually raising the volume of his subculturally meaningful sounds, each trying to "outshout" the other in ethnic symbolism and pride.

During just the past generation, the legal status of blacks in both the U.S. and Canada has significantly improved, as have both the public and private perceptions of black North Americans held by many whites. A quite reasonable conjecture is that the advent of realistic media portrayals of prejudice, coupled with the rise of blacks playing a variety of ethnic-neutral roles in both film and television, has helped to humanize African-Americans for the white majority. Most non-black Americans have seen at least one high-impact portrayal of egregious injustice suffered by sympathetic blacks; although social psychologists may debate the degree of impact of such portrayals on our social behavior, at least most whites are now aware of the range of emotions, family commitments, intellectual talents, and career accomplishments that characterize a diverse black population. A growth of empathy, in simplest terms a change of heart, probably explains much of the change in race relations during a generation. Still, some observers perceive ambivalent feelings in the ambient culture concerning this North American psychic Holocaust, second in carnage only to the experience of the Native Americans. Stories of racial prejudice often

Sal and Mookie in finger-wagging debate only represent the larger truth of the fiery opinions, and racialized tensions, of neighborhood life in Brooklyn, New York, in *Do the Right Thing* (1989).

make for poor intake at the box office—as if Americans do not really want to face the past of naked racial hate and the present of unresolved racial tension. Historically film, challenged to fill a need for escape and fantasy or at least absorbing entertainment, has had trouble drawing most viewers to the most socially significant themes. The pattern holds across time, place, and even population. Assessments of black film viewers, for example, have underscored an interest in escapist diversion, and an unwillingness to patronize films solely because the story line centers on the black experience, or an interracial interaction.

When the black and white dialectic is packaged as part of a engaging story, however, moviegoers respond. Spike Lee's best films are painful, fantasy-free fare yet are self-supporting at the box-office. Representing a similar phenomenon, in *Schindler's List* (1993), Steven Spielberg took the grimmest imaginable subject, made it grimmer still through black and white cinematography, and released a film an hour too long for the attention span of the general audience. Yet its commercial success speaks loudly for the fact that the most compelling drama will find its path into the limelight. In one sense, stark black-on-white is so primordial a theme that it is has, and will, cyclically return in some new set of images. Just when it seemed that there was nothing new to depict concerning the American black-white experience, *A Family Thing* exercised a somewhat fresh twist on old secrets of mixed blood, *A Time to Kill* (1996) evoked the themes of rape and racial hatred with fresh plot development and impact, and *White Man's Burden* attempted to flip conventional race roles, and perceptions, for dramatic effect. *Rosewood* (1997) chronicled the real, yet almost unbelievably gruesome tale of the racist rampage in 1920s Florida that virtually destroyed an entire black community. Another recent film also revisits brutal, historical facts: in *Amistad* (1997) portrayals of slave-trading cruelties and abolitionist battles long worn flat by repeated storytelling again come alive—are forcefully, compelling recreated. Black-on-white will keep coming back, just as the Holocaust has held the popular imagination, returning as a theme time and again.

From South of the Border

Scholars of popular culture and ethnicity, seeking to understand the often Byzantine, even nebulous, yet emotionally electric issue which is ethnic "identity" in the modern context, might spend a productive lifetime exploring and defining the "Hispanic" subculture that co-mingles with the Anglo mainstream (and other subcultures) in the English-speaking Americas. From language to racial ethnicity, from matters of manners to questions of spirit and soul, every issue of the meeting of cultures is exposed or teased out in the examination of the Hispanic world as a minority and culture apart.[6]

So tenacious are the emotional and spiritual currents that run through Hispanic culture that even "light" stories may have weighty subplots and dialogue. In most ways *Fools Rush In* (1996) is a typical product of contemporary Hollywood—cast and filmed attractively, engaging yet predictable. Boy meets girl in everyday circumstances, a romantic electricity produces instant sparks, then curves and twists appear, making the road of romance unnerving, if not tortuous. Standard Hollywood fare—except that here the curves are cultural, as Anglo Alex and Mexican-American Isabel meet in Las Vegas and struggle to connect across the divide. Isabel even offers an apt metaphor during a broadly romantic moment, sunset at the Grand Canyon. Legend has it, she tells Alex, that long ago the earth cleaved and left a group of squirrels divided, some on the North Rim of the Canyon and some on the South Rim. Over time they grew apart in appearance and manner, both adjusting to their own environment, but underneath it all, "even though they look different, and they act different" they remained "the very same squirrel." By the time this scene delivers its gentle philosophical message, the couple has had to stretch across the ubiquitous fault lines: the sacredness of family roots with modern careers, Mexican-style Catholic with Anglo-style Presbyterian religiosity, even representative Anglo with Hispanic tastes in home decoration. "And this canyon between them ... will they ever be able to cross it?" asks Alex hopefully.

Their different social moorings become apparent from the moment that Alex meets the Fuentes family—"You have dinner with your family once a week?" he asks with genuine surprise, en route. "It's like a tradition," replies Isabel. "Why, don't you?" Like many in contemporary Anglo culture, Alex engages with family only on holidays, but he encounters warmth and festivity in the tradition of Fuentes family dinners. "They are great!" he exclaims afterward. "I had no idea that families actually talked at dinner." Not only does the "Hispanic spirit" shine through family gatherings, it is manifest even in Isabel's daily activities, as in one scene where she strikes Alex dumb with admiration as she manages to dance Latin rhythms and prepare a meal at the same time. A modern, charming fairy tale, the film nonetheless digs to the base of cultural foundations, as when Isabel turns to her great-grandmother, still living deep in Mexico, for the wisdom to face the hardest moment of her life. "Abuela" speaks no English, has no knowledge of life in the modern U.S., but her resonant wisdom transcends those facts, and is meant to represent crucial continuities in family life and values.

Largely absent from *Fools Rush In* are the raw issues of prejudice, the marginalization of minority peoples, although Mark's wealthy and very "white" parents show a patronizing ignorance of the Mexican-American subculture. This contemporary portrayal contrasts with the handful of films that chronicle generations of difficult, and sometimes simply brutal relations between the white majority and the "Chicanos." *Lone Star*, also a 1996 release, shines a starkly realistic beam on the past and present ethnic relations of small-town Texas. It follows the twentieth-century history of Hispanic, and black, subcultures in white-run Texas, including such telling characters as Mercedes Cruz, who originally crossed the Rio Grande herself as a "wetback," but is now a conservative, almost reactionary member of the town power structure. "In English!" she exhorts a young Hispanic talking to her in the middle of an emergency, no less. "This is the United States. We speak English," is her refrain. Once when her daughter suggests a family excursion back to the town of her birth—"you must be curious how it's changed"—Mercedes shows a lack of interest close to disdain: "You want to see Mexicans? Open your eyes and look around you. We're up to our ears in them." Mercedes represents at once the fluid history and realities of the border, the sometimes brief historical arc from newcomer to establishmentarian, and the unexpected complexity of Hispanic identity. Who is Mercedes Cruz: an emblem of the "American Dream," a pragmatist comfortable with multicultural realities and unimpressed by slogans, a Mexican rejecting her roots and pretending to be like "Anglos"? A hypocrite? Who?

Her daughter, Pilar, seems comfortably "Mexican-American," relating equally well professionally and personally with the ethnicities at hand. As a public school teacher of history she does manifest an interest in searching for the "truth" about the meeting of ethnicities in Texas, a hazardous quest menaced by the land mines of suspicion, bitter memories, and lingering prejudice on both sides. Pilar's son Amado, experiencing the mushy sense of identity and self-worth characteristic of teen years in modern North America, is ripe for a measure of interest in his "Tejano roots," but his mood is portrayed as part of a larger malaise of small-town, Border region life, charged with just enough remnants of real prejudice to make full assimilation unlikely in the short run. Meanwhile the local black community's quiet search for survival and identity adds to the mix, and bar owner Otis Payne had even built a miniature museum of sorts devoted to the Seminole Indians who had intermarried with Afro-Americans to produce a unique sub-group.

The film does cogently engage the essence of the debate on politically correct representation of Texas history. At a parent-teacher meeting on a controversial curriculum one Anglo woman asserts "If you're talking, about Food and Music and all, I have No Problem with that, but when you start changing Who did What to Whom..." In a classic articulation she reduces cultural difference and cultural history to the immediate and superficial, to the only comfortable forms. "We're not changing anything," protests a teacher, "we're just trying to present a more complete picture." "And that's what's got to stop!" is the reply, perhaps caricature, perhaps more representative of common opinion than we may wish to recognize.

"White" culture dominance and bigotry almost invariably constitute key ingredients in the mix whenever the Hispanic culture operates in a larger Anglo milieu. From the blatant World War II-era racism of the quasi-musical *Zoot Suit* (1981) to the memories of abuse in *My Family, Mi Familia* (1995), the sense of being Hispanic, especially "Chicano" or Mexican-American, is reinforced by the dominant biases which at least have the effect of enhancing Hispanic solidarity. Alongside today's polite public standards for ethnic characterizations, earlier versions were both painfully unfair and almost laughably exaggerated. "This Mexican element," expounds a white "expert" at the frame-up trial in *Zoot Suit*, "all he knows and feels is a desire to use a knife to kill or to at least let blood. This inborn characteristic comes down from the bloodthirsty Aztecs, and when added to the use of liquor or marijuana then we certainly have crimes of violence." Not only can such words lodge in an abused Hispanic psyche, the memory of actions proves more powerful still. In *Mi Familia* Jimmy grows up with the childhood image of his brother gunned down by police, because young Chicanos wanted by the law were considered guilty, dangerous, and expendable. Jimmy's own mother, an American citizen with a family, had years earlier been unceremoniously scooped up in a government raid and shipped deep into Mexico for nothing more than "looking Mexican" in tough economic times, when Mexicans were seen to compete for jobs with "Americans." *Break of Dawn* (1988) presents the success of Hispanic radio personality Pedro Gonzalez in 1920s and 1930s Los Angeles—until his pro–Hispanic advocacy politics run afoul of the local power structure, which painfully reminds him who really rules the city. In *And the Earth Did Not Swallow Him* (1994), a boy's diary of growing up the child of migrant Chicano field hands, the dominant culture is remembered as unfeeling bosses and an obscenely lopsided distribution of wealth, the cause of the degradation that required his family to live in "chicken coops."[7]

In spite of the stifling, demeaning effect of the surrounding Anglo culture, Hispanic life within U.S. American culture maintains both traditional values and an effervescence that transcends the narrow story lines. As seen in these films, a traditional, palpable spirituality sustains Hispanic life in good times and bad as well. Isabel and her mother light candles in church—small, burning prayers to guide the circumstances of daily life in *Fools Rush In*. The young mother in *Mi Familia* is guided by faith during a hazardous journey of months to rejoin her family, believing that God wants her to be with her husband, raising their family together. The mother of a soldier missing in Korea in *And The Earth Did Not Swallow Him* makes repeated appeals by prayer that he be returned safely, but she never loses a grain of faith when the prayers go unanswered. The old Amarante Córdova in *The Milagro Beanfield War* (1988) talks with sincerity and animation to the living—and the dead.

Related to the profound religious traditions of Hispanic culture are belief systems peppered by a faith in the magical, a rejection of the narrowly rational as a closed, excessively "Anglo" way of thinking and being. "I happen to think there's an explanation beyond reason, beyond all logic, that brought you right to this very spot at the exact same time that I showed up at this very spot," asserts Isabel to Alex at their first encounter in *Fools Rush In*. "And why would Fate go to all that trouble?" is his classic, cynical rejoinder. Belief in the non-rational also guides the mother in *And the Earth Did Not Swallow Him* to consult the wisdom of a "seer" as to her son's fate. Signs of the preordained mark the story of *Mi Familia*, as when a white owl appears when an infant is nearly lost in a river crossing, and his death years later is colored with inevitability.

Mi Familia is distinguished by a title that embodies not only its story line but the overarching theme of Mexican-American life as well: virtually every study of the society South of the Border has emphasized the exceptional importance of the family, an importance that many members of the Anglo culture do not easily grasp.[8] When a son participates in a sham marriage to save a Salvadoran woman from deportation, Maria delivers an impassioned rebuke that powerfully wraps together the importance of marriage, family, faith, and tradition. "There are certain things in life that are sacred, "sagradas," and we don't spit on them, because without them it doesn't matter if we live, or die. Marriage is something we don't spit on." The film's dual official title *My Family, Mi Familia* implies that straightforward translation renders the same commodity but experienced observers of Latin American cultures, and the Latin subcultures within North America, know better. (I remember vividly when the wife of the mayor of Mexico's second largest city spoke to me pointedly about the importance of family in her culture, stating that the family more than any institution had allowed her country to cope with the severe economic crisis of the mid 1990s.) The force of family responsibilities shapes life in *And the Earth Did Not Swallow Him* and *Break of Dawn*. A family's emotional meaning haunts even the brutal prison circumstances of *Zoot Suit* or *American Me* (1992), and is tellingly present around the edges of the high school setting of *Stand and Deliver* (1987). Family issues fuel the emotion of the

When daughter Toni of the Mexican-American immigrant Sanchez family reveals her intentions to marry an Anglo ex-priest, she reveals as well that the new generation has traveled a large subcultural distance, in *My Family, Mi Familia* (1995).

Cuban-American story *Fires Within* (1991). The importance of family is felt, convincingly and deeply rooted, across the generations in *The Milagro Beanfield War* and *Lone Star*. And it convincingly touches an intercultural marriage in *Fools Rush In*—Alex and Isabel's elopement enrages her father not because of the marriage itself, but the lack of respect for family that it represents.

Indeed respect, *respeto*, is another phenomenon that translates more easily as language than as a psycho-cultural concept. It is difficult for many Anglos to fully grasp the breadth of the concept in the Hispanic sense, and to understand how *respeto* is interwoven with identity. Much of the gang-driven activity of *American Me* or *Mi Vida Loca* (1994) expresses a misguided quest for respect, and the essence of respect, self-respect, is central to the drive toward achievement in *Stand and Deliver* and fuels the impassioned standoff in *The Milagro Beanfield War*.

The importance of commanding respect and maintaining a sometimes elusive sense of self-respect is not only a natural outgrowth of traditional Hispanic religious, family, and personal codes, but fuses inextricably with issues of identity as members of the subculture attempt to function within their surroundings. At one end of the spectrum is a desire to assimilate into the larger culture, at whatever subcultural cost. "Actually I've never been to Mexico, I've always lived here in Los Angeles, just like yourselves," declares Memo self-consciously in *Mi Familia* to the family of his white, upscale fiancée. He even denies pieces of family history which are too removed from the Anglo experience, such as a relative buried in the back-yard in defiance of dominant-culture custom. His retreat from his mani-festly Mexican roots smacks of going beyond retreat, to rejection, much as Mercedes Cruz displays a distaste for South of the Border grassroots in *Lone Star*. We project that in his marriage the couple—both attorneys—will live a very "U.S. American" life, largely estranged from Mexican moor-ings, devoid of the Spanish language. Other avenues to Hispanic identity in a "white" world afford different psychological outcomes: the narrator of *Mi Familia* has survived on odd jobs while writing the family legend turned screenplay, artistic and expiatory in the same stroke. Grappling with an anguished story of subcultural difference while moving toward a dignified niche in the mainstream forms in fact a noted pattern: the author of the autobiographical *And the Earth Did Not Swallow Him* went on in real-life to a doctorate in literature, and an extremely distinguished career as an university administrator. And towards the far end of the spectrum, (although well short of the self-defeating violence of *American Me* and *Mi Vida Loca*), the sharply cynical, biting *The Puerto Rican Mambo* (1992) lobs a stream of grenades at the dominant culture's mendacity, suggesting that a dignified Puerto Rican-American identity resides in some iconoclastic space outside the reigning hypocrisy. Identity, pride, dignity, success by whatever measure are always haunting issues in these films, while the con-stricting power of the dominant culture is always implicit, if only as an ominous presence in the wings.

Even the modern classic *Stand and Deliver*, featuring Hispanic stars with whites as only bit players, renders the Hispanic struggle within the ambiance of a rich, successful white world. In Los Angeles legendary high school teacher Jaime Escalante drives his largely Hispanic classes toward achievement in math, warning that those who drop out will pump gas for whites for the rest of their lives. The most telling intercultural turn occurs when his students perform superbly on a standardized test, prompting the national board to question the validity, in effect the honesty of the test results. An angry Escalante explodes at the insinuation—to him it's more than just a personal attack on his teaching, it's a racist implication that inner-city Hispanics are incapable of academic excellence. In the odd, and oddly haunting *Mi Vida Loca* not only white figures but adult figures of any ethnicity are strangely absent from an extended-adolescent Hispanic world, in which "by the time our boys are twenty-one they're either in prison, or disabled, or dead." Here again the Anglo world is present only by implication, the dominant milieu that shapes and limits the dead-end, "home-boy" subculture of the barrios.

The deservedly popular *The Milagro Beanfield War* portrays the uniquely flavored New Mexico Hispanic culture, solidly planted in centuries-old traditions, in nose-to-nose conflict with Anglo-style land development. The sense of an Hispanic subculture apart, unique in North America, is invoked while at the same time the more universal Hispanic subcultural themes are wrapped inside an engaging, emotional story. From the opening lines "Thank you, God, for letting me have another day" to the closing triumph of grassroots spirit, the dignity of a people living a substantial distance from the mainstream of modernity stands tested. There are the unpretentious glimpses of family warmth, and the suggestion that even deceased relatives loom large in family and spiritual life. The rootedness, the tradition, of families with three hundred years' history in the valley emerges in stark relief to that of the mobile, fast-profits culture. There is also the sinew of community, albeit a community with warts and divisiveness openly showing, a community predictably more cohesive in the face of assault from the culture of the outside. But most saliently, like a silver thread sewn through the legend, the fiber of religion and magic gives a life force to people and occurrences that further declare a culture apart. Faith, like legs, is what daily life stands upon, and magic is at hand when needed. When the Anglo developers, depicted as avaricious and little more, buy up all the copies of a local muckraking newspaper, a strange wind rescues them before they can be burned, spreads them through the sky, and drops them as if tablets of Truth throughout the town. Religion and magic are present not only in many such an explicit manifestation, but in the memories of a slower, more contemplative style of life, now fading. The old Amarante talks to angels, he admits, in part because "those are the only ones around who get time to spare."

Even thorny political issues of modernity, such as public relations "spin" and information control, basic water rights, and the inevitable clash of aggressive "development" with ecological concerns are laid out as issues of culture and values, if at times too cleanly black and white, good and bad. Yet highly differing shades of loyalty to traditional values are invoked—and gray edges surround all subcultural purity. Nor does the camera blink at parochial thinking, behavior, problems. No lesser a figure than the Hispanic mayor turns away a college researcher when he volunteers to teach locally: "Look, if we don't know it already chances are we're

not interested in learning it." The astute analyst could squeeze almost endless irony and paradox from events, as when Don Amarante buys ammu-
nition—ready to do battle with the dominant culture—with the dominant
culture's food stamps. One line of cynical assessment thus might conclude
that the citizens of Milagro are kidding themselves, are unable really to
live without the charity of the system that many resist, are denying an
inevitable modernity.

In the end the film intends to magnify life onscreen, the emotional
technicolor of proud people up against not only wealthy, powerful interests, but complex, modern dilemmas. The wisdom of Charlie Bloom, an
imported lawyer-journalist who loves the local lifestyle, is welcome, but
he remains an outsider even after several years. "What do you know about
the people here? You are a tourist," a local woman berates Charlie in frustration. "You write your sympathetic articles, but when it gets rough, you
run away to somewhere more comfortable." A reminder that membership
in the emotional community of a subculture is not quickly and easily won,
that subcultural roots may run deeper even than the surface appearance
suggests.

The classic *West Side Story* (1961) now seems quaint while still delivering the lively entertainment of an energy-charged musical, the energy
of cross-cultural electricity. Although *The Puerto Rican Mambo*, satirical
and offbeat, could not differ more from *West Side Story* in superficial style,
it is striking that core Puerto Rican-American perceptions of self have
remained constant across decades: the sense of not belonging to the mainstream, of existing on the margins holds. Additional twists in the road of
cultural self-perception are encountered in *Show of Force* (1990), set in
Puerto Rico and featuring both Anglo-heritage and traditional Puerto
Ricans. Puerto Rico is itself a part of the United States in most ways, yet
not a part of "American life" as we archetypically know it, as the directly
political soul-searching of island residents makes clear. (In the 1990s the
close popular votes over Statehood for the Puerto Rico amply testified to
the conflicted identity issues at play.) "White" journalist Kate Melendez,
the widow of a traditional resident who has raised her children on the
island, experiences the delicacy of defining for them what is, and is not,
an "American," a "Puerto Rican," and any real difference between them.

Fires Within depicts the life of Cuban refugees of The Revolution living in Miami, as Isabel and later her husband Nestor reach U.S. shores.
The powerful and vocal Cuban-American community there constitutes
not only a culture within a society but a political force as well, one
significantly at odds with official U.S. policy, and sometimes law, in its fer-
vor to overthrow Castro. This represents an ironic pattern of subcultural

politics—at times a refugee group takes advantage of the very openness of a society to press political agendas troublesome to the welcoming society. Nestor, finally released from Castro's prisons and reunited with his family, struggles with the temptation to join the U.S.-based counter-revolutionary movement, but he struggles also to adjust, with pride and dignity intact, in a new environment. His wife is now the breadwinner, his daughter has grown up knowing American culture but not knowing him, and Nestor's manhood as well as sense of being culturally Cuban experiences all the thumps inherent in culture shock.

Culture shock lends interest as well to *Nueba Yol* (1995) as Balbuena from the Dominican Republic finally reaches the promised land, well into middle age, having grown up hearing that in New York wealth lies at the fingertips, for the taking. As relatives already living in The City guide his reacculturation, he learns the differences between North American and Dominican ways. Many of the issues pivot on the diminished role that family loyalty appears to play, the "lack of respect" of youth for family, a perceived lack of discipline in the new homeland. Balbuena listens incredulously as his cousin explains that to discipline a child physically in the States is to risk going to jail, to risk even losing custody of the child. The subcultural adjustment is an uneasy one in many ways, the necessity of swallowing dominant-culture rules and methods an uncomfortable price for better economic opportunity. While the innocent, caring personality, even charm of Balbuena enhanced by his romance with Nancy carries the human story, the subcultural story less cheerfully portrays life in the multicultural city, where quality of life deteriorates even as bank accounts are enhanced. Even Nancy, apparently adjusted and successful, has decided that New York is too oppressive for the Dominican soul, that life will be richer again back in Santo Domingo.

"That's the problem with life. It's just so messy," responds immigrant rights worker Toni Sanchez (*Mi Familia*) semi-sarcastically to the dilemma of a Salvadoran woman facing deportation and possibly death, or else the phony marriage arranged to save her life. In many ways the films that address Hispanic subcultures in North America register best when portraying the subtler conundrums, even existential frustration of modern life in conflict with traditional values, such as the job offer of a lifetime far from family (*Fools Rush In*), the "development" of an economically depressed corner of New Mexico (*The Milagro Beanfield War*), or the conflict of domestic comfort with family loyalties (*Nueba Yol*). Yet even terms like conundrum or existential frustration are culturally constructed and may translate as crisis of faith or trust, or as a simple loss of *alma*, soul. A younger and more "sophisticated" generation of Hispanic Americans may reconcile the pressures of modern culture with traditional values in highly individual ways, but the tension inevitably persists.[9]

In large measure, modern Hispanic subcultural identity is forged by that tension, the conflict of timeless roots with changing times. Language composes an element, but not always a telling or consistent element in Hispanic identity: while some "Hispanics" living in the U.S. or Canada speak virtually no English (*Nueba Yol*), others suppress the use of Spanish (*Lone Star*), and many develop a colloquial English peppered with Spanish (or original subcultural) slang (*Stand and Deliver, American Me, Zoot Suit, Mi Vida Loca*). Hispanic solidarity surfaces in the face of anti–Hispanic racism but fades in other settings, in almost predictable patterns: well established communities of Spanish heritage may disdain the recent imports from the South, light skinned Hispanic elites may find little in common with the darker poor, and educated Hispanics may feel little in common with laborers. Numerous ingredients, from family roots, memories, and surnames to religion and moral teachings, from language and slang to customs of food and dress, from experience with discrimination to intercultural marriage all figure in the calculus of the ethnic identity in ways too complex to predict clearly. To "be" or "feel" Hispanic obviously involves the basic sociology of community and family influences. Yet in another sense identity is the most personal of sentiments, a highly individual matter of self-perception, if not choice. In the final analysis we must respect individual declarations of identity, the extent to which a person experiences an Hispanic or Latino identity. Each personal story, like the legends made into films, will sketch the contours of each person's cultural identity, of their dilemmas, their sense of self.

Eastern Spice

"When I know in my bones who I am, then I will be more than ready to risk ... everything" says Geri Riordan in an emotional moment in *The Redwood Curtain* (1995). Her quest for identity is literal, having grown up an adopted child with U.S. Americans, but born in Vietnam to unknown parents. For many of the multicultural Americans of Asian descent, however, genetics and family ties are clear, but a sense of place in the broader white culture is less so. The backdrop of U.S. American (and to a lesser extent Canadian) life has traditionally been anything but Asia-friendly, has instead often proven an alien, although officially open, milieu in which to continue the life from the other side of the Pacific.

Alamo Bay (1985), *China Girl* (1987), *Come See the Paradise* (1990), and

Snow Falling on Cedars (1999) represent the first hurdle of multicultural relations: Is there sufficient openmindedness on both sides to allow for acceptance, if not assimilation, of the newcomers? Certainly not in *Alamo Bay*, where Vietnamese refugees encounter resentment in lieu of the welcome implied in U.S. American mythology. They are considered an odd nuisance at best, a threat to the precarious balance of the Texas Gulf Coast economy at worst. Eminent French director Louis Malle was moved to examine the clash of Vietnamese immigrants with established local fishermen amid racial and cultural intolerance; for all the artistic sophistication that Malle brought to the task the film emerges looking like any other good, and essentially predictable, U.S. domestic treatment of multicultural combat. Racism as a central theme apparently defies New Wave subtlety as surely as it defies cosmetic public relations touch-up—it is as it appears to the naked eye, raw and destructive, the sharpest wedge in creating community fissures. In *China Girl* as well the active ingredient is racism, in equally unadulterated form. "Ever notice that they're squinting, even when it's cloudy?" an Italian youth snidely jokes with friends, one of the tamest insults to local Chinese in the film. The racial divisions tower like steel walls, until an Italian-Chinese couple decide to brave a desperate Romeo and Juliet experience, giving glimmers of interest, and heart, to an otherwise dismal story.

The subtler *Come See the Paradise* and *Snow Falling on Cedars* are nicely conceived World War II period pieces, in which Japanese are imprisoned for mere ethnicity. As in *China Girl*, the love of a white man for an Asian woman drives the dramatic interest; as in all the films involving Eastern subcultures the divide between the "white" and the "yellow" people proves difficult to cross. In *Come See the Paradise* fiery labor organizer Jack McGurn falls for Lily Kawamura while working as a film projectionist in Little Tokyo, Los Angeles, and encounters a father unalterably opposed to the relationship. While protesting a deep and sincere love for the daughter Jack concedes, "What I can never be, not ever, is Japanese," recognizing the simple core of the matter. Nonetheless the love and sensitivity of the couple conquer the vast differences in their backgrounds, differences greatly softened by Lily's status as U.S.-born second generation Japanese, with an understanding of and comfort with both communities. Yet even more than differing cultural practices, the primitive face of bias and inequality looms large: first generation Japanese could not become citizens, or own businesses, and their children's citizenship was no protection against internment in camps in the wake of Pearl Harbor. Racism certainly cuts both ways in these films; the illicit romance in *Snow Falling on Cedars* has no chance to consummate in marriage due to violent (Japanese) parental opposition as well as the onrushing realities of war.

The war may have magnified the gap, but something created uncomfortable distance between Anglo and Asian Americans, not only the Japanese. References in the films to the descendants of the other enemies who were not imprisoned—Italian and German Americans—jolts us to a realization that Japanese appearance, mannerisms, and subcultural solidarity (as well as economic drive and success!), in essence their "inscrutability" to many Westerners, led to one of the great U.S. American injustices.

Chan Is Missing (1981), *The Wedding Banquet* (1993), and *Double Happiness* (1994) present much less traditional prejudice and instead the modern malaise of multicultural identity. *Chan is Missing* spins a tale which, metaphorically at least, pokes with clever dialogue and events at the basic questions: What is "Chinese," and what is "American"; who is the "Other," and who is "Us"? The search for "Chan," who has literally vanished, anchors what passes for a plot while the real interest emerges through a fascinating gamut of Chinese-American identities in San Francisco, seen in both cooperation and conflict. From the F.O.B.—fresh off the boat—to the most established Chinese figures, from Taiwan-born to People's Republic of China-born Chinese, it soon becomes clear that the only quality that Chinese-Americans have necessarily in common is not being Anglo. *Chan Is Missing* ranks deservedly as a modern multicultural classic partly due to paradox and irony that artistically imitate the subcultural condition—what do we *really* know about the life and identity of the invisible Chan? According to whom you asked, Chan was a patriot, a failure, a genius, an eccentric, honest, paranoid, a warrior, and more. Add the theme of thinly veiled play upon the comic detective Charlie Chan to the search for dignity and identity, and the echoes of Pogo come home. We have met the invisibility of Chinese-Americans, and that invisibility is us.[10]

In *The Wedding Banquet* layers of true identity hide beneath layers of public posturing: to keep his parents and their annoying matchmaking at bay, Wai-Tung feigns engagement to the lovely Wei-Wei only to attract an awkward parental visit. In the first of myriad ironies, Wai-Tung's parents assume that the greatest gap between the young couple is that between Taiwanese and mainland Chinese roots, while Wei-Wei is really playing at marriage for a green card, and while Wai-Tung guards a gay identity and a five-year relationship with his Anglo lover, Simon. A gala wedding banquet consummates the farce, with festivity so explosive that a white quest is moved to exclaim "I thought Chinese were meek, quiet, math wizzes." That night in the honeymoon suite, in an atypical, inebriated moment, a child is actually conceived by the couple, surely the outcome longed for by the grandparents-to-be. As the deceit unravels, strands of hope, expectation, need, and disappointment emerge into full view; Wei-Wei, in one

Chinese and U.S. Anglo cultures, Taiwanese and mainland China cultures, and mainstream and gay cultures form a maze of misunderstandings in *The Wedding Banquet* (1993).

touching scene, realizes that the "in-laws" whom she has helped dupe have quickly become surrogate parents, filling a loneliness she has known since leaving her homeland. Through such gentle twists and surprises the Chinese subculture of New York comes into sympathetic life.

Playacting upon the multicultural stage drives *Double Happiness* as well: the engaging Jade must put on a Chinese dutiful daughter's face at home, while enacting a more natural character in the broader social world of Vancouver, British Columbia. The viewer is thus drawn directly into the schism between the traditional Chinese culture, which lives on in parents and elders (Jade introduces the film with the voice-over that her parents "are very Chinese, if you know what I mean...."), and the Chinese-American youth subculture. Much like East and West themselves, the two do not comfortably meet. Jade and her younger sister's sense of being Chinese-American appears based on North American liberal multiculturalism and assimilation: parents and roots are sincerely respected, but an interesting society is available here, now, and is playing in English. Their father fears that a crumbling of traditional ways will sound the death knell of the good that is Chinese: that "we'll be like those white ghosts."

However, Chinese moral perfection itself emerges as staged myth, as layers of posturing peel away—Jade's brother Winston has strayed into a dissolute life while the family's official story recounts his impressive successes, and Uncle Ah Hong conceals an ongoing illegitimate family from his brother's family. Jade's virtually forced date with a young Chinese male reveals his homosexual identity, and his talent at keeping up appearances for the sake of Chinese elders. Emerging from this cauldron of dissimulation Jade chooses the quite unconventional career, at least for a Chinese daughter, of acting, of seeking an artistic identity based on changing personalities. Her quest subtly echoes *Chan Is Missing* because acting roles for young Chinese-American women are missing too, or at the very least prove elusive—there is as much unexpected spin on the expectations of Jade in front of the camera as the expectations of her in real life. Even the actor must act, must fight for identity; for example, if Jade is too Chinese for most roles she must be even more Chinese for others. At one audition she fields the request to feign a Chinese accent; another audition based on her rare status as a bilingual, bicultural actress falls apart when she admits she cannot read the Chinese characters in which her part is written. The problematic nature of her "face" to the camera mirrors the identity struggles of the real social world, but Jade enjoys more control of self-definition in real life and goes so far as to find love with a sensitive white man at film's end.

The young ethnic American woman must do more than define her distance from the traditional; she must negotiate a personal identity, a challenge even without the cross-cultural mix. The modern classic *The Joy Luck Club* (1993), based on a popular novel, poignantly exposes the search for identity that intersects at the crossroads of being Chinese-American and female.[11] Three mothers were born in the old country, three daughters grew up in American "freedom" but fettered by their mothers' emotions and values. Each seeks to be her own woman, but often slumps back to accept elements of "my mother, my self." One mother remembered being raised the old way, "taught to desire nothing, to swallow other people's misery, and to eat my own bitterness. And even though I taught my daughter the opposite … she came out the same way." The messages of family, the echoes of culture sound subtly long after the most audible tones seem to have faded. Born to a tradition in which females should "desire nothing" the daughters are born as well to an ambient culture which desires everything—their loyalties as well as identities easily become tortured in the face of such great expectations.

Like many of the richer multicultural films, *The Joy Luck Club* sits at the cusp of eras, values, and numerous issues. Is it essentially a Chinese quilt, merely embroidered with the contemporary West? A meditation upon Multicultural America, with Chinese moorings merely exemplifying common Old Country patterns? Does culture or gender command the center of its meaning? The epic of mothers and daughters, with (disappointing) males present only on the edges, was long overdue. Many societies, it seems, hide their most heroic characters from view.

For every "serious" film on Eastern subcultures in the West the average film viewer has encountered numerous films that frame Orientals as living and breathing the martial arts. While most are so primitive as to merit no in-depth discussion the phenomenon itself is significant, conjuring up at once questions of the relations of East and West (is martial arts combat merely the metaphorical expression of real, insuperable animosities?), the mystique of Eastern tradition as expressed in coveted skills, and plausibly real differences in levels of physical and psychological discipline. *Dragon: The Bruce Lee Story* (1993) fictionalized the life of the remarkable martial arts master-turned-film-star and in the process illuminated Chinese culture in its American context. Although settled, and citizens, many Chinese considered themselves a society utterly apart. When Lee decided to teach his discipline outside the Chinese community, to members of other ethnic groups, he broke unwritten subcultural law and faced violence and ostracism.

The perception of otherness is often echoed by whites: Lee's prospective Anglo mother-in-law makes clear that American citizenship does not fully make someone "American." What would children of such a union be, she persists, Chinese, white, what? Her question revisits the central issue of where the Oriental-American sits along the continuum of identity. Whether in "Chinatowns" or "Little Saigons" well apart from the broader society, or bending toward the mainstream with some awkward sense of straying from tradition, Eastern subculture offers its own, distinctive notes to the Multicultural Symphony.[12]

American Masala

So broad, varied, and unpredictable have been the U.S. American and Canadian experiences that one folkloric saying insists that, if you stand anywhere in North America and wait long enough, every form of humanity, engaged in almost limitless forms of activity, will pass by. Such unexpected variety is part of the sense evoked by *Mystery Train* (1989), as two young Japanese, as well as an Italian woman and English man, pass through the sleepy yet oddly alive downtown of Memphis, Tennessee. The Japanese youths prove sympathetic and realistic; their reactions show the delightful mixture of confusion in a strange land, their comparisons of the ambiance with home in Yokohama, and their awe at U.S. pop, especially music, culture. Elvis's Graceland, achieving the stature of an international shrine, has brought them to Memphis.

Mystery Train shares with *Mississippi Masala* (1991), *Dangerous Minds* (1995), *Bagdad Cafe* (1988), *Someone Else's America* (1996) and others a sense of life around the margins, evoking a parade of individuals whose lives are several steps removed from the mainline, or at least the fashionably successful, highly visible locations in North American life. *Bagdad Cafe*, in which a middle-aged German woman wanders into a small, desert hamlet in the "middle of nowhere," especially elicits a sense of a "motley America"—eccentric, depressing, fascinating, seedy, and oddly dignified all at one and the same time. For the collection of humanity who live on these margins, the middle of nowhere is actually somewhere, the center of their individual lives and subculture. They live in "someone else's America," the aptly chosen title of Goran Paskaljevic's film that gives remarkable interest, even charm, to an oddly assorted bag of immigrants carving out lives in Brooklyn, New York. A Serbian director orchestrating the interactions (from the old country to the Rio Grande to North America's most diverse central station, New York City) of Spanish, Yugoslavs, Greeks, Chinese, and of course Anglo Americans more than suggests, in the words from an American classic, that we are simply "not in Kansas anymore."

Dangerous Minds, crafted from realism and sensitive acting, may be the best ever of the education-in-the-rough films. LouAnne Johnson, educated and white, finds a position teaching English in urban Northern California and soon develops into an educational missionary, preaching to the unsaved and unwashed. Her inner city school assembles the youth culture within the ambiance of the surrounding barrios, within the broader society; concentric circles of culture must be peeled away to attempt to understand the core of students. Understandably, they find the standard English texts, and those who teach them, much removed from the texts of their lives. "You gonna give me some good advice? Just say no?" jeers Emilio Ramirez in response to LouAnne's declaration of personal concern. "How the hell are you gonna save me from my life?" Belying the image of bravado, the students see their lives as circumscribed, as dead-end streets, at an almost infinite distance from the upbeat, upwardly mobile culture shining in their eyes from all surrounding media. "I ain't raising no doctors and lawyers here," snarls the mother of two black students, insisting that they will not be returning to school. LouAnne's challenge—earning acceptance and respect in an alien ambiance, teaching across cultures without patronizing, and communicating her "culture's" values in ways that resonate with another—remints, with lively variations, the classic intercultural challenge.

Mississippi Masala refers to an East Indian condiment composed of numerous spices, as traditional whites, blacks, and Indians mix in a small town in the contemporary Southern U.S. The Old South was pure salt and pepper, but immigration in multicultural America has reached into nooks, filtered into crannies, and now the mix of cultures everywhere is varied, at times unpredictable. Indians represent an interesting filling between the black and white extremes of the South as racially at half-shade, as a subculture itself concerned with caste and gradations of color. Now, in Greenwood, Mississippi, blacks have another "people of color" with whom to relate, and whites must reconstruct old racial attitudes for a new group.

Mississippi Masala ranks as one of the truly multi-faceted, polyvalent films of the multicultural genre; not only do layer upon layer of subcultural perception and identity unfold, but nagging questions are triggered as well. Do the film's Indians (who used to live in Africa, function as successful merchants, and enjoy more privilege than blacks) represent a soft, subtle white racism, for all their good relations, on the surface, with blacks? If gifted Indian-born director Mira Nair is an obvious choice to construct her culture authentically, why are Indians given the least flattering characterizations in the mix? Are we witness to a liberal overcompensation, a phenomenon with implications for all intercultural film?

The central character, at least, carries a feminist dignity into the center of the wide screen: young Mina assumes the prerogatives of an individual, not merely a young female member of a (male-dominated) group; she speaks her mind, and proves as comfortable with her sexuality as with the numerous subcultures around her. Mina's sympathetic self-assurance advertises the optimistic myth of Multicultural America—a realm where everyone can engage productively with everyone else, if only openmindedness prevails. Behind her apparently effortless cultural multidexterity, however, lies a revealing background: born and raised in Uganda, victim of the Amin pogroms, short-term resident of England, now a resident of the black heritage-white heritage South, she has never visited Indian soil. Is she most comfortable with blacks, who dominated the African landscape she grew up in (and with whom she often spoke Swahili), the whites linked to European culture and her family's language, English, or to the all-enveloping Indian subculture? Such questions, if not surprises and contradictions, lurk around every subcultural corner in the film; while showcasing specific groups interacting, *Mississippi Masala* overall invokes a sense of Multicultural Surprise. If sleepy Greenwood, Mississippi, will now have more spices on the table than merely salt and pepper, what may we expect from livelier, urban communities?

A small Mississippi town confronts a new racial challenge when a community of East Indians settles and negotiates a place between the long entrenched white and black communities, in *Mississippi Masala* (1991). Here Demetrius and Mina love across a large racial and cultural divide.

A Matter of Faith

Differing belief systems, often expressed as religious creed and practice, tend to generate revealing interactions when representatives of those systems meet, whether within or between societies. "Harrison Ford is sensational as the cop who runs head-on into the non-violent world of

Pennsylvania Amish Community," proclaims the box for the commercial video of *Witness* (1985), in unconscious parody of dominant U.S. American cultural style—in which a collision is unfortunately too often the result when a task-oriented official encounters a contemplative, spiritual community. Although mindless disregard for the marginalized culture, in the manner of tanks rolling over flower beds, has often characterized dominant-culture agents with a job to do, the two police thrillers considered here display refreshing layers of subtlety and texture: *Witness* and *A Stranger Among Us* (1992) are distinguished at least by sensitive, pensive, believable portrayals of both the religious subculture and the mainstream characters who interact with it.

In *A Stranger Among Us* a New York policewoman's quest to solve a homicide becomes a quest in personal reassessment as well, when Detective Emily Eden goes undercover, feigning an interest in rediscovering Jewish roots, in the heart of the Hasidic community. The ambiance of a world apart is powerfully presented, from Yiddish speech and Hebrew newspapers and street signs, to segregation of the sexes, to a sense of lives lived more deliberately, more gracefully and graciously, than in the surrounding culture. Emily's lessons begin earlier, upon first contact, as she is ushered in to speak to the head of the community. Aides to the Rebbe, a leader of even greater authority and respect than a Rabbi, rush to cover her shoulders and legs with shawls in respect for orthodox mores. The Rebbe, initially silent, sits with all the presence that Moses must have had, prompting Emily to wonder if direct communication with him will be possible. "The Rebbe speaks eight languages," states his assistant with quiet reverence. "Is English one of them?" ventures Emily.

Emily remains realistically detached yet at once plausibly touched by the kindness, seriousness, and spiritual commitment of her hosts in the world within The City, while a young heir-apparent to spiritual leadership is concomitantly touched by her verve and candor. Although she lives among the Hasidim only to further temporal-world police work, the effect of the all-encompassing spiritual ambiance upon her is almost inevitable, and in ways both superficial and profound she reaches across a cultural gap to communicate. "I got experience, okay, I know human nature," she stresses early on in her investigation. "You will pardon me," replies the Rebbe, "but you do not know *our* nature." Emily comes to know something of that nature, one conversation and one day at a time, in the authentic manner of meeting another way of thinking. Though a police thriller of stock mystery and climax, the film is distinguished by the dignity of the mundane, the centrality of everyday conversation and common detail in defining a people. As in *Seven Years in Tibet*, none of the parties who meet across the divide convert, exactly, but neither are they quite the same after the experience.

Witness likewise lingers on the delicate strokes that paint cultures with differing hues, as a police detective from Philadelphia is forced to take refuge in the Amish country of Pennsylvania. Wounded and in danger from corrupt fellow police, Captain John Book accepts the medical care and nurturance of a people who prefer nothing to do with guns, violence, and the outside world of "The English." In their society it is he, an archetypical figure in Hollywood-style entertainment, who begins to seem odd. The "Amish," usually vaguely, amorphously plural in the American tourist's mind, reveal the flesh of individual personalities, as well as the complexity of maintaining their community. Above all, they represent a trip back in time, as if each moment of their daily lives rises from the set of an old movie. When the big city police chief phones local law enforcement, trying to track down his missing detective by the surname of his host, he's soon disabused of numerous assumptions. "There's your problem, Chief. Your Amishman doesn't live in the twentieth century, doesn't think in the twentieth century.... Since the Amish don't have any telephones, I wouldn't know who to call." "Thanks, it's been an education," sighs the chief finally, a statement that equally applies to the typical viewer, looking inside the Amish community for the first time.

The commercial success of *Witness* may say as much about the contours of U.S. American culture as about the Amish. A contemporary comedy, *For Richer or Poorer* (1997) even chooses Amish country as the haven to which a pair of harried, desperate professionals, needing to dodge modern stresses for a time, escape. Akin to the perennial fascination with Native Americans, a deep-seated pastoralism appears to drive attraction to the simpler time and more sharply carved values which the Amish represent. If the "English" characters in *Witness* lack the purity and honesty of the Amish ones they seem to lack an inner peace as well: few would judge Book's sister Elaine, for example, as happier than the Amish widow Rachel, now also a single mother. A glimpse at the two women reveals both contrast and a feminist sub-text, for both live in male-dominated worlds, albeit quite different ones. Rachel's brush with the elders, even the threat of being "shunned" for her clear affection for the "English" would suggest a much harder path to feminine self-definition in rigid Amish society than in the liberal surrounding one. However counter-arguments hold that guaranteed, quality child care, lifelong relationships, meaningful, respected roles for women, and a community of men who neither smoke, drink, curse, abuse, nor philander provide at least some elements of women's paradise. The analysis of fulfillment in one culture by the standards of another may always invoke apple experts evaluating oranges: how does the feminist text weigh finally when the "non-feminist" central female character brings dignity, a degree of self-reliance within her community's planned interdependence, and qualities as elusively defined as inner peace to the screen? The intercultural near-romance teases the question of Rachel's right place as perhaps in the larger society, with John, exercising women's modern prerogatives. Or is John Book, decent, uncorrupt, yet surrounded by corruption, himself in the wrong place, a closet Amish at heart, tempted to come home?

Immigrants Apart and Cultures Within Cultures

The huge commercial success of *The Godfather* (1972) and its sequels may underscore once more the low common denominators of the movie-going audience—a thirst for intrigue, for a soap opera of betrayal, greed, and murder. But beyond the crudest entertainment values of *The Godfather* lies a powerful subcultural drama, one that evokes a United States of divergent peoples, social systems, and beliefs loosely and sometimes awkwardly functioning under one national system. It should go without saying that the entire Italian-American community should not be tarred with the brush of underworld connections, that Italian-Americans for example have been and are among the most distinguished, incorruptible prosecutors of underworld activity. If to be Italian is by no means to belong to the Mafia, however, the Mafia grew from Italian roots. La Cosa Nostra in *The Godfather* is a subculture within a subculture, an underworld of largely Sicilian roots operating with its own clearly defined mores, laws, and logic. One need only be reminded that crime "families," with structures, systems of succession, and time-honored roles composed La Cosa Nostra for generations, that elaborate codes of conduct were understood, and largely followed, rules perhaps broken no more often than the rules of the larger, enveloping culture. The name speaks for itself: "La Cosa Nostra" literally means "our affair" and more broadly, "our society apart."[13]

Crime as a subcultural way of life also drives the action part of the storyline of *Once Upon a Time in America* (1984), as a group within New York Jewish society develops its particular underworld. The character study across numerous years early in the century, and across several hours of film, firmly reminds us that subcultures exist as powerfully by epoch as any other boundary. In fact, there is little point in discussing the "American character" without heavily weighing the key variables in the mix—the regional and ethnic geography, economic class, and *generation* involved. Almost by definition, to invoke the storyteller's refrain "once upon a time" is to invoke an especial subculture—the commonly held experiences, environment, and beliefs that define a society's boundaries.

"American character" has properly been the subject of myriad analyses which discover a unifying grain, commonalities enough to give the phrase itself the fiber of definition.[14] Within the common system, however, cultural dialects are so pronounced as to strain the limits of a sole, recognizable American character. How much do Jews from New York City really have in common, beyond the English language and a few other shared elements of national culture, with the most remote residents of Appalachia? *Deliverance* (1972) takes the viewer inside the hills of north Georgia to meet a subculture almost frozen in rural time, literally inbred, while *Crossing Delancey* (1988) presents contemporary Jewish culture in New York City, self-contained yet sophisticated. Protagonist Izzy, who works at a serious bookstore, in fact weighs levels of sophistication and excitement in her decision on a mate. One prospect is a stimulating intellect and noted author, the other a seemingly simple Jewish pickle-store owner. While the battle of values and meanings plays out (in a modern morality play addressing feminism, classism, professional snobbism, and more), the richness of Jewish culture remains a thick, heavy, sometimes irritating presence in her life ("You made an appointment [for me] with a marriage broker!?" she asks her grandmother, aghast), but one to which her ties are indissoluble. The subcultural portrayal is much more at arm's length in *Deliverance*, given that the central characters, from outside of Appalachian culture, spend the film in whitewater odyssey on the Cahulawassee river. But as sadists molest them there is no doubt that the attackers are meant to represent an extension of local subculture, albeit an extreme, a minority perversion. James Dickey's intent in the novel may have been a broader re-exploration of the depth of primal sin, but few film viewers will escape without negative images of Appalachian subculture reinforced.[15]

All film no matter how mainstream obviously presents "culture" in some fashion and those drippingly mono-cultural classics, such as *Mr. Smith Goes to Washington* (1939), serve to define central American myths and, by extension, their distance from other traditions. Other traditions in film, from sci-fi to various stripes of modern or new wave, serve notice that new subcultural corners are being turned. *L. A. Story* (1991) pretends to such status as a harbinger film, set in the heart of a "bellweather" state, anticipating the turn of American culture, pushing the limits and poking fun at an America rolling toward New Age extremes. If multicultural film finds its defining tension in the spaces between ethnic groups, *L.A. Story* magnifies the tension within individuals still digging for the pot of gold.

If you've landed in L.A., at the end of the rainbow, and life still doesn't fulfill, where is there left to go?

Actor Steve Martin (as TV weatherman Harris K. Telemacher), a sort of West Coast Woody Allen, may convey a sense of irreverent comedy that intends only to amuse and perhaps to deflate pomposity. Yet beyond entertainment, contradictions and ironies fit packed as tightly as a professor's bookshelves. Our typical L.A. Man, basking in the cult of fun and relaxation, has "had seven heart attacks, all imagined." L.A. residents abuse alcohol and drugs, then torture themselves with health concoctions and pedal madly, yet go nowhere on stationary bikes. The consumer expects every option—at a restaurant table of ten almost everyone orders a different type of coffee—and rates everything—a woman just off a twelve-hour flight gives it an "eight"—yet finds nothing truly satisfying. And everything must entertain, including meteorology: the weather report must bring laughter or lose its air time.

With humor and without pretense *L.A. Story* clearly implies that quantity, novelty, and superficial thrills are quite distinct from quality. A foreign journalist, offered a "cultural tour" of L.A., quips that it should only take "fifteen minutes," although she is proudly shown neighborhoods of historic interest, some boasting houses "over twenty years old." From junk mail arriving in homes by the basketful to impressive electronic gadgets that don't work, one wonders if modern society simply offers "much ado about nothing." Perhaps a prophetic (certainly more than merely eccentric) extension of Western civilization, L.A. Culture here is connected to its roots as several direct echoes of Shakespeare are heard. Even the gravedigger from Hamlet lives on in L.A., burying the entertainers who thought their wit timeless. Yet even if L.A. Man proclaims his city to be the "precious stone set in a silver sea," many of the emotional spaces in his "other Eden" prove dull and jaded. A rescue of sorts, of both the film and the fictional characters within it, comes from magical, "post-rational" events—such as an electric sign that gives a guru's counsel to its readers. For all its apparent comfort, wonders, even excitement, the "demi-paradise" of L.A. Society still needs the magical and the surreal to fulfill.

Towards the Filming of the American Dream

Also set in the quintessential North American city of Los Angeles, *Grand Canyon* (1991) has little to do with the black and white subcultures that co-exist in a major city, and yet has everything to do with those subcultures. Gently magical yet painfully real, essentially a meditation on the complexity and angst of modern life amid apparent comfort, *Grand Canyon* probes around the edges, and as well into the heart, of the confusion of being human. "That's how you get in trouble, by thinking how nice it would be to be happy more," concludes a legal secretary, essentially accepting unhappiness as a norm. Her current fuel for neurosis is a profound attraction to—and irritation with—a married boss who declines to carry on an affair behind his wife's back. "It doesn't have to make sense," she says in finally, tearfully tendering her resignation along with her resentment.

Modern Western life does currently, and will in the foreseeable future spin around philosophical and psychological issues that go far beyond issues of ethnic opportunity and justice. But part of the honesty of *Grand Canyon* is that while social and subcultural concerns recede somewhat before more existential conundrums, the issues of neighborhood, ghetto, black, white, are still there, because in the world as actually experienced they must be. "They almost smoked me," yells teenaged Otis after moving to a largely white neighborhood and accidentally brushing with the police. "See a nigger run around here, they smoke you, ask questions later." His family had made a deliberate decision to leave the ghetto and its pernicious influences— it was sucking Otis inexorably toward gang life—only to encounter awkward, sometimes confusing settings in life outside. For aspiring blacks of modest means where, precisely, is a new and accepting home? The elite whites who dominate the city feel confined as well to certain homelands, and when Mack's BMW stalls in a rough, alien part of Los Angeles, he may as well be stalled on uncharted seas in the middle of a storm. His rescue by a black tow-truck driver is random, serendipitous, leading to the earnest commerce between subcultures that fills empty spaces in modern life.

The opening scenes of the film alone robustly engage contrast and irony, as the camera filters the playground scenes of poor neighborhoods through murky black and white, with black youths looking out through a chain link fence. Though aspiring to basketball greatness they cannot afford to watch their professional idols play in the glitzy ambiance of The Forum, as the camera captures the stunning, technicolor "showtime" of a Los Angeles Lakers game, the athleticism of talented blacks, watched mostly by upscale whites. Police helicopters, ubiquitous over the city, like birds of prey over an ocean of hostile anonymity, fly above all possibility of face-to-face reconciliation: they represent a hi-tech, not a human, response. And the Grand Canyon itself, offered as an ultimate symbol and saving grace, invites respite several hours away from a city in which "chaos" looms as "the central issue in everyone's life." What does the Grand Canyon offer to refugees from an "advanced" North American lifestyle? A temporary escape, an abyss that begs to be filled or at least understood, the distance between lonely perspectives? It seems that life's most gnawing concerns, even burning issues of subcultural identity, are only part of a much wider picture.

Toward Conclusions

In *Lone Star* Otis Payne offered the philosophy, central to both the film and the real multicultural world, of the broad relativity of life when he explained with simple eloquence the relationship of his bar and the local church. "Most choose both," he said. "You see, it's not like there's a Borderline between the Good People and the Bad People. You're not on either One Side or the Other." Blurred lines of moral certainty run parallel with imprecise lines in subcultural identity. Today North Americans define themselves in odd, ever shifting percentages of old cultural roots mixed with membership in the larger society. Subtle shades of attitudes, not just skin pigment or accents, challenge the pollsters of public opinion and the makers of feature film.

Yet as accommodating as the larger cultural pot may be, certain ingredients never truly melt in. U.S. Americans and Canadians tend to believe, often with significant pride, that their countries have historically served as models, even inspiring beacons for Multiculturalism. Symbols like the Statue of Liberty, bearing inscriptions that invite even the poor to a new home, forcefully speak for themselves. More nuanced assessments, such as Walter Nugent's *Crossings: The Great Transatlantic Migration* (1992), in which a broader picture emerges including, for example, patterns of discrimination, back-migration, and the distinct experience of South America, go relatively unobserved except by the professional historian.[16] It is a comforting myth that all the instruments in the multicultural symphony blended productively, from the very beginnings of "American" colonization. Even those political figures (at the turn of the century a majority) who express concern over the contemporary waves of immigration idealize the supposedly egalitarian, multicultural roots from which the contemporary society has grown. They might do well to watch Eli Kazan's *America, America* (1963), a sobering, even depressing reminder of the social dynamics common among ethnic groups only a few generations ago.

The approaching cultural horizon does appear to offer substantially different challenges than the receding one, along both quantitative and qualitative axes. The United States and Canada, beyond their international stature, are gradually becoming World-Countries: United Nations-like conglomerates of cooperating but competing ethnic interests, each with a voice and vote, each contributing to a common political and economic web. In the coming decades populations of Hispanic and Oriental heritage, especially, will evidently make enormous statistical inroads into the concept of an Anglo North America, while myriad other cultural traditions will create increasingly vibrant communities within North American cities. And from statistical trends, to specific immigration problems, to anxious, uncompromising minority demands, there is a sense of problems not only continuing but perhaps escalating (*El Norte, Do the Right Thing, Alamo Bay, Lone Star, Dangerous Minds*). In community and national political arenas, as well as in academic debate, ethnic interests have exerted increasing presence and influence. Issues of ethnic identity and equality have emerged as complex, multi-faceted, thorny and politically delicate. There is sometimes a sense that no treatment, no discussion of these issues could be adequate, that fresh debate will constantly emerge before existing debates can be duly exercised.

The very factors that should elicit caution and humility, however, also stand as reasons to actively engage the challenge of Multiculturalism—it is a delicate yet enormously important social arena, an intellectually rich, subtle, dynamic, and fascinating field. The standard public relations take on Multiculturalism typical of North American corporations, expressed in such themes as "Strength Through Diversity," may be suspect in sincerity but does hint at an overarching truth: Multiculturalism, like virtue, may well include its own intrinsic reward. There is the value-added sheer variety of multicultural communities. An impressive diversity in ethnic food, music, art, and architecture characterizes the meeting of cultures, animating life in multicultural cities. More importantly, human interaction may be leavened by the styles of numerous traditions, as conversation, dialect, and humor all bear distinct subcultural tones (*L.A. Story, The Milagro Beanfield War, Crossing Delancey, Mystery Train, A Family Thing, Bagdad Cafe, Double Happiness*). Most subtle of all is the possibility that differing perspectives may mix to provide a certain wisdom, a level of understanding greater than the sum of the parts.

This broader dimension of Multiculturalism goes far beyond the celebration—reminiscent of tourist literature and restaurant guides—of varied "Ethnic Flavor." Eating at a Chinese restaurant, however authentic, gives precious little insight into Chinese-American character, or the emotional and moral dilemmas confronted daily by members of the subculture. Listening to Mariachi music, or jazz played deep in Harlem, is only a small, first step toward appreciating the culture behind the art. We must see the people in interaction, their actions and values weighed side-by-side with others, to begin to engage their "otherness," and the best multicultural films provide a ringside seat (*Mississippi Burning, Mi Familia, The Joy Luck Club, Chan Is Missing*). More important still, our own reactions to that otherness will tell us volumes about ourselves. Film, like any other entertainment medium, may function as only a shallow means to dabble with the feel of another culture. Or film may be examined and experienced more deeply. Thus in the end multicultural film, like real-life Multiculturalism, challenges us to explore our own preconceptions, to become aware of wider possibilities (*Grand Canyon, A Stranger Among Us, Witness, Mississippi Masala, Trading Places, Fools Rush In*). If there is a greater wisdom to be derived from diverse roots, the Socratic ideal of a deeply examined life finds an excellent expression in the pursuit of multicultural understanding.

Filmography

Film (aka), year, country (language), director, producer/distributor, minutes

Classic Images in Black and White

American History X, 1998, USA, Tony Kaye, New Line Cinema, 117
Amistad, 1997, USA, Steven Spielberg, HBO Pictures, 152
Birth of a Nation, 1915, USA, D.W. Griffith, Epoch Productions, 165
Black Like Me, 1964, USA, Carl Lerner, Continental Films, 105
Boys N the Hood, 1991, USA, John Singleton, Columbia, 107
Conrack, 1974, USA, Martin Ritt, 20th Century–Fox, 107
Courage Under Fire, 1996, USA, Edward Zwick, 20th Century–Fox, 115
The Court-Martial of Jackie Robinson, 1990, TV, USA, Larry Peerce, Turner, 100
The Defiant Ones, 1958, USA, Stanley Kramer, United Artists, 97
Do the Right Thing, 1989, USA, Spike Lee, Universal Pictures, 120
A Family Thing, 1996, USA, Richard Pearce, MGM, 109
48 Hours, 1982, USA, Walter Hill, Paramount Pictures, 92
Ghosts of Mississippi, 1996, USA, Rob Reiner, Sony Entertainment, 130
Glory, 1989, USA, Edward Zwick, TriStar, 122
Guess Who's Coming to Dinner, 1967, USA, Stanley Kramer, Columbia, 108
In the Heat of the Night, 1967, USA, Norman Jewison, United Artists, 109
Introducing Dorothy Dandridge, 1999, TV, USA, Martha Coolidge, HBO, 120
Jungle Fever, 1991, USA, Spike Lee, Universal Pictures, 132
Lily in Winter, 1994, TV, USA, Delbert Mann, MCA/Universal, 94
The Long Walk Home, 1990, USA, Richard Pearce, Miramax Films, 97
Malcom X, 1992, USA, Spike Lee, Warner Brothers, 194
Mississippi Burning, 1988, USA, Alan Parker, Orion Pictures, 128
Murder on the Bayou, 1987, TV, USA, Volker Schlondorff, CBS, 91
Nothing But a Man, 1964, USA, Michael Roemer/Robert Young, Cinema 5, 92

The Pelican Brief, 1993, USA, Alan J. Pakula, Warner Bros., 141
Pinky, 1949, USA, Elia Kazan, 20th Century–Fox, 102
Places in the Heart, 1984, USA, Robert Benton, TriStar, 112
A Raisin in the Sun, 1989, TV, USA, Bill Duke/Harold Scott, Fries Home, 171
Remember the Titans, 2000, USA, Boaz Yakin, Buena Vista Films, 113
Rosewood, 1997, USA, John Singleton, Warner Bros., 140
Shadrack, 1998, USA, Suzanna Styron, Columbia, 86
The Shawshank Redemption, 1994, USA, Frank Darabont, Columbia, 142
Soul Man, 1986, USA, Steve Miner, Balcor Film, 104
A Time to Kill, 1996, USA, Joel Schumacher, Warner Bros., 149
Trading Places, 1983, USA, John Landis, Paramount Pictures, 118
White Man's Burden, 1995, USA, Desmond Nakano, HBO, 89

From South of the Border

Across the Moon, 1994, USA, Lisa Gottlieb, Hemdale Film Corporation, 88
American Me, 1992, USA, Edward James Olmos, Universal Pictures, 125
And the Earth Did Not Swallow Him, 1994, USA, Severo Pérez, Kino Int., 99
La Bamba, 1987, USA, Luis Valdez, Columbia, 103
Break of Dawn, 1988, USA, Isaac Artenstein, Cinewest Productions, 100
Crazy from the Heart, 1991, TV, USA, Thomas Schlamme, DeMann Entertainment, 104
Fires Within, 1991, USA, Gillian Armstrong, United Int., 86
Fools Rush In, 1996, USA, Andy Tennant, Columbia, 109
I Like It Like That, 1994, USA, Darnell Martin, Columbia, 104
Lone Star, 1996, USA, John Sayles, Columbia, 135
The Mambo Kings, 1992, France/USA, Arnold Glimcher, Warner Bros., 100
Mi Vida Loca, 1994, USA, Allison Anders, Cineville Inc., 92
The Milagro Beanfield War, 1988, USA, Robert Redford, Universal Pictures, 118
My Family, Mi Familia, 1995, USA, Gregory Nava, New Line Cinema, 126
Nueba Yol, 1995, Dominican Republic (sp.), Angel Muniz, Cigua Films, 106
The Perez Family, 1995, USA, Mira Nair, Samuel Goldwyn Co., 112
The Princess and the Barrio Boy, 2000, TV, USA, Tony Plana, Showtime, 120
The Puerto Rican Mambo, 1992, USA, Ben Model, Piñata Films, 86
Selena, 1997, USA, Gregory Nava, Warner Bros., 127
Show of Force, 1990, USA, Bruno Barreto, Paramount Pictures, 95
Stand and Deliver, 1987, USA, Ramón Menéndez, Warner Bros., 102
Star Maps, 1997, USA, Miguel Arteta, 20th Century–Fox, 86
Walk Proud, 1979, USA, Robert Collins, Universal, 98
West Side Story, 1961, USA, Jerome Robbins/Robert Wise, United Artists, 151
Zoot Suit, 1981, USA, Luis Valdez, Universal Pictures, 103

Immigrants Apart

The Godfather, 1972, USA, Francis Ford Coppola, Paramount Pictures, 176
The Godfather: Part II, 1974, Francis Ford Coppola, Paramount Pictures, 200
The Godfather: Part III, 1990, Francis Ford Coppola, Paramount Pictures, 161
Once Upon a Time in America, 1984, USA, Sergio Leche, Warner Bros., 139

Eastern Spice

Alamo Bay, 1985, USA, Louis Malle, TriStar, 98
Chan Is Missing, 1981, USA, Wayne Wang, New Yorker Films, 80
China Cry: A True Story, 1990, UK, James F. Collier, Trinity Broadcasting, 101
China Girl, 1987, USA, Abel Ferrera, Vestron Pictures, 90
Combination Platter, 1993, USA, Tony Chan, Arrow Releasing, 85
Come See the Paradise, 1990, USA, Alan Parker, 20th Century-Fox, 138
Dim Sum, 1985, USA, Wayne Wang, CIM, 88
Double Happiness, 1994, Canada, Mina Shum, Fine Line Features, 87
Dragon: The Bruce Lee Story, 1993, USA, Rob Cohen, Universal, 115
Eat, Drink, Man, Woman, 1994, Taiwan (man.), Ang Lee, Central MP Corp., 123
The Joy Luck Club, 1993, USA, Wayne Wang, Hollywood Pictures, 139
Lonely in America, 1990, USA, Pary Alexander Brown, Academy Entertainment, 96
The Redwood Curtain, 1995, TV, USA, John Korty, Hallmark Hall of Fame Prod., 100
Snow Falling on Cedars, 1999, USA, Scott Hicks, Universal Pictures, 126
The Wedding Banquet, 1993, Taiwan/USA, Ang Lee, Central MP Corp., 106

American Masala

Bagdad Café, 1988, USA, Percy Adlon, Island Pictures, 91
Dangerous Minds, 1995, USA, John N. Smith, Buena Vista Pictures, 95
Good Morning, Babylon, 1987, Italy/France, Paolo Taviani, MK2 Prod., 117
Grand Canyon, 1991, USA, Lawrence Kasden, 20th Century-Fox, 134
Macaroni Blues, 1986, Norway, Bela Csepcsanyi, Elan-Norsk, 78
Mississippi Masala, 1991, USA, Mira Nair, Black River Prod., 118
Music of the Heart, 1999, USA, Wes Craven, Miramax, 124
My Own Country, 1998, TV, USA, Mira Nair, Showtime, 94
Mystery Train, 1989, USA/Japan, Jim Jarmusch, JVC Entertainment, 113
Someone Else's America, 1996, France/UK, Goran Poskaljevic, Pandora Cinema, 96

A Matter of Faith

The Chosen, 1981, USA, Jeremy Kagan, 20th Century-Fox, 108
For Richer or Poorer, 1997, USA, Bryan Spicer, Universal Pictures, 115
School Ties, 1992, USA, Robert Mandel, Paramount Pictures, 110
A Stranger Among Us, 1992, USA, Sidney Lumet, Propaganda Films, 110
Witness, 1985, USA, Peter Weir, Paramount Pictures, 112

Cultures Within Cultures/ Defining America

Avalon, 1990, USA, Barry Levinson, TriStar, 126
Back to the Future, 1985, USA, Robert Zemeckis, Universal Studios, 116
Bonnie and Clyde, 1967, USA, Arthur Penn, Warner Bros., 111
A Bronx Tale, 1993, USA, Robert DeNiro, United Int. Pictures, 121

The Burning Bed, 1984, TV, USA, Robert Greenwald, Tisch-Avnet Prod., 95
Crossing Delancey, 1988, USA, Joan Micklin Silver, Warner Bros., 97
Deliverance, 1972, USA, John Boorman, Warner Bros., 109
L. A. Story, 1991, USA, Mick Jackson, TriStar, 95
Liberty Heights, 1999, USA, Barry Levinson, Warner Bros., 127
Mr. Smith Goes to Washington, 1939, USA, Frank Capra, Columbia, 130
Terms of Endearment, 1983, USA, James L. Brooks, Paramount Pictures, 132

Chapter Eight

POPULAR FILM AND INTERCULTURAL STUDIES

"People do not see the world as it is, they see it as they are."
                                                Anna and the King

Stepping Outside Our Experience

Most contemporary humans "travel"—leave the immediate world of their own day-to-day experiences—in a number of ways, from reading escapist novels or absorbing histories to watching the slide shows of returned travelers, from unwinding in front of mindless situation comedies to playing science fiction games on computers. In the relatively few oral-tradition cultures still surviving the principle is the same—the tales of elders around the campfire transport the listener to other times and places, with a little help from the imagination. The great although short-lived days of "radio culture" gave a broad resonance to the traditional journeys of the mind: for a few memorable decades the power of the broadcast word sparked the imaginative reconstruction of exotic locations, of people, motive, and intrigue. Soon came film in black and white, and technicolor, then television—electronic media that wired the mind directly to the studio camera and gave the creation of visual imagery over to full-time mediators.

Few would disagree that feature length film, at its best, is as powerful a medium for slipping into another skin as exists, at its optimum a "next-best-thing-to-being-there" experience. It is perhaps rivaled only by the well-crafted novel and an active individual imagination. Lamentably, the reading of literature seems to have faded somewhat in the mass-media age, replaced

by television and film media that do most of the work. If imaginative readers in partnership with novelists do not "travel" in the numbers they once
did, the film theaters are still packed, and video rental stores have sprouted
like mushrooms after a rain. Granted, full-time screenwriters mediate a
story (often based on a novel) and professional cinematographers mediate
it further, granted, the products are the homogenized, often predictable
outputs of a multi-billion dollar industry, expertly crafted for sensory appeal
to the broadest audience. Yet only an extreme view asserts that commercial
film products are entirely denatured, without the substance of compelling
portrayals and meanings, and only an unwarranted cynicism would hold
that the film's meanings are injected directly into the viewer. The ultimate,
and most meaningful mediation is within the critical faculty of the viewer,
who hopefully draws on the wider experience of travel, reading, conversation, and critical thinking to make reasonable judgments about the authenticity of film portrayals. The very phenomenon of "camp"—that media
clichés from the cannibal's pot to war-whooping American Indian to
bugling cavalry are subject to popular derision—amply demonstrates that
the human critical faculty at least pretends to sophistication. More plausible portrayals may represent a trade-off: less distortion of the "mimetically
accurate" or "real" while, concomitantly, remaining stereotypes are camou-
flaged. The viewer, as film detective, must retain a level of vigilance.

     If excellent films such as *A Passage to India*, *M. Butterfly*, and *El Norte*
offer a feast to the analytical mind, popular, casual fare like *The Golden
Child* offers the pabulum of superficial exoticism—light caricatures in place
of genuine perspective. Movie-goers may need facile, humorous treatment
of dramatic differences to be lured into seeing "intercultural" films, however. Whether such films emerge as net assets or liabilities to broader world
understanding depends, of course, on the mental digestion of the film.

     Superficial exoticism has long appealed widely to a desire for com-
fortable, predictable yet spiced experience. Shallowly exotic film may serve
as a metaphor for tourism itself: millions travel the world each year to stay
in familiar-style hotels, eat familiar foods, speak their native language far
from home, and encounter numerous other experiences packaged to appear
like real, local culture. Millions will proudly announce they have been to
Mexico, Italy, or Thailand, when pictures of Mariachi bands on hotel walls,
the "Italian" food of tourist restaurants, or bellmen in "traditional" Thai
dress represent their deepest points of cultural exposure. A species of light,
travelogue film fulfills the same needs for movie-goers, whisking over the
surface of cultural differences as lightly as the crowded calendars of whirlwind tours. *If It's Tuesday, This Must Be Belgium* (1969), even boils the
essence down to its title: the group must consult the tour schedule to be

sure where it's landed among the maze of roads, gift shops, and hotels that look and feel so much alike. From *Around the World in 80 Days* (1956) to *Death on the Nile* (1978) to *National Lampoon's European Vacation* (1985) "tourism lite" in the flesh and in film proves, if nothing else, that the adventure afforded by wealth and modernity rests forever unsated.

If the condiment of the exotic is overt in films based on travel plots, it emerges more subtly and revealingly in popular film that only incidentally, almost accidentally, features encounters across cultures. *The Last Fling* (1989) illustrates what might be termed the "unthinking intercultural film," because so many touches of ethnicity and exoticism lie around the edges of what otherwise proves a light, monocultural, "all–American" comedy. Phil falls quickly smitten with Gloria and heads off to a romantic encounter in ... Acapulco. Looking for wheels, he's able to buy a (possibly stolen) convertible, cheap, as the first stereotype is played—everything is readily available in Mexico, at a price. After the engine catches fire, he dusts off his high school foreign language skills in seeking help from passers-by. "Excusez-moi. El auto es ... flambé." He and Gloria hop a ride on the passing truck, jammed with Mexican laborers, as other stereotyped cards are dealt one by one. "The only people who travel on roads like this are drug smugglers, revolutionaries, and the Mexican version of the Manson family," she proclaims. Later, Phil, after being locked out and breaking into the beach house one night, is surprised by Mexican police and more surprised still when his self-announced status as an attorney, from the U.S., cuts absolutely no ice. An associate from the States springs him from jail with a bribe, commenting wryly, "Let's just say I paid off the mortgage on the man's home." Other ethnic groups back stateside get still shorter shrift, such as the persons of color working jammed into a hotel kitchen, the stereotyped jealous rages of black and Hispanic boyfriends, the Asians who turn a wedding into a bowing contest.

Also revealing is the brief vignette in which Phil is introduced to the lovely, blond Sonia, who knows only the word "hi" in English. It is not even made clear, not considered relevant where Sonia comes from. Yet the implication of these depictions is resoundingly clear: those outside of U.S. American pop culture deserve humane, even polite treatment, but by no means are as interesting as the persons within it. They need not be taken too seriously unless and until they master being "American." This featherweight comedy nicely exemplifies typical intercultural portrayal in U.S. American film in part because no profound observations were intended, lending the (mis)representations of ethnic groups their own unconscious, popular-culture accuracy. The alert viewer can still learn about Anglos and foreigners, but only by refracted images. The caricatures that clearly please the mainstream audience suggest the extreme in the culturally other, the common denominator in ourselves.

Apparent to the Critical Eye

The best films present much more than the tortured shape of our stereotypes: numerous highly "popular" films, expertly crafted, suggest substantial depth while keeping the casual viewer happy sliding along a slick surface. After reviewing scores of intercultural films that enjoyed commercial success it grows apparent: even in the heart of Hollywood filmmaking artful, realistic scenes find their way in front of the camera. Whether because screenwriters yearn to inject some depth into their popular products, because the best directors have an uncanny sense of realism even while constructing fantasy worlds, or because ethnic actors push for meaningful subtlety, even the glitziest products may have inspired content. The number of compelling scenes that ring authentic, that speak to some critical element of truth, stands as ultimately striking. In the end we infer that the best directors balance their knowledge of the low common denominator targets of commercial film with a sense of their place as film artists, and work masterfully to satisfy the opposing demands.

The exploratory candles lit by these films are all too often ignored by professional film critics. Critics themselves may become mesmerized, lulled to sleep analytically and reacting to the superficial twists of plot or to the relatively unimportant sparks struck by major stars. With a handful of exceptions such as *M. Butterfly* or *White Nights*, it appears that Sunday-supplement critics often miss the point of films set at cultural intersections, ignoring the rich veins of reflective wisdom to be mined. That is not surprising with well-hewn popular film as opposed to commercially marginal cinema: *Dances with Wolves*; *Legends of the Fall*; *Out of Africa*; *Good Morning, Vietnam*; *The Year of Living Dangerously* all dazzle with attractive human and natural scenery, with cleverly engaging moments. The more staid and deliberately paced "thinking person's" film such as *Chan is Missing, Living on Tokyo Time*, and *Praying with Anger* are more easily recognized as intercultural meditations largely due to the lack of distraction, and the semi-documentary *Perfumed Nightmare* or *Iron and Silk* essentially announce their intentions to observe the intersection of cultures. From the slick to the ponderous, they can equally anchor serious study.

Though this book has not explicitly addressed the educational and training uses of these hundreds of films, the commentaries throughout should be suggestive launching points for analysis in myriad settings. The films spotlighted were clearly chosen for depth, but other films exist with still others released each year—merely to scan the copyright dates shows a steadily accelerating production. Late in the process of writing this book new material, too relevant to ignore, kept appearing. *Smoke Signals* and *Naturally Native* added pointedly to portrayals of contemporary Native Americans, both *Seven Years in Tibet* and *Red Corner* enriched the West-meets-China mosaic, and *Fools Rush In* filled an obvious vacuum in films of Multicultural America. Popular film is leavened with ever more cultural crosstalk, and such films will keep coming. The "definitive" book on the subject could never be finished.

Even the discussion of a single, quality film could be seemingly endless. Though discussion in the preceding chapters required brevity, the best films merit copious analysis. University classes focused on cultural or film studies might use *Chan Is Missing, Black Robe, Heaven and Earth, Chocolat, Thunderheart,* or *Moscow on the Hudson* (among numerous others) each as grist for numerous hours. Or consider *Lone Star,* the product of consummate film artist John Sayles, which demonstrates again the coexistence of absorbing entertainment with meaningful exploration of serious issues. No scene of *Lone Star* is less then well crafted, no line of dialogue without purpose. The artistic center of the film is not so much the forty-year old mystery surrounding the murder of despotic sheriff Charlie Wade but complexly coexisting Anglo, Hispanic, and Afro-American communities. Beginning with a story line at the crossroads of the ethnicities—representatives of all three are intertwined in the central mystery—through a screenplay that gives each subculture its own "air time," the film demonstrates further that tone, setting and action may broker ethnic perspectives in balance, yet in colorful counterpoint. The music and language of each community is heard in turn, a reflection of different experiences and mindsets. And though the subgroups lived in the same town their experiences differed sharply: depending on perspective, Buddy Deeds was a hero soldier-turned-sheriff, a fair but dictatorial lawman, a corrupt official, a friend to minorities, a philandering husband, an authoritarian father. Shades of *Chan Is Missing,* we set out to describe a man and end by describing ourselves. Even the smallest events invite different interpretations from the characters, which in turn reveal distinct frames of reference. The late Sheriff Deeds once "employed" a Chicano prisoner to build his patio, an abuse of office in the current sheriff's eyes, yet the old Chicano fondly reminisces about the chance to be "out in the fresh air," eating home-cooked lunches.

Even the broad temporal sense of events is captured in balance, with the force of a highly contemporary "now" set against a past still echoing its importance-and echoing Faulkner: "The past isn't dead. It isn't even really the past." The central mystery begins in the earth, as a skeleton decayed by time rises to the importance of flesh. Modern police science shines up a decades-old sheriff's shield found with the remains, and thus recalls old grudges. With artful camera work Sayles zooms into a basket of tortillas on a table and back out into the same restaurant, with a scene from forty years earlier, and the action of different eras upon the same stage strengthens the sinew of historical links. The frequent, artful cuts that link several stories in a common chain as well convey a wisdom greater than the sum of parallel parts—the estranged ethnic subcultures move on separate paths but their border community, and their inevitable interactions, link them in a common web.

The start-to-finish subtleties of *Lone Star* and films of its caliber suggest a Socratic approach—more pregnant questions emerge than easy answers. Is there a higher morality in the "bribes or bullets" way whites once ran the county, or in Otis Payne's "darktown" bar, sometime site of drug dealing and even violence. Does "blood only mean what you let it," as Otis maintains? How many years of residence gives an immigrant, like Mercedes Cruz, the right to disdain the new generations of "wetbacks"? Does the military represent the ultimate in equality of opportunity, as manifest in the black camp commander, or another misuse of the less powerful by the elite? Is there a clear, objective "truth" to Texas history, or only the subjective political memory of each ethnicity?

Such questions surge with more force and immediacy from film than almost any other medium, questions that invite what is often termed critical thinking. Educators including university presidents should smile upon film that visits variegated settings and viewpoints, underscores the importance of history and contextuality, and ultimately frames the moral conundrums of modern life. Several surveys have shown those very dimensions to be among the intellectual outcomes that presidents most wish for their students.

The value of film as educational grist is underscored when a given film is shown to an interested group and discussed afterward—making clear that the final, constructed meaning of film proves individual. Members of the audience, one by one, absorb the same entertainment and images in distinct ways, imprinted upon their existing patterns of perception. Especially (but not necessarily) if the group is heterogenous, the differing and often surprising reactions grow remarkable. An ideal stage for debate arises, and one line of debate may spawn several equally meaningfully ones.

The possible "takes" on the same dialogue or action seem infinite; any two individuals rarely observe the same scene in exactly the same way. Even when the reactions fall into recognizable patterns, they remind the analyst that myriad perspectives emerge from observers of intercultural scenes, perspectives that reveal both their biases and latent anxieties (as well as the sometimes academic tendency to overcategorize human behavior). The differing reactions may focus on numerous details, or reveal utter differences in worldview. The writer in *The Old Gringo* and the basketball recruiter in *The Air Up There* may only be sympathetic to the audience from which they come. And Japanese viewing filmed versions of *Huckleberry Finn* are often bewildered at Huck's behavior and hero's status. After all, he has defied and abandoned family, run from "responsibility," allied himself with someone from a lower caste, telling myriad lies and breaking numerous laws in the process. Surely this story projects the archetype of pure, unadulterated shame!

After the Curtains Close

When the analysis of a thousand wrinkles is done, what will we have learned from the medium that is larger than life? Will we carry away wisdom from the labyrinth of images and words? Perhaps the most central of all human attitudes is the raw sense of self within a community, manifest in each individual's assumption that his or her own customs, ways, and preferences are "right" and "natural." The irony of the phrase "human nature" may lie in the fact that one constant pervades the attitudes of humans across time and cultures, the paradoxical assumption that there is a "human" nature—the nature constructed by the community into which one has been socialized—and yet that all other natures are at least subtly odd, somehow lacking in validity. In this sense intercultural film may illuminate a broader, less ethnocentric world.

Notwithstanding the variety of content, and of possible reactions, overarching lessons emerge from these films. Once the viewer accepts their personal responses as growing from societal conditioning, tempered by personal experience, they will better recognize that similar processes sculpt the actions, and reactions, of the film's characters. Relativity of experience and meaning thus becomes the foundation for all other conclusions.

Some illumination of power relations will also emerge from encounters across cultures. For example, some pressure almost always weighs on the marginal or foreign party to meet the dominant party more than halfway. Resolutely maintaining a sense of self proves problematic in numerous ways, but so does "going native." As well, the weaker side of a cross-cultural interaction will generally develop sharp perception concerning the stronger, owing largely to self-defense. The dominant party, with less need to truly understand the weaker, will likely have some blind spots; in other instances guilt, a repression of full recognition of the dynamic, will blind the stronger party.

Intercultural film tests theories of universal human attributes and several appear: pride and hubris, social and romantic needs, the drive for self-respect, grief from loss, all arise in some form, just as varied world classics have predicted. Film reveals these universals but hammers home another truth—God and the Devil emerge from the form, and from the details. Old Chu strives intensely to maintain his dignity and pride in *Pushing Hands*, but in a sense that his American daughter-in-law, even his Westernizing son, find difficult to comprehend. Ken in *Living on Tokyo Time* showers social, even romantic flattery upon Kyoko, graced with sincere respect, but falls far short of meeting her needs, which were sculpted by one of the world's most distinctive societies. Not only the devil of intercultural detail but the ubiquity (across time and culture) of "facework" emerges well illustrated by these films—how we continually, instinctively contextualize ourselves and our utterances, even our gestures, in quest of resonance and simple self-respect.

For every emotion we know, other systems of being may have an equivalent, but with manifestations so different as to defy easy recognition. "Embarrassment" across cultures may manifest by blushing, laughter, silence, or rage at personal levels and be expiated by highly differing rituals at the societal. Should we still translate it as "embarrassment" nonetheless? Not only outward manifestations but many social phenomena themselves appear to differ sharply. Both U.S. and Japanese culture recognize "respect" and translate the word freely in both directions. But Jack Elliot in *Mr. Baseball* holds a gunslinger's code of respect while the Japanese imbue the concept with collective importance, woven into the very fabric of their social psychology. Jack's initially disrespectful posture in Japan proves doubly offensive because wearing respect, like wearing clothes in public, shocks with a scandalous nudity in its absence. Every concept, whether respect or embarrassment, success or humility, love or obligation, may have an equivalent even under a similar name cross-culturally, but the commodity may be strikingly different in size or even shape.

For stories that cross cultures to engage their audience, the "other" must be at once much like us, yet distinctly different. How well this contradiction is solved measures a film's success—*Dances with Wolves* made the Sioux deeply Indian yet deeply "us" as well, to tremendous accolades. A longer "director's cut" of the film included a scene in which white poachers were ritually, brutally killed by Sioux, a scene excised from the version released to theaters, upon which the film's reputation was built. It has never been easy to portray the other as a true self, yet sympathetic for the intercultural audience.

It is commonplace to observe that we appear not only projected, but reflected as well on the Big Screen. Does intercultural film serve as a cultural barometer, giving an essentially accurate reading of the state of inter-relations? With the appropriate optical-intellectual corrections, I believe it does. The popular film record of the Natives and New Americans reveals an interest skewed toward the horse-culture plains Indians of earlier centuries, more broadly toward Indians as artifacts and memories, not flesh. These films mirror the common consciousness, including the small but emerging interest in authentic, contemporary Native lives amid the larger society (*Smoke Signals*). While the North and South of the Border body of film spotlights the uneasy, ambivalent interactions between Hispanic and "white" culture, Japanese-focused films have begun to move beyond samurai swords to respect for a broader Japanese character. "Yogi," in Mr. Baseball, even demands and gets exactly that, respect, from the American athletic giant. Films addressing China, India, and the East fasten on exoticism (*Heat and Dust, A Passage to India, Seven Years in Tibet*) and East-West politics (*M. Butterfly, Gandhi*) in roughly the proportions that animate Western interest. The African films, like the Western experience there, are all over the map, but uncover a white (film character and audience) thirst for adventure in the thicket of difference. Russia-meets-the-West film has thawed at about the same rate as real geo-politics. And films seeking to capture Middle Eastern culture can't quite locate their prey, and don't know what to do with it if they do, much like the real relations at play.

Biases and attractions, hopes and fears, warts and all—a careful look at the Screen can reveal them.

CHAPTER NOTES

Introduction

1. Ella Shohat and Robert Stam, *Unthinking Eurocentrism: Multiculturalism and the Media* (New York: Routledge, 1994), pp. 179–82. Although a specific section is cited here, the entire work stands as an exceptionally penetrating and thorough analysis of cultural bias and preconception as transmitted through modern media.

2. For texts which review, and advance, the social science of film viewing, consider the following: Richard Allen, *Projecting Illusion* (New York: Cambridge University Press, 1995); Wheeler W. Dixon, *It Looks at You: The Returned Gaze of Cinema* (Albany: State University of New York Press, 1995); Francesco Casetti, *Inside the Gaze: The Fiction Film and Its Spectator* (Bloomington: Indiana University Press, 1998); Bruce A. Austin, *Immediate Seating: A Look at Movie Audiences* (Belmont, Cal.: Wadsworth, 1989).

3. "Culture" serves as an axial term in this work. In today's academic climate, precise definition of the term itself may be more troublesome than previously; this study simplifies and focuses the meaning of "culture" in two ways. On the one hand the usage is for the generally educated reader, not the academic specialist in a culture-defining discipline. Secondly, to the extent that "culture" is used in learned context, I draw on those theorists who define culture operationally—who are interested in the applied, practical sense by which members of one national or ethnic group may think, behave, and present themselves distinctly from members of another. To this end readers may consult the following seminal sources, among others: Edward T. Hall's *The Hidden Dimension* (Garden City, NY: Doubleday, 1966) and his *The Silent Language* (New York: Anchor Books, 1973); Geert Hofstede, *Cultures and Organizations: Software of the Mind* (New York: McGraw-Hill, 1991); Harry C. Triandis, *Culture and Social Behavior* (New York: McGraw-Hill, 1994).

Chapter 1

1. This topic is obviously huge and multidisciplinary. Readers may begin by consulting Jorge Gracia, *Hispanic/Latino Identity: A Philosophical Perspective* (Malden, Mass.: Blackwell, 2000), esp. pp. 189–92.

2. See Patricia Nelson Limerick, *The Legacy of Conquest: The Unbroken Past of the American West* (New York: W.W.Norton, 1987), and by the same author *Something in the Soil: Legacies and Reckonings in the New West* (New York: W.W. Norton, 2000).

3. Ibid.

4. See Benjamin DeMott's *The Trouble with Friendship: Why Americans Can't Think Straight About Race* (New York: Atlantic Monthly Press, 1995), which explodes the fallacy that polite superficial behaviors genuinely attenuate the deep inequalities often based on race and ethnicity.

5. A film that ends with comic scenes of mass-immigration (to the score of the song "America") should be linked to a cross-border reference. Readers may wish to start with the essays in *Culture Across Borders: Mexican Immigration and Popular Culture*, eds. David R. Maciel and María Herrera-Sobek (Tucson: U. of Arizona Press, 1998).

6. Don Lee Fred Nilsen's *Humor Scholarship: A Research Bibliography* (Westport, Conn.: Greenwood Press, 1993) offers a sense of the variety of this emerging analytical field.

7. *Based on a True Story: Latin American History at the Movies*, ed. Donald F. S. Stevens (Wilmington, Del.: SR Books, 1997). It often proves instructive to review historical detail and compare numerous perspectives on representation when assessing the numerous films that tell "true stories" of strife in Latin America. These essays do not address the *Missing* story directly, but more broadly explore the history-representation link.

8. Texts on Hispanic issues and identity proliferate; the reader may wish to begin by consulting the hard scholarship of Rogelio Díaz-Guerrero, et al., *Understanding Mexicans and Americans: A Mexican-U.S. Communication Lexicon of Images, Meanings, and Cultural Frames of Reference* (Washington, D.C.: Institute of Comparative Social & Cultural Studies Inc., 1985), and Rogelio Díaz-Guerrero, *Understanding Mexicans and Americans: Cultural Perspectives in Conflict* (New York: Plenum Press, 1991).

9. Charles Ramirez-Berg's article "Stereotyping in Films in General and of the Hispanic in Particular" (*Howard Journal of Communication*, 2, 1990) includes additional observations on the intercultural social-psychology of the "Other."

10. Rogelio Díaz-Guerrero, 1985, 1991, ibid.

Chapter 2

1. Edwin O. Reischauer, *The Japanese* (Cambridge, Mass.: Belknap Press, 1995).

2. There are countless references for this point of view; see Renaud de Maricourt's "Japan and Foreign Cultures: Thoughts for Expatriates," *Intercultures*, 22 (July 1993) 79–94, for interesting perspectives.

3. The Shogun myth enjoyed such popularity and impact in our popular culture that it spawned thoughtful analyses. See Henry Smith, ed., *Learning from Shogun: Japanese History and Western Fantasy* (Santa Barbara, Cal.: Program in Asian Studies, 1980); also Michael Macintyre, *The Shogun Inheritance: Japan and the Legacy of the Samurai* (London: William Collins Sons, 1981).

4. Dean Barnlund, *Communication Styles of Japanese and Americans: Images and Realities* (Belmont, Cal.: Wadsworth, 1989), esp. pp. 53–72 and 147–67. See also Barnlund's *Public and Private Self in Japan and the United States: Communicative Styles of Two Cultures* (Tokyo: Simul Press, 1975).

5. Analyzing and "troubleshooting" Western-Asian communication in general and U.S.-Japanese communication in particular has attracted significant focus in recent decades. At the most applied level, readers may consult the (mis)communications modeled in Greg Storti's *Cross-Cultural Dialogues: 74 Brief Encounters With Cultural Difference* (Yarmouth, Maine: Intercultural Press, 1994), esp. passages highlighting U.S.-Japanese interactions on pp. 17, 42, 53, 90, 93, 96, 98, 100, 101, and 102. As well, a host of sources approach the differing communication styles from numerous perspectives. Readers may find it useful to consult not only the sources cited above but also, for example, Robert M. March's *Reading the Japanese Mind: The Realities Behind Their Thoughts and Actions* (New York: Kodansha International, 1996) and *The Japanese Negotiator: Subtlety and Strategy Beyond Western Logic* (New York: Kodansha

International, 1988); also John Condon's *With Respect to the Japanese* (Yarmouth, Maine: Intercultural Press, 1984). For close social-science analysis of personality dynamics which contribute to communication differences, see such articles as Akiko Asai and Dean Barnlund's "Boundaries of the Unconscious, Private, and Public Self in Japanese and Americans: A Cross-Cultural Comparison," *International Journal of Intercultural Relations*, 22:4 (1998) 431–52; also Ryoko Niikara's "The Psychology and Process Underlying Japanese Assertive Behavior: Comparison of Japanese With Americans, Malaysians and Filipinos," *International Journal of Intercultural Relations*, 23:1 (1999) 47–76, a unique commentary in that it compares certain key traits across other Asian cultures as well. The Western hunger to communicate well with the Japanese generates various specialized works, to wit: *Welcoming the Japanese Visitor: Insights, Tips, Tactics*, by Kazuo Nishiyama (Honolulu: U. of Hawaii Press, 1996).

6. Reischauer, ibid.

7. Much literature might serve to sustain this point; especially see Tomoko Tanaka, et al. "Adjustment Patterns of International Students in Japan," *International Journal of Intercultural Relations*, 18:1 (1994) 55–75; also, Reischauer, ibid, p. 399.

8. Dugan Romano, *Intercultural Marriage: Promises and Pitfalls* 2nd edition (Yarmouth, Maine: Intercultural Press, 1997).

9. Although numerous specific references support this assertion, for example, pp. 395–412 of the aforementioned Reischauer text, the point is more broadly lodged in the logic of a culture which is subtly structured, layered, textured, and balanced. Thus the Japanese unease, according to the theory, with those who have lived in a foreign ambiance for enough time to upset the delicate balances of their socialization.

10. Condon, ibid., p. 40.

11. Stella Ting-Toomey, "Facework in Japan and the United States," *International Journal of Intercultural Relations*, 18:4 (1994) 469–506.

12. See Chapter 7, "American Exceptionalism—Uniqueness" and esp. p. 212: "In this chapter, I look at the two outliers, the two developed nations which are most different from each other." Seymour Martin Lipset, *American Exceptionalism: A Double-Edged Sword* (New York: W.W. Norton, 1996).

Chapter 3

Note: The *Film Review Annual* (Englewood, N.J.: J.S. Ozer) reprints the complete text of film reviews.

1. John Anderson, *Newsday*, October 1, 1993, p. 61 (rpt. *Film Review Annual, 1994*, p. 845).

2. Ibid., p. 846.

3. Richard Corliss, *Time*, October 4, 1993, p. 87 (rpt. *Film Review Annual, 1994*, p. 848).

4. J. Hobermann, *Village Voice*, October 5, 1993, p. 49 (rpt. *Film Review Annual, 1994*, p. 848).

5. John Anderson, *Newsday*, ibid.

6. Especially in the early decades of filmmaking, Asians suffered from representations no more flattering, and no more realistic, than those of Native Americans or other sadly caricatured groups. See, for example, Eugene Franklin Wong, *On Visual Media Racism: Asians in American Motion Pictures* (New York: Arno Press, 1978).

7. *New Statesman*, March 3, 1985, p. 31 (rpt. *Film Review Annual*, 1985, p. 1041).

8. Nigel Rapport, *The Prose and the Passion: Anthropology, Literature, and the Writing of E. M. Forster* (Manchester, U.K.: Manchester University Press, 1994).

Chapter 4

1. Winner of a Pulitzer Prize, Jared Diamond's *Guns, Germs, and Steel: The Fates of Human Societies* (New York: W. W. Norton, 1997) resoundingly makes the case for

environmental factors as determinants of "economic development" in the modern sense. It offers well-documented counterpoint to the insidious suggestion that a pre-modern mentality is responsible for slow economic and social evolution.

2. A sense of the complexity of Africa, historically and currently, is afforded by Kwame Anthony Appiah and Henry Louis Gates, Jr., eds., with *Africana: The Encyclopedia of the African and African American Experience* (New York: Basic Civitas Books, 1999).

3. Athol Fugard, *Master Harold—and the Boys* (New York: Alfred Knopf, 1982).

4. The reader may wish to consult Marianna Torgovnick's *Primitive Passions: Men, Women, and the Quest for Ecstasy* (New York: Alfred Knopf, 1997), pp. 88–97, for intelligent ruminations on Fossey's real-life story and media image.

5. A cold, even pessimistic assessment of the problems and challenges of the African continent, which may be useful in contextualizing these film treatments, is found in George B. N. Ayittey's *Africa in Chaos* (New York: St. Martin's Press, 1998).

6. See Y. Y. Kim's *Communication and Cross-Cultural Adaptation: An Integrative Theory* (Clevedon, England: Multilingual Matters, 1988).

7. Kwame Anthony Appiah's *In My Father's House: Africa in the Philosophy of Culture* (New York: Oxford University Press, 1992) explicates depths of African culture that few films or novels reveal effectively, but which serve as a framework within which to analyze stories of Africa. Yale Richmond and Phyllis Gestrin's *Into Africa: Intercultural Insights* (Yarmouth, Maine: Intercultural Press, 1998) provides a more practical, applied look at the Africa fictionalized in these films.

8. Another respected work which serves well to contextualize Africa vis-à-vis modernity is *Perspectives on Africa: A Reader in Culture, History, and Representation*, eds. Roy Richard Grinker and Christopher B. Steiner (Cambridge, Mass: Blackwell, 1977).

Chapter 5

1. From Hedrick Smith's *The Russians* (New York: Ballantine, 1984) and *The New Russians* (New York: Random House, 1990) to Yale Richmond's more specialized *From Nyet to Da: Understanding the Russians* (Yarmouth, Maine: Intercultural Press, 1992), a readable, accessible literature offers insight into the individual and collective character of Russians.

2. Literally an immigrant's handbook, *Living in the U.S.A* by Alison Lanier and C. William Gay (Yarmouth, Maine: Intercultural Press, 1996) refers to a host of mundane but important issues for immigrants, many of which are touched upon in this film.

3. David Denby, *New York*, April 16, 1984, p. 90 (rpt. *Film Review Annual, 1985*, p. 910).

4. Sheila Benson, Los Angeles *Times*, November 22, 1985, Calendar, p. 1 (rpt. *Film Review Annual*, 1986, p. 1499).

5. Pam Cook, *Monthly Film Bulletin*, April, 1986, p. 121 (rpt. *Film Review Annual*, 1986, p. 1504).

6. Rex Reed, New York *Post*, November 22, 1985, p. 21 (rpt. *Film Review Annual*, 1986, p. 1503).

7. David Denby, *New York*, November 22, 1985, p. 115, (rpt. *Film Review Annual*, 1986, p. 1503).

8. Yale Richmond, ibid., esp. pp. 105–12.

9. Highly respected, *The Cultural Atlas of Islam*, by Isma'il R. Al-Faruqi and Lois Ibsen Al-Faruqi (New York: Macmillan, 1986), suggests the depth, breadth, and subtlety of Islamic studies.

10. Samuel Huntington *The Clash of Civilizations and the Remaking of World Order* (New York: Simon and Schuster, 1996).

11. Kevin Thomas, Los Angeles *Times*, July 29, 1994, Calendar, p. 10 (rpt. *Film Review Annual*, 1995, p. 512).

12. See Edward C. Stuart and Milton J. Bennett, *American Cultural Patterns: A Cross-Cultural Perspective* (Yarmouth, Maine: Intercultural Press, 1991), esp. pp. 32–84.

13. Kazuo Ishiguro, *The Remains of the Day* (Boston: Faber and Faber, 1989).

14. Hamid Mowlana, *Global Information and World Communication* (Thousand Oaks, Cal.: Sage, 1997).

15. Ibid., esp. pp. 96–100.

Chapter 6

1. Michael Hilger's *From Savage to Nobleman: Images of Native Americans in Film* (Lanham, Md.: Scarecrow Press, 1995), suggests the fascinating historical trajectory of representations of the Indian.

2. Such contemporary works as *Hollywood's Indian: The Portrayal of the Native American in Film*, ed. Peter C. Rollins and John E. O'Connor (Lexington: University Press of Kentucky, 1998); Ward Churchill's *Fantasies of the Master Race: Literature, Cinema, and the Colonization of the American Indian* (San Francisco: City Light Books, 1998); and Jacquelyn Kilpatrick's *Celluloid Indians: Native Americans and Film* (Lincoln: U. of Nebraska Press, 1999), further analyze the range of Native American representations.

3. For further perspective on natives of the Far North in film see Ann Fienup-Riordan's *Freeze Frame: Alaska Eskimos in the Movies* (Seattle: U. of Washington Press, 1995).

4. See Lee Clark Mitchell's *Westerns: Making the Man in Fiction and Film* (Chicago: U. of Chicago Press, 1996), p. 10. Also see the novel, Robert Gessner's *Broken Arrow* (New York: Farrar & Rinehart, 1933).

5. Harry W. Lawton, *Willie Boy: A Desert Manhunt* (Balboa Island, Cal.: Paisano Press, 1960).

6. The very title of Ralph E. and Natasha A. Friar's *The Only Good Indian: The Hollywood Gospel* (New York: Drama Book Specialists, 1972) suggests the white-culture drive to exterminate the race. Also, see *The Hunt for Willie Boy: Indian-Hating and Popular Culture*, by James A. Sandos (Norman: U. of Oklahoma Press, 1994).

7. Georgia Brown, *Village Voice*, May 19, 1992, p. 60 (rpt. *Film Review Annual, 1993*, p. 654).

8. Some critics, such as Dan Georgakas writing for *Cineaste* (28: 2, [1991] 51; rpt. *Film Review Annual*, 1992, p. 317), lambasted the film for inaccuracies in "history and sociology." More common, however, were critics drawn to the film in spite of themselves; typical was M.S. Mason (*Christian Science Monitor*, Dec. 7, 1990, p. 12; rpt. *Film Review Annual*, 1992, p. 316). He noted not only incongruities but "clichés" that "pour out in buckets," yet expresses high praise—"The complexities of leaning across the barriers of language and culture [director] Costner captures with grace"—and concludes that the effort achieves "a sense of community that crosses cultural craters." While Native American reviewer Edward D. Castillo (*Film Quarterly*, 44: 4 [Summer, 1991] 14; rpt. *Film Review Annual*, 1992, p. 320) notes foolish departures from the realistic, he focuses largely on the film's contributions to humanizing Natives: "The screenplay, without preaching, engenders understanding, acceptance, and sympathy for Lakota culture."

9. Marianna Torgovnick, *Primitive Passions: Men, Women, and the Quest for Ecstasy* (New York: Alfred Knopf, 1997), esp. pp. 150–52.

10. Deconstructing the remarkable Grey Owl myth is a growing cottage industry especially in light of the Richard Attenborough film, which one critic called "more fraudulent than anything Archie Belaney ever concocted"; see Kevin Michael Grace, *Report Newsmagazine* (National Edition), Oct. 25, 1999, p. 52. The film holds some fascination, but should be considered soberly in light of the biographical record; readers may wish to consult Donald B. Smith's *From the Land of the Shadows: The Making of Grey Owl* (Saskatoon, Canada: Western Producer Prairie Books, 1990).

Chapter 7

1. Judith Roof and Robyn Wiegman, eds. *Who Can Speak?: Authority and Critical Identity* (Urbana: U. of Illinois Press, 1995).

2. Numerous popular textbooks, such as Vincent N. Parrillo's *Strangers to These Shores: Race and Ethnic Relations in the United States*, 6th edition (Boston: Allyn and Bacon, 2000), broker factual and sociological contexts for the evaluation of popular cultural representations.

3. The essays in *Hollywood as Mirror: Changing Views of "Outsiders" and "Enemies" in American Movies*, ed. Robert Brent Toplin (Westport, Conn.: Greenwood Press, 1993) support the reflection metaphor in commenting on films through several decades. Additional historical analysis is found in *Ethnic and Racial Images in American Film and Television*, eds. Allen L. Woll and Randall M. Miller (New York: Garland Publishing, 1987). Readers may wish as well to consult *Mediating History: The Map Guide to Independent Video by and about African American, Asian American, Latino, and Native American People*, eds. Barbara Abrash and Catherine Egan (New York: New York University Press, 1992).

4. For the broadest perspective on the mass media representation of African-Americans, see Donald Bogle's *Blacks in American Films and Television: An Encyclopedia* (New York: Garland, 1988) and his *Toms, Coons, Mulattoes, Mammies, and Bucks: An Interpretive History of Blacks in American Film*, 3rd edition (New York: Continuum, 1994). *Slow Fade to Black: The Negro in American Film 1900–1942* by Thomas Cripps (New York: Oxford University Press, 1993) takes a look at the especially dismal early years of that representation.

5. The film generated a book of essays in *Spike Lee's "Do the Right Thing,"* ed. Mark A. Reid (New York: Cambridge University Press, 1997).

6. *Latino Cultural Citizenship: Claiming Identity, Space, and Rights*, eds. William V. Flores and Rina Benmayor (Boston: Beacon Press, 1997), is only a recent example of texts which broadly explore Latino identity and "citizenship" issues. For an interesting example of popularized discussion, see the article "Inter-Latino Dating" in *Latina* (November, 1997, pp. 57–59) for a look at topical conceptions of difference among Latino subgroups.

7. Although a select number of films are considered here, many texts broadly examine the portrayals of U.S. Hispanics in the film medium; for example, Arthur G. Pettit, *Images of the Mexican American in Fiction and Film* (College Station: Texas A&M University Press, 1980); Chon A. Noriega, ed., *Chicanos and Film: Essays on Chicano Representation and Resistance* (New York: Garland, 1992); Luis Reyes, *Hispanics in Hollywood: An Encyclopedia of Film and Television* (New York: Garland, 1994); Alfred Charles Richard, *Contemporary Hollywood's Negative Hispanic Image* (Westport, Conn.: Greenwood Press, 1994); Christine List, *Chicano Images: Refiguring Ethnicity in Mainstream Film* (New York: Garland, 1996).

8. For a superior and very readable text on Mexican cultural psychology see the English translation of the eminent Mexican social-psychologist Rogelio Diaz-Guerrero—*Psychology of the Mexican: Culture and Personality* (Austin: U. of Texas Press, 1975). While he obviously studies only one national culture, it is generally held that other Latin cultures show roughly similar characteristics along basic axes such as family values.

9. David Abalos's *Latinos in the United States* (Notre Dame, Ind.: U. of Notre Dame Press, 1986) posits tensions so profound that he calls for nothing less than a conscious "transformation"—a new, redefined sense of being Latino within a largely alien Anglo milieu.

10. For an interesting treatment of the subculture see Benson Tong's *The Chinese Americans* (Westport, Conn.: Greenwood Press, 2000).

11. Amy Tan, *The Joy Luck Club* (New York: Vintage Books, 1991).

12. For a contemporary overview of Asian-American representation see Jun Xing's

Asia America Through the Lens: History, Representations, and Identity (Walnut Creek, Cal.: AltaMira Press, 1998).

13. Perspectives on Italian U.S. Americans within the larger society are conveyed by the essays in *Beyond the Margin: Readings in Italian Americana*, eds. Paolo A. Giordano and Anthony Julian Tamburri (Madison, N.J.: Fairleigh Dickinson University Press, 1998).

14. Examinations of American character are worth revisiting for context. See such modern classics as David Reisman's *The Lonely Crowd: A Study of the Changing American Character* (Garden City, N.Y.: Doubleday, 1953); Philip Slater's *The Pursuit of Loneliness: American Culture at the Breaking Point* (Boston: Beacon Press, 1970); Robert Bellah's *Habits of the Heart: Individualism and Commitment in American Life* (Berkeley: U. of California Press, 1985); also, Edward C. Stuart and Milton J. Bennett's *American Cultural Patterns: A Cross-Cultural Perspective* (Yarmouth, Maine: Intercultural Press, 1991) provides an unusually rigorous analysis of American culture vis-à-vis other national patterns.

15. For a broad, interesting look at the "hillbilly" in popular culture and film, see J.W. Williamson's *Hillbillyland* (Chapel Hill: U. of North Carolina Press, 1995).

16. Walter T.K. Nugent, *Crossings: The Great Transatlantic Migrations, 1870–1914* (Bloomington: Indiana University Press, 1992).

SELECTED BIBLIOGRAPHY

This book verges on numerous broad and complex questions, from ethnic identity to the impact of media on social psychology, from the history to the psychology of numerous nation-states, from the protocol of international encounter to the deeply emotional messages transmitted, willingly or not, by myriad intercultural interactions. Obviously this study cannot and does not pretend to account for the immense body of research and commentary relevant to all of those questions and disciplines. Likewise, the body of research and commentary about film is large and steadily increasing. It is not unusual to encounter articles or full-length texts focused on highly specific targets, for example, "American Fantasies of the South Pacific as Seen in Film," and the like. And the representation of major groups in the media, such as Mexican-Americans, Asian Americans, or Jewish Americans, is amply discussed in almost countless venues.

The focus here remains primarily the *interactions* of representatives of different cultures, as depicted in popular, accessible film. Beyond references specific to that mission, therefore, this bibliography has been purposefully selective, limited to those texts that may serve readers as convenient launching pads for exploration of numerous specialties, or avenues of interest. The list is intended as suggestive, not encyclopedic. Those recommended texts themselves, almost invariably, will include the bibliographic support to take readers as far as time and interest permit.

Abalos, David, *Latinos in the United States*. Notre Dame, Ind: U. of Notre Dame Press, 1986.

Abrash, Barbara, and Egan, Catherine, eds., *Mediating History: The Map Guide to Independent Video by and about African American, Asian American, Latino, and Native American People*. New York: New York University Press, 1992.

Al-Faruqi, Isma'il R., and Al-Faruqi, Lois Ibsen, *The Cultural Atlas of Islam*. New York: Macmillan, 1986.

Allen, Richard, *Projecting Illusion*. New York: Cambridge University Press, 1995.

Appiah, Kwame Anthony, *In My Father's House: Africa in the Philosophy of Culture*. New York: Oxford University Press, 1992.

_____, and Gates, Henry Louis, Jr., eds. *Africana: The Encyclopedia of the African and African American Experience*. New York: Basic Civitas Books, 1999.

Asai, Akiko, and Barnlund, Dean, "Boundaries of the Unconscious, Private, and Public Self in Japanese and Americans: A Cross-Cultural Comparison," *International Journal of Intercultural Relations*, 22:4 (1998) 431–52.

Austin, Bruce A., *Immediate Seating: A Look at Movie Audiences*. Belmont, Cal.: Wadsworth, 1989.

Ayittey, George B. N., *Africa in Chaos*. New York: St. Martin's Press, 1998.

Barnlund, Dean, *Communication Styles of Japanese and Americans: Images and Realities*. Belmont, Cal.: Wadsworth, 1989.

_____, *Public and Private Self in Japan and the United States: Communicative Styles of Two Cultures*. Tokyo: Simul Press, 1975.

Bellah, Robert, *Habits of the Heart: Individualism and Commitment in American Life*. Berkeley: U. of California Press, 1985.

Bogle, Donald, *Blacks in American Films and Television: An Encyclopedia*. New York: Garland, 1988.

_____, *Toms, Coons, Mulattoes, Mammies, and Bucks: An Interpretive History of Blacks in American Film*, 3rd edition. New York: Continuum, 1994.

Brislin, Richard W., *Cross-Cultural Encounters, Face-to-Face Interactions*. New York: Pergamon Press, 1981.

Casetti, Francesco, *Inside the Gaze: The Fiction Film and Its Spectator*. Bloomington: Indiana University Press, 1998.

Churchill, Ward, *Fantasies of the Master Race: Literature, Cinema, and the Colonization of the American Indian*. San Francisco: City Light Books, 1998.

Condon, John, *Good Neighbors: Communicating with the Mexicans*, 2nd edition. Yarmouth, Maine: Intercultural Press, 1997.

_____, *With Respect to the Japanese*. Yarmouth, Maine: Intercultural Press, 1984.

Condon, John, and Saito, Miksuko, eds., *Communicating Across Cultures for What? A Symposium on Humane Responsibility in Intercultural Communication*. Tokyo: Simul Press, 1976.

Condon, John, and Yousef, Fathi, *An Introduction to Intercultural Communication*. New York: Macmillan, 1987.

Cripps, Thomas, *Slow Fade to Black: The Negro in American Film 1900–1942*. New York: Oxford University Press, 1993.

DeMott, Benjamin, *The Trouble with Friendship: Why Americans Can't Think Straight About Race*. New York: Atlantic Monthly Press, 1995.

Diamond, Jared, *Guns, Germs, and Steel: The Fates of Human Societies*. New York: W. W. Norton, 1997.

Díaz-Guerrero, Rogelio, *Psychology of the Mexican: Culture and Personality*. Austin: U. of Texas Press, 1975.

_____, *Understanding Mexicans and Americans: Cultural Perspectives in Conflict*. New York: Plenum Press, 1991.

_____, et al., *Understanding Mexicans and Americans: A Mexican-U.S. Communication Lexicon of Images, Meanings, and Cultural Frames of Reference*. Washington, D.C.: Institute of Comparative Social & Cultural Studies Inc., 1985.

Dixon, Wheeler W., *It Looks at You: The Returned Gaze of Cinema*. Albany: State University of New York Press, 1995.

Fienup-Riordan, Ann, *Freeze Frame: Alaska Eskimos in the Movies*. Seattle: U. of Washington Press, 1995.

Flores, William V., and Benmayor, Rina, eds., *Latino Cultural Citizenship: Claiming Identity, Space, and Rights*. Boston, Beacon Press, 1997.

Friar, Ralph E., and Natasha A., *The Only Good Indian: The Hollywood Gospel*. New York: Drama Book Specialists, 1972.

Fugard, Athol, *Master Harold—and the Boys*. New York: Alfred Knopf, 1982.
Geertz, Clifford, *The Interpretation of Cultures: Selected Essays*. New York: Basic Books, 1973.
_____, *Local Knowledge: Further Essays in Interpretive Anthropology*. New York: Basic Books, 1983.
Gessner, Robert, *Broken Arrow*. New York: Farrar & Rinehart, 1933.
Giordano, Paolo A., and Tamburri, Anthony Julian, *Beyond the Margin: Readings in Italian Americana*. Madison, N.J.: Fairleigh Dickinson University Press, 1998.
Goffman, Irving, *Forms of Talk*. Philadelphia: U. of Pennsylvania Press, 1981.
_____, *Frame Analysis: An Essay on the Organization of Experience*. Cambridge: Harvard University Press, 1974.
_____, *Interaction Ritual: Essays in Face-to-Face Behavior*. Chicago: Aldine Publishing Co., 1967.
Gracia, Jorge, *Hispanic/Latino Identity: A Philosophical Perspective*. Malden, Mass.: Blackwell, 2000.
Grinker, Roy Richard, and Steiner, Christopher B., eds., *Perspectives on Africa: A Reader in Culture, History, and Representation*. Cambridge, Mass: Blackwell, 1977.
Hall, Edward T., *The Hidden Dimension*. Garden City, NY: Doubleday, 1966.
_____, *The Silent Language*. New York: Anchor Books, 1973.
Hall, Ivan P., *Cartels of the Mind: Japan's Intellectual Closed Shop*. New York: W.W. Norton, 1998.
Harrison, Lawrence E., and Huntington, Samuel P., eds., *Culture Matters: How Values Shape Human Progress*. New York: Basic Books, 2000.
Hilger, Michael, *From Savage to Nobleman: Images of Native Americans in Film*. Lanham, Md.: Scarecrow Press, 1995.
Hofstede, Geert, *Cultures and Organizations: Software of the Mind*. New York: McGraw-Hill, 1991.
Huntington, Samuel, *The Clash of Civilizations and the Remaking of World Order*. New York: Simon and Schuster, 1996.
Ishiguro, Kazuo, *The Remains of the Day*. Boston: Faber and Faber, 1989.
Kilpatrick, Jacquelyn, *Celluloid Indians: Native Americans and Film*. Lincoln: U. of Nebraska Press, 1999.
Kim, Y.Y., *Communication and Cross-Cultural Adaptation: An Integrative Theory*. Clevedon, England: Multilingual Matters, 1988.
Lanier, Alison, and Gay, C. William, *Living in the U.S.A.* Yarmouth, Maine: Intercultural Press, 1996.
Lawton, Harry W., *Willie Boy: A Desert Manhunt*. Balboa Island, Cal.: Paisano Press, 1960.
Limerick, Patricia Nelson, *The Legacy of Conquest: The Unbroken Past of the American West*. New York: W.W. Norton, 1987.
_____, *Something in the Soil: Legacies and Reckonings in the New West*. New York: W.W. Norton, 2000.
Lipset, Seymour Martin, *American Exceptionalism: A Double-Edged Sword*. New York: W.W. Norton, 1996.
List, Christine, *Chicano Images: Refiguring Ethnicity in Mainstream Film*. New York: Garland, 1996.
Maciel, David R., and Herrera-Sobek, María, eds., *Culture Across Borders: Mexican Immigration and Popular Culture*. Tucson: U. of Arizona Press, 1998.
Macintyre, Michael, *The Shogun Inheritance: Japan and the Legacy of the Samurai*. London: William Collins Sons, 1981.
March, Robert M., *The Japanese Negotiator: Subtlety and Strategy Beyond Western Logic*. New York: Kodansha International, 1988.
_____, *Reading the Japanese Mind: The Realities Behind Their Thoughts and Actions*. New York: Kodansha International, 1996.
Maricourt, Renaud de, "Japan and Foreign Cultures: Thoughts for Expatriates," *Intercultures*, 22 (July 1993) 79–94.

Mitchell, Lee Clark, *Westerns: Making the Man in Fiction and Film*. Chicago: U. of Chicago Press, 1996.

Mowlana, Hamid, *Global Information and World Communication*. Thousand Oaks, Cal.: Sage, 1997.

Niikara, Ryoko, "The Psychology and Process Underlying Japanese Assertive Behavior: Comparison of Japanese with Americans, Malaysians and Filipinos," *International Journal of Intercultural Relations*, 23:1 (1999) 47–76.

Nilsen, Don Lee Fred, *Humor Scholarship: A Research Bibliography*. Westport, Conn.: Greenwood Press, 1993.

Nishiyama, Kazuo, *Welcoming the Japanese Visitor: Insights, Tips, Tactics*. Honolulu: U. of Hawaii Press, 1996.

Noriega, Chon A., ed., *Chicanos and Film: Essays on Chicano Representation and Resistance*. New York: Garland, 1992.

Nugent, Walter T.K., *Crossings: The Great Transatlantic Migrations, 1870–1914*. Bloomington: Indiana University Press, 1992.

Parrillo, Vincent N., *Strangers to These Shores: Race and Ethnic Relations in the United States*, 6th edition. Boston: Allyn and Bacon, 2000.

Pettit, Arthur G., *Images of the Mexican American in Fiction and Film*. College Station, Texas: A&M University Press, 1980.

Ramirez-Berg, Charles, "Stereotyping in Films in General and of the Hispanic in Particular," *Howard Journal of Communication*, 2, (1990).

Rapport, Nigel, *The Prose and the Passion: Anthropology, Literature, and the Writing of E.M. Forster*. Manchester, U.K.: Manchester University Press, 1994.

Reid, Mark A., ed., *Spike Lee's "Do the Right Thing."* New York: Cambridge University Press, 1997.

Reischauer, Edwin O., *The Japanese*. Cambridge, Mass.: Belknap Press, 1995.

Reisman, David, *The Lonely Crowd: A Study of the Changing American Character*. Garden City, N.Y.: Doubleday, 1953.

Reyes, Luis, *Hispanics in Hollywood: An Encyclopedia of Film and Television*. New York: Garland, 1994.

Richard, Alfred Charles, *Contemporary Hollywood's Negative Hispanic Image*. Westport, Conn.: Greenwood Press, 1994.

Richmond, Yale, *From Nyet to Da: Understanding the Russians*. Yarmouth, Maine: Intercultural Press, 1992.

_____, and Gestrin, Phyllis, *Into Africa: Intercultural Insights*. Yarmouth, Maine: Intercultural Press, 1998.

Rollins, Peter C., and O'Connor, John E., eds., *Hollywood's Indian: The Portrayal of the Native American in Film*. Lexington: University Press of Kentucky, 1998.

Romano, Dugan, *Intercultural Marriage: Promises and Pitfalls* 2nd edition. Yarmouth, Maine: Intercultural Press, 1997.

Roof, Judith, and Wiegman, Robyn, eds., *Who Can Speak?: Authority and Critical Identity*. Urbana: U. of Illinois Press, 1995.

Sandos, James A., *The Hunt for Willie Boy: Indian-Hating and Popular Culture*. Norman, U. of Oklahoma Press, 1994.

Shohat, Ella, and Stam, Robert, *Unthinking Eurocentrism: Multiculturalism and the Media*. New York: Routledge, 1994.

Slater, Philip, *The Pursuit of Loneliness: American Culture at the Breaking Point*. Boston: Beacon Press, 1970.

Smith, Donald B., *From the Land of the Shadows: The Making of Grey Owl*. Saskatoon, Canada: Western Producer Prairie Books, 1990.

Smith, Hedrick, *The New Russians*. New York: Random House, 1990.

_____, *The Russians*. New York: Ballantine, 1984.

Smith, Henry, ed., *Learning from Shogun: Japanese History and Western Fantasy*. Santa Barbara, Cal.: Program in Asian Studies, 1980.

Stevens, Donald F. S., *Based on a True Story: Latin American History at the Movies.* Wilmington, Del.: SR Books, 1997.

Storti, Greg, *Cross-Cultural Dialogues: 74 Brief Encounters with Cultural Difference.* Yarmouth, Maine: Intercultural Press, 1994.

Stuart, Edward C., and Bennett, Milton J., *American Cultural Patterns: A Cross-Cultural Perspective.* Yarmouth, Maine: Intercultural Press, 1991.

Tan, Amy, *The Joy Luck Club.* New York: Vintage Books, 1991.

Tanaka, Tomoko, et al., "Adjustment Patterns of International Students in Japan," *International Journal of Intercultural Relations,* 18:1 (1994) 55–75.

Tasker, Peter, *The Japanese: Portrait of a Nation.* New York: Penguin Books, 1987.

Ting-Toomey, Stella, "Facework in Japan and the United States," *International Journal of Intercultural Relations* 18:4 (1994) 469–506.

Tong, Benson, *The Chinese Americans.* Westport, Conn.: Greenwood Press, 2000.

Toplin, Robert Brent, ed., *Hollywood as Mirror: Changing Views of "Outsiders" and "Enemies" in American Movies.* Westport, Conn.: Greenwood Press, 1993.

Torgovnick, Marianna, *Primitive Passions: Men, Women, and the Quest for Ecstasy.* New York: Alfred Knopf, 1997).

Triandis, Harry C., *Culture and Social Behavior.* New York: McGraw-Hill, 1994.

Williamson, J.W., *Hillbillyland.* Chapel Hill: U. of North Carolina Press, 1995.

Woll, Allen L., and Miller, Randall M, eds., *Ethnic and Racial Images in American Film and Television.* New York: Garland, 1987.

Wong, Eugene Franklin, *On Visual Media Racism: Asians in American Motion Pictures.* New York: Arno Press, 1978.

Xing, Jun, *Asia America Through the Lens: History, Representations, and Identity.* Walnut Creek, Cal.: AltaMira Press, 1998.

INDEX